LOUIS M. KYRIAKOUDES

The Social Origins of the Urban South

RACE, GENDER,

AND MIGRATION

IN NASHVILLE AND

MIDDLE TENNESSEE,

1890–1930

The University of North Carolina Press

Chapel Hill & London

frontispiece: Library of Congress

Library of Congress Cataloging-in-Publication Data
Kyriakoudes, Louis M.
The social origins of the urban South : race, gender, and migration in Nashville and middle Tennessee, 1890–1930 / Louis M. Kyriakoudes.
p. cm.
Includes bibliographical references (p.) and index.
ISBN 0-8078-2811-4 (paper) — ISBN 0-8078-5484-0 (pbk.: alk. paper)
1. Rural-urban migration—Tennessee—Nashville—History. 2. Women—Employment—Tennessee—Nashville—History. 3. Nashville (Tenn.)—Race relations—History. 4. Nashville (Tenn.)—Economic conditions. I. Title.
HT384.U52 N375 2003
307.2'4'09768'55—dc21

2003001893

cloth 07 06 05 04 03   5 4 3 2 1
paper 07 06 05 04 03   5 4 3 2 1

The Social Origins of the Urban South

FOR LISA,

HELEN, KATHERINE,

AND MICHAEL

Contents

Acknowledgments   xvii

Introduction   1

1   The Grand Ole Opry and the Urban South   7

2   City and Hinterland   19

3   The Countryside   40

4   Turning to Urban Markets   58

5   Leaving the Countryside   73

6   Going to Nashville   96

7   Men's Work   115

8   Women's Work   136

Conclusion   157

Appendix: Middle Tennessee and Nashville
            Net Migration Estimates   161

Notes   167

Bibliography   201

Index   221

Illustrations

Uncle Dave Macon   9

Lasses and Honey   15

DeFord Bailey   17

Map of the Booster Club's 1924 trip to
   Nashville's hinterland   20

Cartoon showing Nashville's wholesalers as
   a magnet to merchants   26

An eroded Tennessee farm   55

A woman feeding chickens on a farm   64

Advertisement for cream separators   66

Tennessee farmers who also worked
   as tie hackers   69

The one-room schoolhouse   91

Tennessee tenant farmer, c. 1930   93

Advertisement for a commercial
   laundry   140

Tables

3.1. Tenancy Rates of Middle Tennessee Farms, by Geographical Region, 1890–1930   46

3.2. Number of Middle Tennessee Farms, by Geographical Region, 1890–1930   51

5.1. Tennessee-Born Blacks Residing in Other States, by Census Region, 1890–1930   83

5.2. Tennessee-Born Whites Residing in Other States, by Census Region, 1890–1930   84

6.1. Estimated Net Migration of U.S.-Born Population to Nashville, Tennessee, 1890–1930   102

6.2. Gross Migration of U.S.-Born Males, Ages Twenty-One to Thirty-One, to Nashville, Tennessee, 1917   106

7.1. Occupational Rank of Nashville Males, Ages Twenty-One to Thirty-One, by Migration Status, 1917   116

7.2. Occupational Rank of White Nashville Males, Ages Twenty-One to Thirty-One, by Migration Status, 1917   121

7.3. Occupational Rank of Black Nashville Males, Ages Twenty-One to Thirty-One, by Migration Status, 1917   122

7.4. Occupational Rank of White Nashville Male Migrants, Ages Twenty-One to Thirty-One, by Region of Birth, 1917   123

7.5. Occupational Rank of Black Nashville Male Migrants, Ages Twenty-One to Thirty-One, by Region of Birth, 1917   124

7.6. Occupational Rank of White Nashville Male Migrants, Ages Twenty-One to Thirty-One, by Size of Birthplace, 1917   125

7.7. Occupational Rank of Black Nashville Male Migrants, Ages Twenty-One to Thirty-One, by Size of Birthplace, 1917   125

8.1. Percentage of Nashville Women Age Ten and Older Gainfully Employed, 1900–1930   137

8.2. Occupational Distribution of Nashville Women, by Race, 1900–1930   138

Figures

3.1. Tenancy Rates of White Tennessee Farmers, by Age, 1900–1920   47

3.2. Tenancy Rates of Black Tennessee Farmers, by Age, 1900–1920   48

3.3. Middle Tennessee Farmland Values, 1890–1930   52

3.4. Distribution of Middle Tennessee Farms, by Size, 1890, 1910, and 1930   53

5.1. Estimated Net Migration Rates of U.S.-Born Population from Rural Middle Tennessee, by Sex and Race, 1890–1930   81

5.2. Age Structure of Net Migration of U.S.-Born Population from Rural Middle Tennessee, by Sex and Race, 1890–1900   85

5.3. Age Structure of Net Migration of U.S.-Born Population from Rural Middle Tennessee, by Sex and Race, 1900–1910   86

5.4. Age Structure of Net Migration of U.S.-Born Population from Rural Middle Tennessee, by Sex and Race, 1910–1920   87

5.5. Age Structure of Net Migration of U.S.-Born Population from Rural Middle Tennessee, by Sex and Race, 1920–1930   88

6.1. Estimated Net Migration Rates of U.S.-Born Population to Nashville, Tennessee, by Sex and Race, 1890–1930   103

6.2. Age Structure of Net Migration of U.S.-Born Population to Nashville, Tennessee, by Sex and Race, 1890–1900   104

6.3. Age Structure of Net Migration of U.S.-Born Population to Nashville, Tennessee, by Sex and Race, 1900–1910   104

6.4. Age Structure of Net Migration of U.S.-Born Population to Nashville, Tennessee, by Sex and Race, 1910–1920   105

6.5. Age Structure of Net Migration of U.S.-Born Population to Nashville, Tennessee, by Sex and Race, 1920–1930   105

Maps

2.1. Nashville's Correspondent Banks, 1890   28

2.2. Nashville's Correspondent Banks, 1925   29

3.1. Middle Tennessee Study Area and Agricultural Subregions   41

6.1. Place of Birth of Tennessee-Born Male Migrants to Nashville, 1917   108

Acknowledgments

It is with great pleasure that I am able to acknowledge the colleagues, institutions, and organizations that have offered me support, advice, criticism, and encouragement during the research for and writing of this book.

I have relied heavily upon librarians and manuscript curators. This study could not have been completed without the assistance of the staffs of the Tennessee State Library and Archives, the Southeast Regional Branch of the National Archives and Records Administration, the Archives of Appalachia at East Tennessee State University, and the University of North Carolina's Southern Historical Collection, Howard W. Odum Institute for Research in Social Science, and Carolina Population Center Library. I am especially grateful to Dr. Wayne Moore of the Tennessee State Library and Archives, who has generously shared with me his unmatched knowledge of rural Tennessee history over the years I have worked on this project.

Grants from Vanderbilt University, the University of Southern Mississippi, and the Economic History Association facilitated initial research and writing. My colleagues at the University of Southern Mississippi provided a supportive environment conducive to good scholarship. I was able to complete the final revisions of the manuscript while I served as a National Institute of Child Health and Human Development postdoctoral fellow at the Carolina Population Center at the University of North Carolina at Chapel Hill. I am indebted to Tom Swasey and Brian Frizzelle for their help with illustrations and maps and to Barbara Entwisle, Carolina Population Center director, for funding the making of the index.

The arguments in this book have been presented before the Andrew Mellon Foundation's Seminar on Population Movement and Urbanization, the Agricultural History Society, the International Country Music Conference, the Organization of American Historians, the St. George Tucker Society, the Social Science History Association, the Southern Association of Women's Historians, and the Southern Historical Association. At each occasion, I have been the beneficiary of thoughtful and penetrating criticism from many individuals. In particular, I would like to thank Fitzhugh Brundage, David Carlton, Leon Fink, Gilbert Fite, Wayne Flint, Lacy Ford, Jimmie Franklin, Michele Gillespie, LuAnn Jones, Jonathan Liebowitz, Bill Mansfield, Robert Margo, Mark Schultz, Rebecca Sharpless, Marjorie Spruill, Cecilia Tichi, and Don Winters for their comments on this work. Lewis Bateman, formerly of the University of North Carolina Press, first approached me when this book was but an exploratory essay. David Perry, Mark Simpson-Vos, and Mary Caviness have skillfully shepherded this through the review, editorial, and production processes.

One's greatest debts are always listed last. This book began as a seminar paper in Don H. Doyle's social history seminar at Vanderbilt University. From that grew the dissertation upon which this book is drawn. This is just one of a number of books to have emerged from professor Doyle's workshop. It is my hope that it lives up to the high standards of its predecessors.

It has been my great good fortune to have been first a student and then a friend of Peter A. Coclanis. His unfailing support and encouragement have meant a great deal to me, and the standard he has set as a scholar has given me an ideal for which to strive.

The dedication of this book scarcely acknowledges the love and patience that my wife, Lisa Eveleigh, has shown over the years. She has challenged me to sharpen my arguments and strengthen my prose. For her skills as a writer and scholar, and for her love and support, I will be forever grateful.

The Social Origins of the Urban South

Introduction

In 1923 a Vanderbilt University undergraduate and aspiring poet began attending the informal meetings of a group of local writers who called themselves the Fugitives. Robert Penn Warren had come to Nashville from Guthrie, Kentucky, a small town just over the Tennessee border that was best known for the Black Patch War, a violent struggle of tobacco farmers against the American Tobacco Company. The move from country to city came as quite a shock to the young aspiring poet. Nashville, he later recalled, "seemed like a perfectly huge city to me. I was much impressed by its grandeur and scale, [and] by its hurry and bustle." Warren would graduate in 1925, study at Berkeley, Yale, and Oxford, contribute an essay to *I'll Take My Stand*, the manifesto of the Southern Agrarians, and then go on to an illustrious career as a poet, novelist, and literary critic.[1]

In that same year of 1923, Sidney Harkreader, a lanky, twenty-five-year-old Middle Tennessee farm boy and fiddler, wandered into Melton's Barbershop, a well-known hangout for Nashville's growing community of traditional, or "old-time," musicians. Like Warren, Harkreader was a son of the country, but the circuitous route that brought Harkreader to Nashville belied his more humble origins in the farmlands of Middle Tennessee's Wilson County. During World War I, he left his father's farm to work at a newly constructed DuPont munitions plant just outside of Nashville. Taking advantage of the strong wartime labor market and seeking some adventure, he headed to Cincinnati. At the war's end, he came back home to Wilson County to farm. After a few seasons trying to scratch a living from the soil, he returned again to Nashville. At Melton's Barbershop, Harkreader met Uncle Dave Macon, a banjo-playing vaudevillian who liked the young fiddler and promptly asked Harkreader to join his act. The two toured the southern vaudeville circuit. By the fall of 1925 Fiddlin' Sid Harkreader was regularly performing on Nashville's newly inaugurated WSM radio station on the Barn Dance variety program that would soon be renamed the Grand Ole Opry.[2]

Certainly at first glance, Warren and Harkreader seem to have little more in common than having been in the same city at the same time. Yet each reveals a different facet of a massive, but largely unexamined, migration of population from the southern farms and hamlets to the region's growing cities, a migration that transformed both the rural and urban South. Across the South tens of millions of rural people—blacks and whites, men and women—left the southern countryside to live and work in southern cities. This "southern great migration" came to transform the region, laying the foundations for today's modern, urban South.[3] The foundations for this migration were laid during the period between the economic depressions of the 1890s and 1930s, a period of sustained urbanization in the region. In 1890 a bit more than 10 percent of the region's population lived in urban areas; by 1930 this figure had swelled to nearly 33 percent.[4] Not only did the size of the South's urban population increase sharply, the region also saw the rise of a new class of fast-growing interior cities that eclipsed in size and importance the coastal port towns that had dominated the antebellum urban hierarchy. Atlanta, Birmingham, Dallas, Houston, Memphis, and, of course, Nashville, small or nonexistent before the Civil War, grew rapidly afterward and laid the foundations for the region's modern urban system.[5] Attracting few foreign immigrants or domestic migrants from beyond the South, the region's cities could only grow by pulling population from the farms and hamlets of the southern countryside.

This book explores the process of migration from the perspective of migrants themselves and probes its causes and consequences for both the rural and urban South. The focus is on Nashville and its Middle Tennessee hinterland. The diversified, highly self-sufficient, general farming regime that late-nineteenth- and early-twentieth-century agricultural reformers thought would improve farm life in the cotton South was deeply embedded in Middle Tennessee life. If the yeoman farmer ideal could exist in the South, Middle Tennessee would be its home. By the same token, Nashville's economic leadership, never tied to myths of defeat, eagerly sought New South economic development. If the promise of the New South boosters would ever ring true, it would be in Nashville. The city also gave birth to two of the South's most creative cultural responses to migration and modernity in the circle of writers and critics who came to be known as the Southern Agrarians, and in the old-time music radio program that came to be known as the Grand Ole Opry.

Robert Penn Warren and his fellow Southern Agrarians offered a broad critique of New South economic development and industrial capitalism in an attempt to create an alternative to the modernizing trends sweeping the region. To fellow Agrarian Andrew Lytle, the "urbanization of the countryside" was shorthand for the spread of profit-oriented, progressive agriculture and consumerist values that were undermining the white yeoman culture that the Agrarians idealized as the essence of southern distinctiveness. That nearly all the Agrarian critics had forgone rural life to live, work, and write at one of the South's first modern urban research universities was an irony not lost to the group's critics. The Southern Agrarians needed urban life and urbanity. Nashville provided the necessary vantage from which they could view the region as a whole.[6]

Harkreader, no learned critic of literature, history, or regional development, was a genuine product of the upcountry white yeoman culture the Agrarians idealized. Yet, much more than anything expressed in the polemics of the Agrarians, his career as a musician illustrates the complex and contradictory ways in which rural southerners faced the modernizing changes that were sweeping across the rural and urban South. While fiddle and banjo players had always been a staple of vaudeville, Harkreader was one of a pioneering generation of traditional performers who took advantage of new technologies—the phonographic disc and radio—to build careers as performers. As an early performer on the radio program that would evolve into the Grand Ole Opry, Harkreader helped define the emerging forms of what would later be known as country and bluegrass music. He did so from a radio program founded and owned by a Nashville insurance firm eager to build goodwill and demand for its products throughout the South.[7] Hence, a new technology that spearheaded the dissemination of an urban-based consumer culture in the rural South also became an agent of artistic preservation of that rural culture.

David Goldfield, pioneering historian of southern urbanization, was the first to draw our attention to these complex rural-urban relationships. He argued that southern cities needed to be understood in the context of the rural South that shaped the unique and distinctive characteristics of southern cities.[8] In order to understand southern rural-urban migration, however, one must appreciate the powerful influence the region's cities exerted over their rural hinterlands. One historical study, William Cronon's *Nature's Metropolis*, has shown how Chicago's growth was fueled by its entrepreneurs' ability to impose capitalistic order over the rural countryside. Demographers' recent studies of the developing world have found strong relationships between rural development, urbanization, and migration.[9]

Historians have also examined closely the northward migration of black southerners that comprised the World War I–era Great Migration.[10] That movement, however, was part of a much broader exodus of blacks and whites from southern agriculture. Placing migration in the context of social, economic, and demographic change in Nashville and its rural hinterland allows us to understand the connections between urbanization and agricultural change. Doing so also allows us to appreciate the complexity of migration as individuals and families circulated between countryside and city in an attempt to cope with the rapid economic and social changes that swept the early-twentieth-century South.

This study begins with the Grand Ole Opry. The development of this rural radio minstrel show, which Chapter 1 examines, illustrates the complex changes that were sweeping both the rural and urban South and the ways in which southerners navigated those changes. Chapter 2 explores Nashville's economic growth. The city's business leadership saw in Middle Tennessee the raw materials and markets to build the city into a major manufacturing and commercial metropolis. While the city's economic development failed to live up to boosters' expectations, the industries that did thrive, such as lumber and wood-products, flour-milling, and meatpacking, did so thanks to access to markets and raw materials in the city's hinterland.

Chapter 3 examines Middle Tennessee agriculture and the mounting pressures on farm families. Beginning in the 1890s and continuing through the 1920s, the diversified agricultural regime that characterized most of Middle Tennessee entered a period of sustained crisis. However, this crisis did not stem from market pressures generated by a commercialization of agriculture. Instead, increasing population pressures and shrinking acreage undermined small farms in Middle Tennessee and dissuaded more and more young adults from entering farming. Middle Tennessee farm families responded in two ways to these pressures. As shown in Chapter 4, they first turned to new products of field and forest, shifting to truck and fruit crops, poultry, dairy products, and livestock. They also logged the remaining old-growth forests for the city's lumber and wood-products manufacturers. Rather than being oppressed by the cash economy, Middle Tennessee farm families also took advantage of new market linkages between Nashville and the countryside to bolster their livelihoods, especially after 1900. In this way, Nashville's development helped serve as a prop for many Middle Tennessee farm families.

The viability of these linkages was short-lived, however. Chapters 5 and 6 show how the interactions of city and countryside led to migration to Nashville. Chapter 5 shows how moving was a well-established response to economic change, and young, unmarried men had long worked as migrant timber or agricultural workers before returning to their communities to marry and settle down to farm as tenants or owners. Attempts by progressive reformers to stem the flow from the farms through public school reforms and highway construction in the 1910s and 1920s were unsuccessful and hastened the movement. Chapter 6 shows how these circular migration patterns came to include work in northern cities, as well as southern cities like Nashville. Mobilization during World War I drew thousands of rural people to Nashville, particularly women, to labor in war-related industries. By the 1920s, migration from Middle Tennessee had become an exodus, and rural men and women poured into the city.

This study concludes by examining critical facets of rural migrants' urban experience. Chapter 7 examines the relationship between Nashville's labor market and migration, showing how rural migrants' support for organized labor influenced the rise and fall of trade unions during and immediately after World War I. Chapter 8 explores the experiences of the female migrants that flooded into Nashville in the 1920s seeking some measure of independence from the travails of rural life.

The Grand Ole Opry
and the Urban South

One Saturday evening in 1927, George D. Hay, the program director of Nashville radio station WSM, was preparing to introduce the evening's local program, the WSM Barn Dance. Not really a barn dance at all, the program's succession of what was then called "old-time" or "hillbilly" musical acts interspersed with comedy routines made it more akin to vaudeville or minstrelsy. Hay had begun the program soon after arriving at the then one-month-old station in November 1925, and the heady brew of traditional string band music performed by musicians drawn from Nashville and its hinterland proved extremely popular with radio audiences across the South. On that night, the Barn Dance followed an NBC network presentation of symphonic music from New York. The conductor Walter Damrosch, stating over the airways that he was making an exception to his rule that "there was no place in the classics for realism," ended his program with a performance of a brief orchestral composition depicting a locomotive. When Hay's Barn Dance program went on the air, Hay announced that "for the next three hours we will present nothing but realism. It will be down to earth for the earthy." Thereon, DeFord Bailey, harmonica virtuoso and the sole African American performer of the program, laid into a rousing rendition of "Pan American Blues." After Bailey's opener, Hay sought again to differentiate his program from its high culture predecessor and bragged that "for the past hour we have been listening to music taken largely from Grand Opera, but from now on we will present 'The Grand Ole Opry.'" And that is how the "mother church" of country music, and Nashville's best-known and most enduring contribution to the nation's popular culture, got its name.[1]

Hay understood why listeners tuned into the Opry, and he was adamant in claiming folk music status for the program. A 1929 press release boasted that the Grand Ole Opry was where "the folk tunes of the Tennessee hills are put on direct from the soil." Waxing fulsomely in his memoirs, Hay explained how the program "tapped the vein of American folk music which lay smouldering [sic] and in small flames for about three hundred years."[2] There was much truth to Hay's claim. The program's early performers, such as Uncle Dave Macon, Sid Harkreader, DeFord Bailey, the Fruit Jar Drinkers, and Dr. Humphrey Bate and his Possum Hunters, all had roots in Middle Tennessee's rich rural folk culture. Even the Fugitive poet and Agrarian critic Donald Davidson, a keen observer of the commercial country music industry that was springing up literally blocks from his Nashville home, begrudgingly saw in the early Opry powerful expressions of southern folk music tradition. Davidson had become quite critical of the intense commercial incentives that pushed the popular "hillbilly singer and his 'band'" to degrade traditional folk song by composing "*new* songs—quasi-folk songs or frankly popular ditties—which will bring him royalties from phonograph records and music sheets." Nonetheless, for Davidson, the early Opry "began at the genuine folk level."[3]

At first glance, the Grand Ole Opry stands as the clearest example of how, as one prominent historian of the urban South has argued, "rural values dominated southern cities."[4] Few institutions in modern America so completely reflect the culture and sensibilities of the white rural South as the Opry. Despite the diversity of its performers over the years, the Opry has consistently developed a stylized vision of white rusticity leavened by a powerful strain of Protestant Christian fatalism—what Curtis Ellison has described as "from hard times to heaven." This vision has been the core of the Opry's appeal.[5] After World War II, Opry stars like Roy Acuff helped spawn a recording industry that broadcast what was dubbed "country music" well beyond the region.[6] What greater example is there of the dominance of rural ways in twentieth-century Southern life?

Yet the story is more complex. When one looks closer at the Opry's origins, it becomes clear the Opry functioned as an urban institution that worked to reshape rural culture, developing as it did out of the close interaction between the culture of the rural South and imperatives of twentieth-century business enterprise. The radio program was both a product of and an agent in the modernization of the countryside, fostering what Southern Agrarian Andrew Lytle termed "the urbanization of the countryside." In creating a rural vaudeville show for the radio, Opry founder George D. Hay constructed a radio stage upon which white rural southerners could project their nostalgia for elements of a fading rural culture without actually surrendering their desire for the products and ways of modernity.[7]

Recent scholars have pointed out that Hay was not quite forthright in his characterization of the Opry as "genuine to the core." Both Curtis Ellison

Uncle Dave Macon (right), a vaudevillian and the first star of
the Grand Ole Opry, with his son, Dorris (Southern Folklife
Collection, University of North Carolina, Chapel Hill)

and Richard Peterson have shown that artifice and show-business manipu-
lation shaped the developing format and conventions of the Opry. Peterson
has been the most emphatic on this point, arguing that the "authenticity"
that country music performers prided themselves on and that their audiences demanded was based upon a fabricated vision of rural life—a "mis-
remembered" past manipulated by Hay to build an image of rural white
rusticity on the radio.[8]

The hayseed image of the Opry and its performers was largely Hay's creation. As the Barn Dance program of the mid-1920s grew into the Grand
Ole Opry, Hay consciously developed hillbilly personas for his leading acts.
To be sure, most of the early performers were country-born, but they all
had experienced urban life. Uncle Dave Macon had spent his formative ado-
lescent years living in downtown Nashville, where his parents operated a
hotel catering to traveling vaudevillians. It was here that Joel Davidson, a
prominent late-nineteenth-century vaudevillian, taught Macon the banjo.

Macon was a seasoned veteran of the southern vaudeville circuit well before his joining the radio program. Sid Harkreader and DeFord Bailey both migrated to Nashville from rural Middle Tennessee as young men in search of work and were living in the city when WSM began broadcasting string band music in 1925. Humphrey Bate was called "Doctor" because of his Vanderbilt University M.D. degree. The other "day jobs" of Opry performers included such urban occupations as barber, insurance salesman, railroad dispatcher, automobile mechanic, and watchmaker. At first, performers insisted upon arriving at the studio sporting their Sunday best. Only later did Hay encourage the acts to devise corny names such as the Fruit Jar Drinkers, Clodhoppers, and Possum Hunters, and then pose them alongside hay bales and pigsties wearing overalls and wide-brimmed straw hats before the publicity photographer.[9]

The origins of WSM radio illustrate the urban roots of the Grand Ole Opry. WSM radio's beginnings lay in the decision of Edwin Craig, an executive with the National Life and Accident Insurance Company, to establish a radio station in 1925 in order to, in Craig's words, "serve the South and create good will for the Company." While National Life did not begin direct radio advertising until the early 1930s, it always maintained close ties to the station, even to the point where the call letters—WSM—came from the company slogan, "We Shield Millions."[10]

Changes in the insurance industry moved the executives of National Life to turn intensively toward rural markets, and WSM and the Opry played a significant role in that strategy. In the 1920s, the company expanded from its original business of industrial insurance—a form of income-replacement disability insurance aimed at the waged-labor market—into what was then termed "ordinary" life insurance (similar policies are called "whole" life today) with premiums paid on an affordable monthly, rather than annual, basis and containing a cash value investment annuity. This expansion opened a vast market among southern rural households, particularly in the predominantly white, upcountry regions such as Middle Tennessee. The Opry and WSM brought the message of the National Life and Accident Insurance Company to this new market.

The rising interest of southern farmers of modest means in financial investments such as life insurance indicates a profound change in their attitudes toward work, money, and security. Owning land and creating a large family were the traditional routes farm families pursued to guarantee their economic security. That changed in the early twentieth century. Southern farmers faced harsh economic pressures that seemed to cast a pall over the viability of farming, as well as a rising propensity for their children to migrate out of rural areas and out of agriculture. Furthermore, religious strictures against life insurance waned. No longer did people view life insurance as a sacrilegious wager against God's "divine function of protection." By the late 1920s, southern farmers increasingly envisioned security in financial terms, just as did their urban, wage-earning counterparts.[11]

Selling to the rural farmer was now the same as selling to the urban wage worker, and National Life executives sought to exploit this development in their marketing plans. Company advice to its agents on "selling farmers life insurance" noted that "along with good roads, electricity, and many other improvements, the farmer is making more real income and has a greater need for Life Insurance than any other occupational group we can think of." The company explicitly linked religion and life insurance, explaining to its sales staff that just as "an unsaved man is never ready to receive salvation . . . until he is convinced that he is lost without it," so is an "uninsured man" unwilling to purchase a policy "until he is convinced that he and his dependent ones are liable to suffer unless he has proper protection." National Life executives understood that this rural market was growing because of a fundamental change in the mentality of rural southerners brought on by their closer integration with an urban economy and urban culture. National Life advised its sales force that the farmer's "contact with the outside world through press and radio has given him all the desires of the average industrial worker. He and his family want all the conveniences and better things of life just like the city dweller." National Life's marketing strategy linked WSM radio, the Grand Ole Opry, and insurance. "You can depend upon the finest entertainment [on WSM], just as you depend on the Shield Man for your security and peace of mind—through insurance," noted a WSM promotional booklet distributed widely by its agents. The rural elements of the Opry disguised a very modern business strategy.[12]

The performances on the early Grand Ole Opry also reveal the urban origins of the program. The early Opry acts owed much to the conventions of vaudeville, burlesque, and minstrelsy. The earliest broadcasts often featured popular vaudeville acts that happened to be passing through town and whose participants wanted to advertise their performances over the airways. Crooner Nick Lucas—whose signature song was "Tiptoe through the Tulips"; the Ray-O-Vac twins; Chief Kiutus Tecumseh; Ken Hackley and His Cowboys; Happy Jack Haines; and ukulele artist Chester Zahn all appeared in the early years. A bowed musical saw virtuoso and at least three different Hawaiian bands—the Maunakia Hawaiian Serenaders, Fields and Martin, and the Silver String Hawaiians—also appeared on the program.[13] Rather quickly, the Opry settled on a format that stressed "old-time music."

Yet, even then, veteran vaudevillians Uncle Dave Macon, Ed McConnell, and the blackface duos of Lasses and Honey and Jamup and Honey remained some of the most popular performers on the program.

Old-time music made the Grand Ole Opry immensely popular with its southern audiences. A 1926 letter writer from northern Alabama praised the program for airing "those old tunes [that] carry us back to the days gone by." Another letter suggested that listening to the Opry was a communal event: "There are from eight to twenty here [at my home] every Saturday night, and your old dance pieces and your barn-dance programs are fine." C. J. Johnsonious, a National Life salesman in Paris, Tennessee, wrote that "the programs of WSM are gaining in popularity here, and . . . are going to mean much to the Company and the public."[14]

However, the popularity of old-time music on the Opry was not rooted solely in nostalgia for times long past. The program's musicians often addressed rural southerners' ambivalence toward modernization, alternately praising and damning the changes sweeping the countryside. In doing so, the Opry performers stood at the forefront of a larger trend of creating a new southern music that had roots in the region's rural past but spoke to the concerns and anxieties of a present undergoing rapid change.[15]

Opry musicians frequently sang about the automobile, ownership of which was spreading rapidly in the countryside and which embodied autonomy and escape for younger rural people. Sam and Kirk McGee, sometime partners of Uncle Dave Macon, sang of the almost sensual pleasure of driving in the tune "Chevrolet Car." Giving in to the seductions of speed, they sang, "I give her the gun, look out boys and let me pass" and "I love my baby, but I'm crazy 'bout my Chevrolet."[16]

Uncle Dave Macon's treatment of the automobile in his songs illustrates rural southerners' uncertainty about change. Sometime around 1900, a full twenty years before Macon embarked upon a show business career, he began a freight-hauling business, the Macon Midway Mule and Wagon Transportation Company, between the Middle Tennessee towns of Woodbury and Murfreesboro. The business lasted until 1920, when Macon retired the line in the face of competition from motorized trucks and automobiles, whose travel was facilitated by hard-surfaced roads. Only then did Macon turn to a new career as a performer. His local performances led to engagements with the Loew's and Kieth-Albee vaudeville circuits. The automobile and improved roads, the very technology that drove Macon's wagon line out of business, made possible his concert tours through the rural and small-town South. Macon sometimes praised the automobile, as in the tune "New Ford Car": "Lord, Lord, you ought to take a ride, get in a Ford with your donnie by your side." But mostly he damned the automobile. In "From

Earth to Heaven" he sang: "Well, gonna tell you just how I feel; I'd rather ride a wagon and go to heaven, than to hell in an automobile." In "Farm Relief," he complained that the automobile undermined traditional community; country people "used to go to church for to hear them shout, telling the good Lord what 'twas all about. Now the congregation is all so far, riding around in a new Ford car." In another tune, he sang bluntly, "The autos ruined the country; let's go back to the horse and buggy and try to save some money."[17] Macon also echoed a common antipathy toward the new taxes southern farmers began paying in the 1920s to finance the construction of the hard-surfaced roads that trucks and automobiles demanded. In "We're up against It Now," Macon sang, "Since the highway's come, they've taxed the farmer down. The road's so slick that his team can't travel when he has to go to town."[18]

Nowhere were these tensions between modernity and tradition more evident than in the Opry's twofold emphasis on blackface minstrelsy and music of the "folk." From minstrelsy's beginnings in the 1830s, the act of blackening up highlighted the performer's and the audience's white identity by creating an "elaborate cultural disguise" that stressed the fact that "whiteness really mattered." In the antebellum urban North, minstrelsy helped build a common racial identity among an ethnically and culturally divided working class. In the early-twentieth-century South, minstrel shows acted as a stage upon which much more homogeneous white audiences could project their fears and anxieties about a rural social and economic order undergoing rapid change. In combination with a growing regional consumer culture that relied upon racially explicit messages that reinforced racial privilege, the Opry was part of a larger cultural process of what historian Elizabeth Hale has called "making whiteness."[19]

Blackface acts continued to draw large crowds on the southern vaudeville circuits even as the form lost its appeal in the North. Itinerant medicine shows remained popular in the South into the early 1930s. In the mid-1920s, Nashville's vaudeville houses hosted itinerant acts like the "Coontown Divorcons," who featured both cross-dressing and a blackface comedian whose signature song was "Roses of Picardy." The Al G. Fields Minstrels, from which the Opry would later attract the blackface duo of Lasses and Honey, regularly included Nashville on its tours. Passing through the city in 1920, the troupe featured Bert Swob, an "old time minstrel and one of the best impersonators of negro characters on the American states."[20]

The role of blackface minstrelsy is usually mentioned and then quickly dismissed as peripheral to early country music and the Opry. In fact, "blacking up" was central to the creation and popular appeal of both the musical genre and the radio program. Pioneering country artists regularly included blackface singers, dancers, and comedians in their acts. Vernon Dalhart, the first country performer to sell a million records, toured regularly with blackface fiddling virtuoso Adelyne Hood. Hood's mammy persona eventually attracted the attention of the Quaker Oats Company, who hired her to play "Aunt Jemimah" on the radio. Alton and Rabon Delmore, popular Opry stars of the early 1930s, also included a blackface duo in their tours.[21]

Racialized humor formed the foundation of George D. Hay's career well before he moved to Nashville to begin the Opry. An Indiana native born in 1895 and raised in Chicago, Hay first attracted notice in the early 1920s as a court reporter for the Memphis *Commercial Appeal*, penning a weekly humor column called "Howdy Judge." He claimed that the material came from his coverage of the Memphis Police Court but admitted that "the imagination was called upon at times." The column was pure minstrelsy in print. Hay built each column around dialogue between a white judge and a succession of clownishly portrayed black defendants. Hay built his humor around re-creations of black dialect and a cruel, racist ridicule of the misfortunes and supposed failings of black folk. In one column, a black defendant complains to Judge L. T. Fitzhugh: "I feels so bad wheah dey busted me on de haid I cain't hahdly stuh 'roun' much, jedge." The judge dismisses the defendant's claims of police brutality and offers a stern rebuke, accusing him of laziness: "I don't see a thing. You've been sleeping so long you have a headache." Another column takes delight in the humiliation of "Sam Blow—Preachin' Man," who is accused of playing the "policy," or numbers racket. Hay ridicules the bivocational tradition among black clergy when the defendant tells the judge, "I ain't pastorn' jes' now, jedge. I'se got me a bahbah shop, but I takes on call now an' den to preach." Hay's characterizations in "Howdy Judge" are crude, even by the contemporary standards of minstrelsy.[22]

"Howdy Judge" launched Hay's career, landing him a brief stint with Chicago's WLS National Barn Dance program, the first major radio review and the model for the WSM Barn Dance. When National Life executives brought Hay to Nashville in 1925 to re-create the success of the Chicago program, Hay quickly integrated the material from his "Howdy Judge" columns into on-air blackface skits. Typically, veteran vaudevillian Ed McConnell, speaking in black dialect as "Uncle Wash," was brought before "Judge Hay" and the two would engage in a dialogue inspired by his columns.[23] Hay sought to capitalize on his new celebrity by republishing his "Howdy Judge" columns in a volume dedicated "to my radio friends." In the race-obsessed minstrelsy of his "Howdy Judge" newspaper column lay the origins of Hay's Grand Ole Opry radio persona, "The Solemn Old Judge." Hay placed his

Lasses and Honey, WSM and Grand Ole Opry black
face minstrels (from *Lasses White's Book of Humor
and Song* [1935])

on-air nickname beneath his real name on the title page of his book to ensure no mistake was made about the connection between "Howdy Judge"
and his Nashville-based radio celebrity.[24]

Hay ended his impromptu minstrel skits when he added the professional
blackface duo of Lee Roy "Lasses" White and Lee David "Honey" Wilds in to
the Opry lineup in 1934. The duo was popular. They had hosted their own
Friday night program on WSM since 1932. The station had featured Lasses
White and His All Star Minstrels in trade publications geared toward spon-
sors, pointing out that the program "not only entertains, but lends itself to
adroit merchandising . . . and happy hearted identification with the product." As part of the Opry, Lasses and Honey and its successor, Jamup and
Honey, continued to be one of the show's more popular acts on radio and
on tour.[25]

Lasses and Honey's routines, which featured comical dialogues and
parodies set to popular songs, played upon rural southerners' growing integration into a national consumer and political culture. "A Cigar Poem,"
opening with the line "Mr. 'Bull Durham' met Miss 'Fatima,'" spoofed nationally advertised tobacco and cigarette brands. Another routine parodied
the jumbled advertising messages broadcast on a succession of dilapidated
roadside billboards: "This is what greeted my eye: smoke the 'Coca-Cola,'
Drink 'Essolene' cigarettes, See 'Greta Garbo' wrestle with a box of 'Cas-

carets.'" Lasses and Honey mocked the consumer products that were now available in even the most remote corners of the rural South when they sang, "The 'Gold Dust Twins' met 'Mary Garden' and 'Camay' in the drug store show case one night." They also offered unstinting praise to Franklin D. Roosevelt and the New Deal programs that were so popular with rural folk. In a parody of the popular song "After the Ball," they sang about a poor, crippled, fatherless child whose mother says, "You may get cured now—after these years, we've got a friend dear—who heard our call. . . . God help us keep Mr. Roosevelt, after the ball." In "The New Deal," a parody of the alphabet soup of New Deal programs, they crooned, "My hat's off to Mr. F.D.R. We're seeing signs again—Wanted—Men for Hire, he put through a deal called the N.R.A. . . . For prosperity's coming P.D.Q."[26]

Reflecting upon his career in the 1970s, Lee Davis "Honey" Wilds defended racialized humor by pointing out that "Jamup and Honey were as popular with blacks as whites" and that "they [blacks] filled the balconies up at almost every show. We didn't think we were making fun of [black people]." Perhaps we can take Wilds at his word. Like minstrels stretching back to T. D. Rice in the 1830s, Wilds was careful about being both "authentic" to his subjects and sympathetic, almost to the point that they identified with his characters.[27]

As with its minstrelsy, the structure of the Opry's musical programming projected a reassuring cultural message that the modernizing changes in the region would not disrupt elements of white southern identity. The biracial origins of upcountry string band traditions have been well established by musicologists and folklorists. The statements of early Opry stars confirm them. Humphrey Bate, Uncle Dave Macon, and Sid Harkreader, for example, all acknowledged the important role of African American teachers and traditions in their early musical training. DeFord Bailey described his own musical roots as "black hillbilly music."[28] These biracial musical traditions, so vital to the nineteenth- and early-twentieth-century upcountry South, did not survive when old-time music first became a saleable commodity in the 1920s. One can interpret Uncle Dave Macon's comments that he "learned the tunes of the darkies" as symbolic blackface. Macon did not literally wear a mask, but his claims of black influence had the same effect of allowing him to briefly and temporarily transgress the color line. Indeed, Piedmont bluesman John Jackson, who knew the Opry only through the radio, grew up believing that Uncle Dave Macon was black.[29]

DeFord Bailey's presence on the early Opry stood as a formal acknowledgment of the biracial elements of old-time music. Bailey was central to the Opry—his harmonica performances were among the most popular performances on the program—and the radio did not directly indicate his race.

The. Wizard of the Harmonica, DE FORD
BAILEY, who plays the Pan-American Blues
that even L. & N. men think it's the real
Pan-American being broadcast over WSM as
it is each evening at 5:40! De Ford knows
his stuff and does his audience like it?

DeFord Bailey, harmonica virtuoso of the early
Grand Ole Opry (Southern Folklife Collection,
University of North Carolina, Chapel Hill)

But Hay refused to accept him as an equal member of the Opry, referring
to Bailey as "a little crippled boy . . . [who] was our mascot." Hay typically
required Bailey to play alone and restricted him to a limited repertoire; he
was fired, ironically, for not learning new tunes.[30] Bailey's allotted role in the
Opry, then, was not as a trailblazing integrator but, as Hay intended, a mascot. Like many of the pioneering white Opry performers, Bailey also hailed
from the rich musical culture of rural Middle Tennessee, and he was descended from a long line of locally prominent musicians. Bailey was caught
between his biracial string band tradition, to which he was devoted, and the
emerging mass media definitions of what was white and what was black.[31]

The Opry, then, was a complex cultural institution that engaged its rural
audience in a subtle cultural dialogue about the meaning of modernity. The
early Grand Ole Opry can stand as a metaphor for the process of urbanization, rural-urban migration, and modernization in the twentieth-century
South. Beneath the patina of the Opry's country culture lay a modern corpo-

ration pioneering the use of radio in the forefront of modern mass-product advertising. The Opry provided an outlet for southerners' ambivalence about modernization while it defined what was white and southern for city dwellers and country folk alike. The experience of rural southerners migrating to the region's cities paralleled the development of the Opry. While themselves products of the rural South, their lives in the countryside were transformed by the economic and social changes embodied in urbanization. As the city beckoned, migrants responded to economic and social change by leaving the farm and forging new lives in the city. Once in town, rural people generally adapted well to urban life. But they did so in an urban social and economic order that reinforced and extended the racial distinctions of the rural South. Thus, like the modern business enterprise behind the Grand Ole Opry, beneath the migrant's country folk patina lay the modern urban dweller.

CHAPTER 2

City and Hinterland

In the spring of 1917 a contingent from Nashville's Booster Club boarded a special train for the thirteenth annual "Booster Trip" through the city's hinterland. The merchants, manufacturers, and businessmen that comprised the Booster Club sought, as they had on their thirteen previous annual excursions, to "renew the friendship with the merchants in each town" who purchased the various goods manufactured in and distributed through the city. The boosters' six-day itinerary took them east over the Tennessee Central and Southern Railroads to Knoxville. They then turned south to Chattanooga before heading back to Nashville on the Nashville, Chattanooga & St. Louis Railroad, "visiting all towns thereon." While America's entry into the European war in April prompted the boosters to add promoting preparedness for the war effort to their stated purpose of "boosting Nashville," the goal of this annual promotional excursion remained unchanged—to foster closer commercial ties between Nashville's merchants and manufacturers and their customers, the smaller wholesale and retail merchants in the towns and hamlets in the economic orbit of the city.[1]

Nashville's businessmen understood that Middle Tennessee, with its numerous towns and hamlets, its natural resources, its varied agriculture, and its teeming population was vital to the city's ongoing growth and prosperity. While geographers have carefully explored the function of metropolitan hinterlands in fostering urban growth, these businessmen knew from their very practical business experience that winning a dominant position in their city's "trading territory" was essential not only to the success of their own businesses but also to the continued economic health of their city. Nashville's businessmen strove to make their firms masters of the commercial and financial economy of Middle Tennessee, to achieve what the geographers characterize as "control of exchange."[2]

Nashville's businessmen also understood that the boundaries of their trading territory were not fixed. Hinterlands could be won or lost, and the collective efforts and will of the business community—boosterism—were

A map of the Booster Club's 1924 trip that helps define the city's
hinterland (*Nashville Tennessean*)

necessary to maintain and extend Nashville's commercial influence and
thus to foster the city's growth. By strengthening the links between city
and hinterland, Nashville businesses brought the city and its goods to the
countryside and contributed to the transformation of rural life that would
lay behind rural outmigration.

The first booster trip in 1903 was a "river trip" that carried businessmen along the Upper Cumberland River. Subsequent trips, all by rail, took
the boosters into eastern and western Tennessee, south central Kentucky,
northern Alabama, and northeastern Mississippi. On each of these trips,
however, the bulk of the booster train's stops were in Middle Tennessee,
the region immediately surrounding Nashville.[3]

Middle Tennessee was much more than just a market to be plumbed by
Nashville's numerous wholesaling and jobbing firms. It was the primary

source of both economic and demographic growth of this Upper South city from 1890 to 1930. It was the chief market for many of the goods produced in Nashville. And the city's banking and insurance firms conducted a large part of their business here as well. Middle Tennessee served as the source of the raw materials for many of the city's most important industries. Its forests supplied the cedar, oak, hickory, and poplar for Nashville's extensive lumber and wood-products manufacturers. Its farms supplied not only a sizable portion of the grain for Nashville's extensive milling industry but also the cattle, hogs, and sheep for the city's livestock markets and meat-packers, the hides for its tanneries, and the tobacco for its snuff and cigar industry. Abundant phosphate deposits nearby fostered the growth of fertilizer manufacturing. In fact, so central to the prosperity of Nashville was its surrounding countryside that one of the local newspapers wrote, "It is the largest single resource of the city."[4]

Nashville owed its growth to its position as a gateway between the Deep South and the Midwest, as well as its preeminent position in Middle Tennessee. The city prospered as an important wholesale and jobbing center, and by the first decades of the twentieth century, Nashville was able to overcome regional capital disadvantages to develop a large banking and insurance sector. The city developed a varied manufacturing base, producing a wide variety of manufactured goods for markets in its more immediate hinterland and the wider South, as well.

Nashville's development, however, showed many of the weaknesses of the southern economy as a whole and that of its immediate hinterland in particular. Late-nineteenth-century southern manufacturers had to compete in a national market against more efficient northern producers who were more skilled and experienced in marketing goods in an increasingly integrated national market.[5] Nashville's merchants and manufacturers sought to overcome this disadvantage by focusing on markets close to home, thus taking advantage of lower transportation costs, raw materials, and close wholesale marketing connections with their city's hinterland.

Great disparities in industrial development existed between Nashville and its hinterland. Middle Tennessee did not experience the diffused pattern of industrialization that characterized the textiles-dominated Georgia and Carolina Piedmont. Industrial development in Middle Tennessee was highly concentrated in Nashville, with little spilling over beyond the city limits. What industry did develop beyond the city's confines, such as lumbering, was extractive, low-value-added, and low-wage. The hinterland upon which Nashville came to depend for its prosperity and growth was beset by an increasingly stagnant agriculture and offered limited opportunities in any endeavor outside of farming. Outmigration from the rural districts of

Middle Tennessee was heavy and sustained during the period of this study, and much of it was directed to Nashville. But Nashville's pull on the rural population was uneven. Its peripheral position in the national economy and its resulting specialization in local and regional markets limited the city's ability to employ all those leaving the countryside.

Late-nineteenth- and early-twentieth-century Nashville was a merchant's city. Commerce and finance comprised the city's leading economic activities, and its merchants and financiers served as the city's economic and political leaders.[6] Nashville's position as a commercial and financial center rested partly on geographic factors: its location between the Midwest and the Deep South and its access to the Ohio and Mississippi Rivers via the Cumberland River. Nashville competed with other southern cities for control of the wholesaling trade of the mid-South. Chief among these were Louisville and Cincinnati to the north; Memphis to the west; Atlanta and Chattanooga to the southeast; and Birmingham to the south, but it was able to emerge as the dominant wholesale market for Middle Tennessee, and the city also enjoyed some influence in southern Kentucky and northern Alabama. Its success relative to other southern cities as a wholesale market was also a product of history: its early start in the commerce of the mid-South, a relatively benign Union occupation, its excellent railroad connections, and the preferential freight rate policies of the leading rail lines serving the city.

Nashville's position as a leading southern wholesale market reached back to the mid-1850s, when the completion of the Nashville & Chattanooga Railroad (later the Nashville, Chattanooga & St. Louis) in 1854 and the Louisville & Nashville in 1859 gave the city's merchants access to the Midwest, as well as the markets of Middle and East Tennessee. Bolstered by its new railroad connections, Nashville's trade grew sharply in the decade before the Civil War. In 1850, before the city enjoyed rail service, the city's three wholesale dry goods houses did a business of some $375,000. On the eve of secession, Nashville's twelve wholesale dry goods firms shipped some $2.25 million in goods. The wholesale grocery business also expanded, by 1860 reaching a trading area that included Middle and East Tennessee, southern Kentucky, and northern Alabama and stretching into Georgia.[7]

During Union occupation, while other southern cities' commerce was disrupted and their infrastructure laid waste by destruction or neglect, Nashville suffered only briefly after its bloodless fall to the Union army in the winter of 1862 and then went on to experience something of a boom, as the Union army used the city as the primary distribution point for its forces in the western theater. Nashville's railways escaped the destruction and neglect that befell railways farther south. The main line into Nashville from the north, the Louisville & Nashville, reaped generous profits from its war traffic and, unlike other southern railroads, emerged from the war in healthy financial and physical condition, ready to expand.[8]

After the Civil War, Nashville's business leaders resumed their efforts to make their city *the* wholesale market for the mid-South. In the late 1870s and 1880s, as the southern railway network began to emerge, Nashville gained connections south to Alabama with the construction of the Nashville & Decatur (Ala.) Railway and to Montgomery with the South & North Railway. Incorporated into the Louisville & Nashville system in the 1880s, these lines linked Nashville to the Deep South through Birmingham and to Chicago and the Midwest via Louisville. The Nashville, Chattanooga & St. Louis Railroad connected Nashville to Memphis in the west, Hickman and Paducah, Kentucky, to the northwest, and Chattanooga and Atlanta to the southeast. The Tennessee Central penetrated the Cumberland Plateau, east of Nashville. Although the L&N acquired controlling interest in the NC&StL in 1881, the larger railroad never merged the operations of the two lines.[9]

These railroad connections allowed Nashville merchants access to northern manufacturers, as well as to the markets in the central South. By 1906, the *Nashville Banner* estimated Nashville's wholesale jobbing trade at some $152 million, dealing in nearly every imaginable line of goods.[10] The agents of Nashville's jobbing and wholesale firms scoured Middle Tennessee and the central South, supplying small-town merchants with all manner of goods from agricultural implements, coffee, hardware, and lumber to tobacco and printed goods.

These "commercial travelers" were the backbone of Nashville's wholesaling economy. While studies of boosterism and urban rivalry have centered on who won or lost the trading regions, the role of the men who actually drummed up the business that kept the city's merchants and manufacturers busy—drummers, traveling salesmen, and other itinerant agents—has largely been ignored. These men were the first links on the wholesale distribution chain that connected Nashville to its commercial hinterland. While mail-order business became important throughout rural America, including the South, after the introduction of rural free delivery in 1896, new products typically reached the countryside through the commercial travelers' order books. Traveling salesmen took advantage of the city's excellent railroad connections, combing the countryside, visiting small-town and country merchants, soliciting the orders that moved goods out of Nashville's warehouses and factories, and building the customer base among Middle Tennessee merchants that was the foundation of Nashville's success as a commercial and manufacturing city.

Nashville's commercial travelers thought in terms of territory. They viewed their job and the trade of their city in essentially geographic terms. Traveling salesmen viewed the sales territory as the fundamental unit of business, an area throughout which they traveled constantly, building trading relationships and contacts with the numerous country and small-town merchants. While Nashville's boosters were fond of claiming dominance in a trading territory, commercial travelers understood that most of their sales territories were constantly contested terrain. Representatives from other Nashville firms and, more commonly, from firms in other cities all competed for the wholesale trade of the country and small-town merchants. Nashville's commercial travelers used martial metaphors to describe the inter-urban competition for dominance in trading territories. They were an "army of commercial travelers." Their comings and goings were reported in a column in the *Nashville Tennessean* titled "Rank and File." When out in their territories soliciting orders, they were on the "Firing line."[11]

Nashville's businessmen believed that the commercial travelers' skills and tenacity set the boundaries of the city's trading area and thus contributed to the growth of the city. "Traveling men have [the] power to make a bigger and better city," reported the *Nashville Tennessean*, adding that the "efforts of every traveler will result in [the] growth of Nashville."[12] Nashville wholesalers and manufacturers "all have their live up-to-date men out covering every town, village and hamlet in the South." The grocery wholesaler "keeps his men scouring his territory with a fine-tooth comb." The city's Board of Trade noted that "the frequency with which these Nashville salesmen call upon the retailers [in the countryside] largely aids in the development of Nashville's trade."[13] Nashville's wholesalers "are the most important factor in building a city," claimed one paper; "Nashville has on the road, covering a large part of the South like the dew, an army of high class men who are daily sounding the praises of Tennessee's capital."[14]

The actual territory covered by Nashville's commercial travelers by the 1910s and 1920s tended to vary with particular lines of goods. Low-value, bulk, or perishable goods tended to be traded close to home. One representative for a hat dealer was reported as "having a fine business in the upper Cumberland territory."[15] Another salesman for the Dowell-Hawes Clothing Company sold in West Tennessee.[16] Sam F. Knott, of Spurlock-Neal, a wooden spoke and handle manufacturer, was well established in the territory covered by the Nashville and Chattanooga railroad southeast of Nashville.[17] W. R. Montcrief of the Huggins Candy Company was reported as having arrived in town from just outside of Nashville with a "dandy bunch of orders."[18] R. E. McElroy represented Robert Orr & Company, a wholesale grocer, "in the Sparta [Tennessee] territory." In the early 1920s, the Cherokee mills, one of the city's largest flour mills, had a wider reach, selling its flour "over a territory for two hundred miles east, west, and south of Nashville."[19]

Higher-value products tended to have a wider distribution. The Phillips & Buttorff Stove works sold its stoves throughout the South. It was reported in March of 1917 that its vice president had just returned from a "successful trip through the [Mississippi] Delta Territory."[20] The Gray & Dudley Company, a hardware and agricultural implements manufacturer and wholesaler, employed a force of fifty-five to sixty salesmen who traveled "through the central, southern, southwestern and southeastern states."[21]

Not all wholesaling was conducted through traveling commercial men. Merchants from the outlying towns and the countryside made periodic buying trips to Nashville to stock the shelves of their stores back home. The *Nashville Tennessean* reported that "there is a continuous stream of merchants coming to the Nashville market to buy merchandise" to supply the "immense volume of consumers" in Middle Tennessee.[22] The comings and goings of the more important country merchants were recorded in the press. In spring 1917, for example, the *Tennessean* reported that O. T. Reynolds, "a prominent merchant of Dover, Tennessee," conducted his business in Nashville's wholesale market. Likewise, the newspaper stated that a representative of the Jere Whitson Hardware Company, "one of the Cumberland Plateau's largest and most enterprising mercantile concerns and . . . a strong friend of the Nashville market," purchased stock in Nashville.[23]

In an effort to advance such wholesale purchases, Nashville's merchants sponsored promotions such as Buyer's Week to attract hinterland merchants. By the early 1920s, to maintain the city's position in an increasingly competitive environment, Nashville's merchants were offering to refund railroad fares of merchants who traveled to Nashville to purchase their stock. Fares of merchants living within 50 to 100 miles were refunded if they purchased at least $500 worth of goods, while merchants beyond 100 miles were so rewarded if they purchased $1,000 worth of goods.[24]

How, then, can Nashville's hinterland be defined? If one were to follow the pronouncements of its businessmen and booster press, it would be large, indeed. The Nashville Board of Trade claimed in 1909 that the city's wholesale trade territory stretched from "Virginia to Texas, from Indiana, Illinois, and Missouri and all the states between."[25] Nearly fifteen years later the *Nashville Tennessean* claimed that "as a central distributing point [Nashville] is without equal" because it stood at "almost the exact geographical center of a circle that includes Buffalo on the northeast, Dallas on the southwest, Des Moines on the northwest and Jacksonville on the southeast."[26]

Such extravagant claims were, of course, so much wishful thinking. As

This cartoon, which appeared in the *Nashville Tennessean*, shows how Nashville's wholesale merchants envisioned the city's relationship to its hinterland in the mid-1920s.

the annual booster trips and trade patterns discussed above suggest, Nashville's economy was tied closely to rural Middle Tennessee. For analytical purposes, this study defines Nashville's hinterland as the forty-two counties of Middle Tennessee, from the Tennessee River in the west, reaching into the Cumberland Plateau to the east. While Nashville's influence spread farther, especially into northern Alabama and central Kentucky, this represents the area in which Nashville's economic pull was greatest.

The scale and scope of Nashville's hinterland can be charted systematically by looking at the development of its banking industry, which began in the early nineteenth century and did not mature until the early twentieth century.[27] After 1900, Nashville's banks competed successfully with the banks of other southern cities, especially Louisville, for banking dominance. The scope of Nashville's banking industry was highly regional, its reach primarily limited to Nashville's trading territory. The source of prosperity among Nashville's banks was not domination of the entire South but, instead, dominance within its more restricted hinterland of Middle Tennessee.

One can measure the increasing dominance in Tennessee of Nashville-based banks by tracing correspondent linkages between rural and small-town banks in the state and larger urban banks in Nashville and other southern cities. Banks would establish correspondent accounts with banks in larger cities to facilitate financial transactions. Larger banks would compete for the correspondent accounts of hinterland banks.[28] Virtually all of Tennessee's state and nationally chartered banks followed standard practice in maintaining correspondent accounts with one of the larger New York banks, reflecting the reality that New York was the banking hub of the entire nation. However, small-town Tennessee banks also maintained one additional correspondent account with a bank in a regional banking center to facilitate local and regional transactions. As Nashville's banks grew from 1890 to the 1920s, they held an increasing number of the correspondent accounts of Tennessee's small-town banks. The trend in correspondent linkages was clearly toward Nashville-based banks and away from banks based in other banking centers such as Louisville, St. Louis, Cincinnati, and Memphis. Neither Atlanta nor Birmingham, two leading southern banking centers, had much of a presence in Tennessee, as measured by correspondent linkages. Nor did Nashville have much of a presence in Kentucky or Alabama.

In 1890 Louisville was Nashville's chief rival for the dominant banking position in Tennessee, and especially Middle Tennessee. Of the 128 Tennessee banks that maintained a correspondent account with a regional bank in 1890, 41 held their accounts with a Louisville bank and 40 held accounts with a Nashville bank. The remaining banks maintained their correspondent accounts with banks based in other cities: 15 held accounts in Cincinnati, 9 in Knoxville, 7 in Memphis, 6 in St. Louis, 3 in Chicago, 2 in Chattanooga, and 1 each in Baltimore, Kansas City, New Orleans, Philadelphia, and the hamlet of Sparta, Tennessee.

On the surface, it appears that Louisville and Nashville were about even in their competition for the correspondent accounts of Tennessee banks in

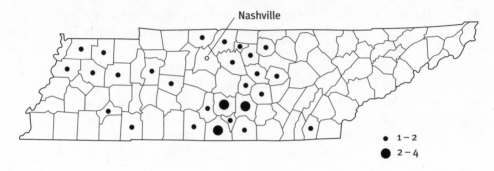

Map 2.1. Nashville's Correspondent Banks, 1890

1890, reflecting the rivalry between the two original termini of the Louisville & Nashville Railroad. Louisville, however, enjoyed the advantage of
holding correspondent accounts of much more heavily capitalized banks
than those held by Nashville's banks. The average capitalization of the Tennessee banks with correspondent accounts in Louisville was $79,559, nearly
twice the average capitalization ($40,144) of the Tennessee banks that main-
tained correspondent accounts in Nashville banks. In 1890, the largest
banks in Middle Tennessee towns maintained accounts with Louisville-
based banks, while Nashville dominated the business of the smaller, less
capitalized banks in the smaller towns (see Map 2.1).[29]

This differential eroded as Nashville's banks grew in size. By 1904 Nashville's banks held the correspondent accounts of sixty Tennessee banks, primarily in Middle Tennessee. Louisville, on the other hand, held correspondent accounts from only twenty-seven, albeit heavier capitalized, banks.
The banks that continued to hold their correspondent accounts with Louis-
ville-based banks were primarily located in the tobacco-dominated Black
Patch, which was closely tied to Louisville's tobacco industry. After Nashville and Louisville, the leading cities competing for the correspondent
accounts of Tennessee's banks were Knoxville, with twenty-four banks,
St. Louis, with thirteen, Memphis, with twelve, and Chattanooga, with
seven. As in 1890, however, Louisville's banks were roughly twice as heavily
capitalized as Nashville's, reflecting Louisville's dominance among banks
based in larger towns and cities of the state. Louisville's average capitalization was $55,902, while the average capitalization for Nashville's banks was
$30,436.[30]

By the 1920s, a decade of sustained expansion of the city's banks, Nashville emerged as the dominant banking city of Tennessee, its position augmented by its recently acquired Federal Reserve branch. By 1925 Louisville

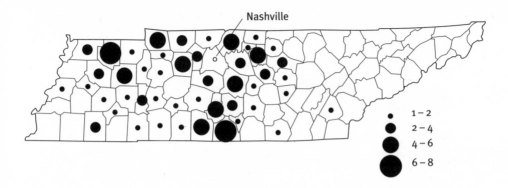

Map 2.2. Nashville's Correspondent Banks, 1925

held correspondent accounts of only three relatively small banks in Middle Tennessee. Nashville, on the other hand, held correspondent accounts from 130 of the 189 banks in the state. After Nashville, only Memphis, with correspondent accounts of twenty-four banks, maintained an appreciable role in Tennessee banking. Nashville's preeminence among the numerous small-town banks in Tennessee was nearly complete (see Map 2.2).[31]

Nashville's emerging banking power in Tennessee was a source of prosperity not only for the city's banks but for its credit-hungry wholesale houses as well. This fact did not go unnoticed by local observers. Acknowledging the close connection between banking and commerce, the *Nashville Banner* claimed that the city's banking industry "has greatly increased since the Booster expeditions were first started."[32] The regional emphasis of Nashville's banking industry was closely tied to the reach of its wholesale commerce.

Insurance was the other branch of Nashville's formidable finance industry, emerging soon after the Civil War with the founding of the Nashville Life Insurance Company in 1867. That company sought to capitalize on sectional pride and fears of economic domination from the North by directing its efforts to southerners seeking insurance from a company that would "invest in their state or section" and would not discriminate against writing insurance for southerners living in purportedly unhealthy Deep South climates, as some northern insurance companies were accused of doing.[33]

However, Nashville's early start in insurance was limited and it failed to lead to the development of a substantial industry. The Nashville Life Insurance Company seems to have expired sometime in the 1880s. There were other, smaller companies based in Nashville as well, but they were undercapitalized and did not survive the depression of the 1890s. Not until the early twentieth century did Nashville's insurance industry develop into a substantial regional power and an important sector of the city's economy. It did so with the founding in the early 1900s of two life insurance companies that would come to dominate the insurance industry of the city and the South as well: the National Life and Accident Insurance Company and the Life and Casualty Company. Both companies emerged when the South's insurance industry began a sustained take-off, and both initially focused primarily on regional markets.[34]

National Life grew out of a Huntsville, Alabama–based benevolent association founded in 1897 and devoted to selling "industrial insurance." By 1900 the company had moved to Nashville, selling life and disability insurance policies to working families. Before World War I, National Life also built a strong business among southern blacks, selling relatively low-cost disability and death benefit plans.[35]

Early on, unlike many of Nashville's businesses, National Life expanded in a limited way beyond its original territory of Tennessee, Alabama, and Kentucky, into markets north of the Ohio River, opening an Evansville, Indiana, branch in 1903.[36] By 1909 the company was conducting business in nine states, mostly in the South.[37] In the 1920s National Life and Accident emerged into a national concern with offices in twenty-one states stretching from Pennsylvania to California, although the heart of its business was still in the South. The company employed some 2,350 agents and office workers across the country and was rapidly expanding upon its $8.5 million assets. By 1930 the company had assets of $29.6 million.[38]

Life and Casualty Company emerged as the chief Nashville-based competition for National Life. Smaller than National Life—its assets in 1930 stood at $12.2 million—before World War I it concentrated strictly on selling insurance in Tennessee. In the 1920s it expanded to a wider southern market, with 1,500 employees selling insurance throughout the South and working in its Nashville home office.[39]

Smaller companies bolstered Nashville's insurance industry. They, too, focused their efforts on regional markets. The Independent Life Insurance Company, founded in 1908, had offices in thirteen southern cities and assets of just under $900,000. The Lincoln Fire Insurance Company, begun in 1913, specialized in the African American market, selling "fire protection to the laboring man on the small payment plan." The Southern Insurance Company, established in 1909, also did an extensive business in the region.[40]

Thus, Nashville developed commercial and financial industries that engendered economic growth in the city by relying upon primarily regional markets to which it gained access with its army of commercial travelers. Its wholesale commerce, banking, and insurance concerns carved a niche for themselves by concentrating on markets close to home.

Nashville's business leaders saw their hinterland as central to the city's manufacturing industry. In the 1870s and early 1880s, Nashville's leading businessmen, imbued with a strong sense of self-interested regional and civic boosterism, and bolstered by the rhetoric of a New South of business and industry, envisioned that Nashville's position in a region rich in the products of field and forest, mill and mine, destined the city to emerge as a leading southern industrial metropolis. In 1874, Joseph B. Killebrew, a prominent New South propagandist born just outside the city, predicted that Nashville's access to natural resources "will make Nashville, in time, a great manufacturing center . . . ring[ing] with the hum of industry."[41] An 1890 promotional publication claimed that "one secret of the expansion of Nashville's manufactures [is that] the elements of iron, wood, and cotton . . . are convenient of access."[42] A booster history published that same year attributed Nashville's "progress and good name" to the fact that "the agricultural and mineral resources of that portion of the State tributary to Nashville are practically inexhaustible" and suggested that the city's economic prospects were similarly limitless.[43]

Two of those natural resources that might build Nashville into a great manufacturing city were coal and iron ore. Iron ore deposits of varying quality were located along the western Highland Rim, and coal deposits were ample east of the city beneath the Cumberland Plateau. Indeed, there had been a vigorous, small-scale, charcoal-based iron industry west of the city before the Civil War.[44] In the 1880s New South boosters argued that access to these deposits and expanded access to iron and coal deposits to the east would lead to the development of a modern iron industry near or within the city. Advocating the completion of the rail line between Nashville and Knoxville, the *Nashville Daily American* predicted that it would give Nashville easy access to "the coal of Kentucky on the north, that of the Cumberland coal fields on the east, and that of Alabama on the South, all within convenient distance, and, including the near western belt of iron deposits, more iron within convenient distance than any other city in Tennessee, or, perhaps, the United States." Indeed, the *American* argued that the mid-South metropolis had access to "a larger variety and greater quantity of ores within a compass of three hundred miles than Pittsburg [sic] has within a range of at least one thousand miles."[45]

Nashville's natural advantages for developing into a center for iron production turned out to be less than ideal, however. The brown ore beneath the western Highland Rim was of poor quality and unsuited for modern blast furnace methods.[46] Coal from the east was not forthcoming, either, as the eastward railroad link through the Upper Cumberland Plateau called for in 1881 had to wait until 1902, when the Tennessee Central railroad was completed. Even then, the Tennessee Central, persistently short of capital, was unable to build the spur lines and acquire the rolling stock necessary for the full development of coal mining in the Cumberland Plateau. Although the Nashville-based Tennessee Coal, Iron & Railroad Company operated coke ovens and blast furnaces southeast of Nashville in Cowan and Tracy City, Tennessee, the focus of its operations quickly shifted to northern Alabama and Birmingham in the 1880s.[47]

By the 1890s the locus of southern iron production had bypassed Nashville and was firmly planted in the Birmingham district. What iron production continued in Tennessee centered in and around Chattanooga, and even this industry floundered after 1900. Plagued by outdated equipment, a lack of capital, and competition from more efficient Birmingham firms, Tennessee's iron industry went into a steep decline in the early years of the twentieth century, with the last Chattanooga blast furnace closing in 1919.[48]

While Nashvillians failed to see blast furnaces arise in their city's midst, Nashville did, nonetheless, develop an important foundry industry, manufacturing all manner of iron products from agricultural implements to stoves. The largest concerns, Phillips & Buttorff and Gray & Dudley, manufactured a wide array of inexpensive copper, tin, and sheet-metal products, along with coal and wood stoves. Phillips & Buttorff was particularly successful, growing into the South's largest manufacturer of stoves by the turn of the century. By the 1920s Phillips & Buttorff's 400 workers produced about 100,000 stoves annually. Gray & Dudley also employed about 400, a large number of them inmates at the state penitentiary.[49]

While Phillips & Buttorff and Gray & Dudley distributed their goods throughout the South, and even beyond the region, they were the exception among Nashville's iron-products manufacturers. As with Nashville's wholesalers, the city's foundry industry concentrated on serving local markets. Nashville's iron-products concerns produced for local and regional markets in Middle Tennessee and the mid-South, relying upon the city's advantageous location and low freight rates to compete with other southern and midwestern manufacturers and distributing their products primarily through the city's wholesale network. The firm of B. G. Wood, a manufacturer of boilers, tanks, and other sheet-iron goods, was typical of the regional market of Nashville's iron industries. "The trade of the firm extends over Middle and West Tennessee, Southern Kentucky, and North Alabama," reported one observer in 1890.[50] This market pattern remained the same for Nashville's foundries through the 1920s. The firms of John Beachard &

Sons and Jakes Foundry sent 90 percent of their output of cast-iron pipes, manhole covers, and other foundry products to cities in the South through Nashville-based jobbers in the 1920s.[51]

Nashville's merchants and boosters also looked to textiles to develop the city's manufacturing base soon after the Civil War, and the first large factory began operating in 1872. With 400 looms and nearly 14,000 spindles, the Tennessee Manufacturing Company employed some 268 workers—202 of them women—in the production of "heavy brown sheetings." By 1890 the plant had prospered enough to expand into a second building, increasing its capacity to 35,000 spindles and 1,018 looms and employing some 800 workers.[52] Three more mills—the Nashville Woolen Mills, the Nashville Cotton Mills, and the National Manufacturing Company—followed in the late 1870s and 1880s.

But by the mid-1880s, at the moment that the textile industry was beginning to expand in the Carolina and Georgia Piedmont, it slowed in Nashville. By the turn of the century, Nashville was home to just two mills: the Nashville Woolen Mills and the Morgan & Hamilton Mills, successors of the Tennessee Manufacturing Company. By 1920, there were just three cotton textile mills and one hosiery mill in Nashville and textiles accounted for only a small portion of the city's manufacturing base.[53]

Thus, while textiles always maintained a presence in Nashville's industrial economy, it was not a strong one. As with the iron industry, Nashville's natural advantages for cotton goods production touted by the city's boosters were less than ideal.[54] The broad expanse of the Cumberland River offered few opportunities to harness water power, and Nashville was too far from important markets for cotton textiles in the Northeast. Finally, the potential sources for investment in textiles may have been limited, since Nashville's economic diversity—including banking, insurance, or other manufacturing concerns—presented many competing investment options. Consequently, by the 1920s, the city's surviving firms concentrated on the manufacture of cheap cotton and burlap bagging and hosiery to be sold primarily in the South.[55]

Textiles, Nashville's business leaders realized, were not much of a city builder, either. Mill villages tended to be small and were generally located away from metropolitan areas where there was little competition for labor. Indeed, by the 1920s many of Nashville's leading businessmen interested in developing the city's manufacturing base had soured on textiles, noting that isolation and low wages of textile jobs offered little benefit to the city's economy. A. M. Burton, president of the Life & Casualty Insurance Company—perhaps prompted by difficulties in getting millworkers interested in life insurance—expressed this sentiment during a meeting of the Industrial Committee of the city's chamber of commerce, arguing that cotton mills "bring very little wealth to a community" because the mill operatives "are usually locked up in their mill villages where commissaries are provided and little if any business gets beyond the village."[56] As with the iron-products industries in the city, textiles were an important but only secondary component of Nashville's industrial base.

Heavy industry never took root in the city. Instead, light manufactures —wood products, grain milling, and meat processing—formed the backbone of industrial Nashville. All three industries depended upon supplies of raw material or markets in the city's hinterland and the wider South and served regional markets. Nashville's access to the old-growth forests of the Cumberland Plateau spurred the development of an extensive wood-products industry, which included makers of barrel staves, lumber, spokes, and handles and furniture factories. Nashville sat in the middle of a veritable kingdom of virgin forest in the late nineteenth century, one ripe for development at precisely the time the white pine stands of the Great Lakes region had been cut over. Before the Civil War, Nashville's timber industry centered around the production of white oak barrel staves, which were exported to the breweries and wineries of Europe via New Orleans. In addition, untold millions of board-feet of red cedar were exported from the forests of Middle Tennessee to be used as railroad crossties. Red cedar, valued for its rot-resistant qualities, continued to be logged heavily in the 1870s and 1880s for fence wood, telegraph poles, and buckets.[57]

As northern hardwood stocks became exhausted in the 1870s, demand for Tennessee hardwood timber increased. Timber scouts began scouring the forests of Tennessee and Kentucky, purchasing the largest, highest-grade black walnut, white oak, yellow poplar, and ash trees.[58] Massive trees were so plentiful that loggers only bothered to take the trunks below the first branch, leaving the rest behind. Poplar trees typically "squared" twenty-four inches, with thirty-four-inch diameters; and they would easily yield 10,000 or more board-feet of lumber. Payment to the landowner was typically "fifty cents a foot across the stump," so a tree with a diameter of nearly three feet would earn the farmer $1.50.[59] In the early 1880s, some 15 million board-feet of yellow poplar, the leading species in the Nashville market, were being rafted down the Cumberland River each year. Most timber reached Nashville during the spring and fall, when high water swelled the rivers and tributaries to the Upper Cumberland. By 1900 the volume of timber and lumber entering Nashville made the city the nation's leading hardwood lumber market.[60]

Nashville developed an extensive lumber and wood-products industry to process the raw lumber arriving from the Upper Cumberland. Most of the mills sat along the gently sloping bank of the Cumberland River opposite the city center in East Nashville, and they incorporated the manufacture of a variety of finished goods along with the processing of the logs into lumber. The firm of Liebermann, Loveman & O'Brian, one of the largest buyers of hardwood timber along the Upper Cumberland River in the 1890s, employed some 225 hands in the manufacture of hardwood flooring, shingles, boxes, and other building materials, in addition to operating a mill that could produce more than ten million feet of lumber a year. Nashville's leading furniture maker in the 1890s, the Edgefield and Nashville Manufacturing Company, a manufacturer of inexpensive home and commercial furniture, employed some 400 employees in its East Nashville plant. The lumber and wood-products industries accounted for 24 percent of all manufacturing employment in 1890.[61]

Yet, at the very point that Nashville emerged as the leading hardwood timber and lumber market, employment in wood-products industries entered a period of decline as the once bountiful timber in the city's hinterland, especially along the Upper Cumberland, became scarce. While the number of firms remained stable from 1890 to 1920, at twenty-six and twenty-nine, respectively, the number of operatives employed by them actually declined steadily from 1,979 in 1889, to 1,288 in 1909, to 1,041 in 1920. By 1930, there were so few lumber and wood-products manufacturers in Nashville that the census did not provide separate employment figures for them.[62]

By the early 1920s, Nashville's larger lumber concerns were already moving their operations to timberlands in Arkansas, Mississippi, and Louisiana. Nashville could no longer claim to be Tennessee's leading lumber and wood-products city, having fallen behind Memphis in both the wholesale hardwood lumber trade and the manufacture of wood products. City leaders sought to convince themselves in the 1920s that the wood was not running out, arguing that virgin timber remained plentiful in the Upper Cumberland, and even in Nashville's own Davidson County, but the reality was that the hardwood lumber industry was moving west. The city's wood and lumber industries had declined, never to return to their former prominence. Indeed, Southern lumber production as a portion of that of the nation's peaked in 1921; after 1928, the center of the nation's lumber industry shifted to the old-growth forests of the Pacific Northwest.[63]

As with its wood-based industries, Nashville's substantial flour milling industry arose as a result of an advantage that proved to be transitory. Unlike that of the lumber and wood-products industries, the advantage that built the milling industry in the city was man-made. The Louisville & Nashville Railroad, in a deliberate policy to build Nashville into the "Minneapolis of the South," pursued a preferential rate policy that gave Nashville-based millers a cost advantage over other Tennessee and mid-South millers. The milling industry prospered as a result. When the Interstate Commerce Commission overturned Nashville's favored position in the L&N rate structure in the 1920s, its milling industry declined.

Wheat was an important crop for Middle Tennessee farmers, and since the early nineteenth century they had sent their annual harvest of grain to Nashville to be milled. As early as 1817, Nashville was home to a steam-powered flour mill. The industry expanded rapidly in the 1870s after the L&N railroad began its rate policy. In the 1880s, Nashville's mills took the lead in the South in building large, capital-intensive mills employing the latest technology and supplying much of the central South with flour. In 1881 Nashville's Lanier Mill Company was the first southern plant to convert to the more modern and efficient roller process, increasing its milling capacity from 300 to 500 barrels of flour per day. Although the number of mills in the city declined in the 1880s, the capacity of the city's milling industry actually increased as the larger, more heavily capitalized mills replaced the older, smaller mills. By the 1890s the city's largest mill, the Nashville Mill Company, was producing 1,000 barrels of flour per day.[64] By 1919 six mills were in operation in the city. With the wartime boom, they continued to prosper into the early 1920s. E. C. Faircloth Jr., the manager of the Cherokee Flour mills, one of the city's largest, with a daily capacity of 2,000 barrels of flour, reported in 1923 that he was running his mill twenty-four hours per day at full capacity to meet demand. He expected "the coming twelve months will be the most prosperous since war-time days." The city's other mills also were reported as operating "at capacity."[65]

As mentioned above, however, the success of Nashville's flour millers rested on their advantageous freight rates. The city's millers had long ago outstripped Middle Tennessee's grain production, and as early as the 1880s, these mills were relying on northern-grown grain.[66] The series of Interstate Commerce Commission decisions that culminated in the Southern Freight Rate Investigation of 1925 undermined the L&N's preferential rate structure. Nonetheless, in 1930 Nashville was home to nine mills, three more than in 1919, producing $3.6 million worth of flour for a primarily southern market. Nashville's mills specialized in flours geared toward southern tastes, producing low-gluten, or soft-wheat, flours, as well as self-rising flour. Like Nashville's iron products and foundry industries, the market for the city's flour was primarily restricted to the South and the more immediate hinterland of the city.[67]

Nashville's vigorous livestock market and meat processing industry also depended upon the produce of the city's hinterland in Middle Tennessee. Stock raising had long been a mainstay of Middle Tennessee agriculture, and the region was famous for its mules and horses, the former shipped to farms of the South, the latter to the farms of the Midwest.[68] By 1873 the city's stockyards posted receipts for some 21,000 cattle, 35,000 hogs, and 18,000 sheep; seven years later the city claimed five stockyards and three pork-packing concerns, although throughout this early period most of the livestock entering the city was reshipped to other markets, usually farther south.[69]

By 1910 Nashville's position as the leading southern livestock market was assured. The *Nashville Banner* noted that Middle Tennessee was raising over $30 million in livestock each year and that "there is hardly any limit to the livestock that might be grown in Middle Tennessee."[70] These predictions for growth rang true. The number of cattle received at the city's now con-solidated Union Stockyards increased by one-third from 1916 to 1920. The number of hogs received increased by 64 percent and sheep, by 141 percent during the same four-year period. In 1920 the city's stockyards received 98,773 cattle, 614,523 hogs, and 129,172 sheep and earned cash receipts of over $90 million.[71] While only one-quarter of the livestock received at Nashville was slaughtered and processed at the city's meatpacking houses in 1920, by 1940 the proportion of livestock locally slaughtered and pro-cessed increased to 75 percent of all livestock received at Nashville.[72]

Like the city's other industries, Nashville's meatpackers produced for lo-cal and regional markets. Nashville's largest meat processor, the Neuhoff Packing Company, sold its cured meats primarily in the South through its force of twenty-seven traveling salesmen. While the firm enjoyed "a fine big business in the city of Nashville [and] surrounding territories," it also sent eighteen to twenty-five railroad cars of products "to Birmingham, Atlanta, through[out] North and South Carolina, and Virginia."[73]

But Nashville's livestock industry did not simply enrich the city by provid-ing profits for its livestock dealers and employment for its citizens. As one of the local papers pointed out, the high prices offered at the city's livestock markets attracted sellers from a wide area and "put money into [farmers'] pockets," much of it being spent in Nashville. The *Nashville Tennessean* ex-horted that "the citizenry of Nashville should well appreciate the rapid de-velopment of this great enterprise as it brings thousands of people here all through the year who sell their cattle, hogs and sheep for cash."[74]

Other manufacturing industries that relied on easy access to raw materi-als and served local or regional markets developed in Nashville in the 1910s and 1920s. A vigorous fertilizer industry emerged on the western fringes of the city, bolstered by southern farmers' increasing use of commercial fertilizers and by the extensive phosphate deposits in nearby Williamson, Giles, Maury, and Hickman Counties. Middle Tennessee and central Kentucky's dark-fire tobacco came into the city to be manufactured into snuff at the Weyman & Bruton Company. The city was also an important printing and publishing center, particularly of religious materials. The maintenance facilities of the city's two railroads also employed large numbers of men.[75]

Thus, while in many ways Nashville's manufacturing economy was strong and diversified, two characteristics of Nashville's industrial development bore directly upon the patterns of migration in Middle Tennessee. First, industrial development was highly concentrated in Nashville and surrounding Davidson County—much more so than it was in the textile-dominated Georgia and Carolina Piedmont. As a result, industrial development in the counties surrounding Nashville lagged as capital and labor were drawn to the city. Rural and small-town flour milling and lumber concerns were particularly hard hit as more efficient, capital-intensive processes displaced them. In a process resembling Gunnar Myrdal's "backwash" effect, Nashville's industrialization encouraged migration from the city's hinterland by undermining opportunities for rural off-farm employment.[76]

The fact that Nashville's manufacturing industries tended to specialize in simple, low-value-added production primarily for regional and local markets also affected migration patterns in Middle Tennessee. The city's industrial base rested upon a foundation of wood-products manufacturing, grain milling, and meat processing, along with some textiles, printing, and fertilizer manufacturing. This thin manufacturing base meant that the city was unable to absorb all those who were leaving rural Middle Tennessee. Hence, industrial development in Nashville and Middle Tennessee helped to promote migration from rural Middle Tennessee, yet it could not provide opportunity for all those leaving the farms in the region.

The disparities in manufacturing development between the rural counties of Middle Tennessee and Nashville in the late nineteenth and early twentieth centuries are striking. Per capita value added by manufacturing in Davidson County in 1890 was $65.98, while in the forty-one rural Tennessee counties that comprised Nashville's hinterland, it was only $6.46. This disparity stayed constant throughout the entire period under consideration. In 1929 per capita value added in Davidson County had increased $3^{1/3}$ times (in unadjusted dollars) to $289.04, while that of the counties of Nashville's hinterland increased at nearly an equivalent rate to $28.36. No other single county approached the level of development of Nashville's Davidson County. Among hinterland counties in 1890, Houston County held the highest figure at a mere $21.87, and twenty-one out of the forty-one hinterland counties had levels of per capita value added by manufacturing of less than $10.00. The range was similar in 1929. After some forty years, twenty-nine of the rural Middle Tennessee counties exhibited per capita value-added figures of less than $50.00. In the terminology of developmental economics, Nashville was certainly a "growth pole," or core, attracting capital and labor—much of it at the expense of its hinterland.[77] But Nashville developed a relatively weak pole and a relatively low density core.

Nashville's limited manufacturing development stemmed from the city's, and the entire South's, peripheral position in the national economy in the nineteenth and early twentieth centuries. American industrialization began in the antebellum Northeast and expanded in a series of westward spreading industrial regions, forming the modern American manufacturing belt by 1880. The South, failing to develop a significant manufacturing region before the Civil War, found itself unable to compete with more established, more efficient, and more capitalized northern firms. Furthermore, the natural resource endowment of Middle Tennessee and the South as a whole paled before the richness of the Midwest, with its fortuitous combination of oil, coal, and iron ore, all easily transported by the Great Lakes and a topography well suited to the railroad. Thus Nashville shared the South's dilemma of being unable to move beyond local resources and local markets.[78] As a consequence, despite efforts to develop iron and textile industries, the city concentrated on a variety of relatively low value-added industries for primarily southern and hinterland markets.

The hopes that Nashville would emerge as the South's leading iron or textile center were never realized. While the city did develop other industries based upon access to the raw materials and markets in its hinterland—lumber, wheat, and livestock—these resources did not develop the city into a great manufacturing center. During the first thirty years before the onset of the Great Depression, the most dynamic sectors of its economy lay in commerce and finance. The pattern of uneven development between Nashville and its hinterland stunted off-farm employment opportunities, contributing to the decision of thousands to leave rural Middle Tennessee. In the end, Nashville's pull on the rural population was uneven. As we shall see, by the 1920s, women rather than men and whites rather than blacks could expect to find greater opportunities in Nashville.

CHAPTER 3

The Countryside

The rural hinterland that Nashville's business leaders looked to as the source of their city's growth and prosperity entered the twentieth century in an increasing state of economic and social crisis. Rooted in the increasingly bleak prospects that Middle Tennessee agriculture faced after the 1890s, this crisis shaped rural dwellers' perceptions of future opportunities as farmers, persuading thousands to abandon agriculture and the countryside.

Middle Tennessee's burgeoning farm population faced a population crisis that placed harsh pressures on the household economy and disrupted the social organization of the region's general farming regime. As more and more rural Middle Tennesseans entered an already crowded agricultural sector, increasing competition for land pushed farm values upward, and Middle Tennessee farmers found it ever more costly to acquire farms suitable for supporting their families. Farms tended to grow smaller, and young people found it more difficult to gain access to farmland, start their own families, and continue in agriculture. For young people coming of age after the turn of the century, the price of entering the livelihood of their parents and grandparents was rising, and rising sharply.[1]

Nashville's Middle Tennessee hinterland—its "largest single resource," as the city's booster press frequently referred to it—reached across three physiographic sections: the Central Basin, the Highland Rim, and the Cumberland Plateau.[2] Each section had its own distinctive geographic features, crops, market orientation, and soil characteristics, and these influenced the primary components of each section's agriculture.

The heart of Nashville's Middle Tennessee hinterland was the Central Basin. A fertile agricultural region of rolling hills and shallow valleys stretching across some sixteen counties, including Nashville's Davidson County, the Basin's fertile brown and red loam soils supported a varied and productive agriculture, earning it the epithet "Garden of Tennessee."[3] The Basin contained Middle Tennessee's most fertile soils, and its farmers were

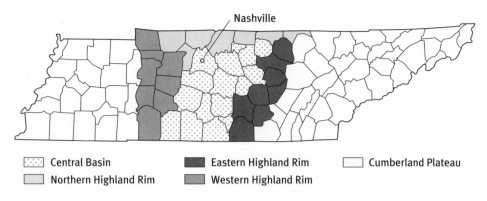

Nashville

Central Basin **Eastern Highland Rim** **Cumberland Plateau**
Northern Highland Rim **Western Highland Rim**

Map 3.1. Middle Tennessee Study Area and Agricultural Subregions

accustomed to harvesting the highest crop yields in the region. In 1889, for example, Central Basin farmers harvested an average of 24.4 bushels of corn per acre, more than the harvests of Highland Rim or Cumberland Plateau farmers.[4]

Railroad connections to Nashville provided most of the Basin with easy access to the city. In 1890 only Trousdale County lacked a rail line to Nashville, but it had access to the city via the Cumberland River.[5] The Central Basin's railroad connections gave the region easy access to markets, and its farmers tended to be the most commercially oriented of Middle Tennessee farmers. The Basin's leading crops—corn and wheat—were usually shipped either to the mills of Nashville or to those in other sections of the South. Its farmers also raised large amounts of the minor grains: barley, rye, and oats. Truck farming and dairying were extensive closer to Nashville. Farther from the city, stock-raising and hay crops were important, and most of the Basin's hogs, cattle, and sheep made their way to Nashville's stockyards and slaughterhouses.[6]

The Highland Rim encircles the Central Basin, rising some 400 feet above it. Also characterized by rolling hills and stream-eroded valleys and plains, this region was more rugged and generally less productive than the Basin. Its richest soils could be found along the river bottoms of the western section of the Tennessee River and among the limestone soils of the Rim's outer western reaches. On the other hand, large sections of the inner portion of the Highland Rim bordering the Central Basin were known as the "barrens" because of the predominance of sandy, unproductive soils. The best of these thin, sandy soils were cultivated, whereas the poorest soil, found in the "flatlands," especially to the southwest of Nashville in Lewis, Dickinson, and Perry Counties, were left to scrub timber.[7]

The Highland Rim was poorly served by railroads. Nine counties in that region had no rail transportation in 1890; seven were located northeast of Nashville along the Upper Cumberland River and its tributaries, and two were west of the city. The Highland Rim's steep elevations and rough topography made railway building difficult and expensive, and the sparse population and lack of any major towns offered little incentive to surmount these obstacles.[8]

In the areas of the Highland Rim remote from railroads, such as the eastern portion, farmers raised primarily corn and livestock. Cash-crop production for the market was entrenched in the dark-fire tobacco-growing counties of the northern Highland Rim—the Black Patch of Kentucky and Tennessee—and the peanut- and corn-growing areas of the more fertile sections of the western Highland Rim.

Highland Rim crop yields were highest in the Rim's western portion, where in 1890 farmers harvested an average of twenty-five bushels of corn per acre. Yields were slightly lower in the northern Highland Rim, where farmers harvested an average of twenty-four bushels per acre, and lowest in the hillier and more remote eastern Highland Rim, where farmers in 1889 harvested on average only approximately twenty-one bushels of corn per acre.[9]

Although the soils of the Highland Rim were not as rich as those of the Central Basin, the region was rich in virgin timber in the late nineteenth century, much of it oak, hickory, cedar, and poplar. Coal deposits of varying quality were plentiful in limited sections of the eastern Rim, especially in White and Putnam Counties, and low-grade iron deposits existed on the western Rim.

The Cumberland Plateau was the most isolated section of Nashville's hinterland in the late nineteenth century. Geologically part of the Appalachian Plateau, which extends from northern New York through Pennsylvania, West Virginia, eastern Kentucky, and into Tennessee, the Cumberland Plateau climbs some 900 to 1,200 feet above the eastern Highland Rim. It is comprised of gently rolling hills and valleys interspersed with large sections of rough and irregular topography. The thin, sandy soils of the region made farming there a difficult endeavor.

The northern counties of the Plateau and adjacent eastern Highland Rim counties—collectively referred to as the Upper Cumberland—depended upon the erratic and difficult-to-navigate Cumberland River and its numerous tributaries for transportation. The Cumberland's navigable stretch snaked from the city of Burnside in southeastern Kentucky down through the Highland Rim to Nashville, before turning northwesterly to meet the

Ohio River near Paducah, Kentucky. By the 1890s the Cumberland River was the great highway of commerce to this isolated region. Like the Highland Rim, the Cumberland Plateau was rich in timber, and the Cumberland River was the chief means of getting that timber to the sawmills, lumber yards, and wood-products factories in Nashville. The Cumberland River and its tributaries remained an important commercial artery until the 1920s, when steamboat navigation finally succumbed to competition from railroads and trucks. By 1930 the river's traffic consisted almost entirely of vessels carrying local shipments of sand and gravel.[10]

The Cumberland Plateau marked the eastern frontier of Nashville's commercial hinterland. The first railroads to penetrate eastern Tennessee followed the north-south direction of the Tennessee River valley, and they closely tied the Plateau to Cincinnati to the north and Chattanooga and Atlanta to the south. In the 1890s the construction of the Tennessee Central Railroad linked Nashville to the counties along the western section of the Cumberland Plateau. The Tennessee Central, the only east-west line connecting Nashville to eastern Tennessee, opened up a large portion of the previously isolated eastern Highland Rim and Cumberland Plateau to Nashville's markets.[11]

Despite the variation in Middle Tennessee's physiography, most of the region's farmers—with the notable exception of those on the dark-fire tobacco farms of the northern Highland Rim and the peanut farms of Humphreys County in the western Highland Rim—practiced what contemporaries called "general farming." A diversified agriculture based primarily upon corn cultivation augmented by wheat, tobacco, hay, and livestock, this type of farming was characterized by high levels of household production and of landownership.

The lack of individual-farm production data for the years after 1880 makes a precise, systematic accounting of farm production by farm size and tenure status impossible. The best data available are county-level measures that obscure differences in production between owners and tenants, as well as between large and small farms. But other studies of mid-nineteenth-century Tennessee agriculture that draw upon earlier extant agricultural census data show that even in isolated, marginal areas with few market connections, significant disparities in wealth distribution and farm size existed.[12]

County-level data may not be able to account for variations in production by farm size and tenure, but it does offer a general guide to the characteristics of Middle Tennessee agriculture. These data also provide a strong indication of trends affecting production and tenure and support the contention that, on average, farms in even the most marginal sections of Middle Tennessee produced large and varied amounts of food crops for both home consumption and sale.

Row crops like cotton and tobacco played an important role in Middle Tennessee agriculture, but their cultivation was highly concentrated within Middle Tennessee. On average in 1889, Middle Tennessee farmers planted 1.6 acres of cotton and harvested just one-third of a bale per farm. Central Basin farmers each planted an average of nearly three acres of cotton but harvested only half a bale. Middle Tennessee's five leading cotton-growing counties—all in the Central Basin—accounted for 87.8 percent of all the cotton harvested in Middle Tennessee in 1889.[13]

Middle Tennessee tobacco production outside Black Patch, a dark-fired-tobacco region that sat astride Tennessee and Kentucky, was negligible. In the eastern Highland Rim and Cumberland Plateau farmers on average harvested, respectively, only 9.8 and 6.0 pounds of tobacco per farm. The Central Basin farmers were more committed to tobacco, producing, on average, sixty-one pounds per farm. In the counties of the Black Patch, however, tobacco was a major crop. Northern and western Highland Rim counties produced, respectively, 1,970.6 and 258.3 pounds of tobacco per farm in 1889. Middle Tennessee's five leading tobacco-growing counties—all in the Black Patch—accounted for 86.1 percent of all the tobacco grown in Middle Tennessee in 1889.[14]

Corn farming comprised the foundation of Middle Tennessee agriculture. Ground into meal or boiled into hominy or grits, corn was the dietary staple. Farmers would "pull fodder"—the "blades of the corn"—for livestock feed.[15] Middle Tennessee's farmers, particularly those in the Central Basin, had long shipped corn surpluses southward to the cotton-dominated Black Belt.[16] More land was devoted to corn than any other crop. In 1889 Middle Tennessee farmers each planted an average of anywhere from a high of 19.9 acres of corn per farm in the Central Basin to a low in 15.0 in the Cumberland Plateau. The average per-farm harvest of corn that year ranged from 545.2 bushels in the Central Basin to 271.0 in the Cumberland Plateau.

Middle Tennessee was also "a powerful wheat country," recollected one former Bedford County resident of his childhood region in the late 1880s and early 1890s.[17] On average, Middle Tennessee farmers planted some 6.1 acres of wheat and harvested 62.2 bushels. In the more rugged western Highland Rim and Cumberland Plateau farmers planted on average two acres or less of the grain per farm. The broad plains of the Central Basin south of Nashville were at the heart of Middle Tennessee's wheat production. There, farmers in 1889 planted an average of some 8.1 acres of wheat per farm and harvested 87.2 bushels. Williamson and Bedford Counties led in 1889 wheat production, each county reaping about half a million bushels.

Livestock—present on even the most remote Middle Tennessee farms—provided an important component of household production. Middle Tennessee's reputation as the premier stock-raising section of the South had been established before the Civil War, and hogs were especially plentiful on the region's farms. The typical farm in 1890 possessed an average of anywhere from 14.3 hogs in the Central Basin to 11.5 in the eastern Highland Rim. These numbers are especially notable because 1889 was a difficult year for Tennessee hog farmers; many lost as much as 30 percent of their herds to disease.[18] Farms of all sizes and tenure status counted large numbers of hogs largely because Tennessee law protected the practice of raising hogs on the open range until the late 1920s. Subsisting on the open range, these hogs would "run out . . . on the mast" feeding on the thick layer of "acorns and nuts of different kinds" in local forests. Middle Tennessee farmers who kept these "mountain hogs" usually had "only a vague notion of the number of such hogs they own[ed] until the hogs [were] driven from the forests and actually counted." Open-range hogs provided an important, low-cost source of meat and income for farmers, especially tenants and owners who farmed small plots. In the fall and early winter throughout Middle Tennessee, hog killings were an annual community event where "the neighbors came in to help" and later sang or told stories.[19]

Middle Tennessee farmers also raised chickens. The average number of chickens per farm in Middle Tennessee ranged from 82.8 on Central Basin farms to 49.8 on Cumberland Plateau farms. Milk cows, though less common, provided an important component of household production and an important part of Middle Tennessee diets. Farms throughout the region averaged around two milk cows per farm, producing anywhere from 599 to 663 gallons of milk per farm each year. Peas, greens, and other vegetables from kitchen gardens rounded out family diets. Geese, prized for their feathers and down, were also common on Middle Tennessee farms.

Middle Tennessee's general farming regime rested upon a foundation of widespread landownership. Late-nineteenth-century Middle Tennessee farm families understood that owning land offered the surest guarantee of family security. Most white Middle Tennessee farmers owned the land they tilled, and those who did not, in time, expected to join the ranks of the landowning. Young white men entering farming in the late nineteenth and early twentieth centuries held the hope of acquiring the means to buy land and continue in their fathers' footsteps.

Middle Tennessee's low rate of tenancy, at least among whites, and the tendency of tenancy to be concentrated among younger farmers are evi-

Table 3.1. Tenancy Rates of Middle Tennessee Farms, by Geographical Region, 1890–1930

Section	1890	1900	1910	1920	1930
Central Basin	30.8%	38.4%	39.4%	41.5%	46.5%
Northern Highland Rim	18.8	34.8	37.2	40.2	46.6
Eastern Highland Rim	22.2	30.7	31.4	32.6	36.1
Western Highland Rim	26.8	35.7	35.0	35.2	41.7
Cumberland Plateau	24.1	31.4	29.3	23.6	21.5
Total	26.6	35.6	36.4	37.7	42.3

Source: U.S. Agriculture Census, 1890–1930.
Note: Davidson County is excluded from figures.

dence of this pattern. In 1890 just over one-quarter of Middle Tennessee farmers farmed as tenants, as shown in Table 3.1. The depression of the 1890s caused tenancy rates to shoot upward to 35.6 percent by 1900, but rates then remained stable at roughly that level until the 1920s, when they increased to 42.3 percent. Tenancy rates rose most dramatically in the northern Highland Rim, spurred by the increasing dependence upon tobacco monoculture.[20]

Among white farmers, tenancy was closely related to the rural life cycle. Young men overwhelmingly farmed as tenants, while older farmers worked their own land. The integrated public-use samples of the decennial federal population census allow a cross-tabulation of farm tenure and age. The age structure of tenancy among white Tennessee farmers in 1900 summarized in Figure 3.1 (no such figures are available for 1890 or 1930) shows that the rate of tenancy progressively declined from a high of 81 percent for farm operators under the age of twenty-five to a low of 5.6 percent among those sixty-five and older. Young white Middle Tennessee farmers at the turn of the century observed that most of the older farmers around them owned land, and the idea of having to climb an agricultural ladder leading one from a tenant to an owner appeared to be a distinct reality.[21]

White farmers found ascending that agricultural ladder more difficult after 1900. In the decade 1900–1910, tenancy among white Middle Tennessee farmers increased from 32.1 to 38.1 percent. As Figure 3.1 shows, in all age categories tenancy rates increased sharply. Most significant is the sharp rise in the rates among the twenty-five to thirty-four and the forty-five to fifty-four age groups, which increased some ten percentage points each. These upward shifts in the tenancy rate are all the more significant considering that the first decade of the century saw a recovery from the low prices

Figure 3.1. Tenancy Rates of White Tennessee Farmers, by Age, 1900–1920

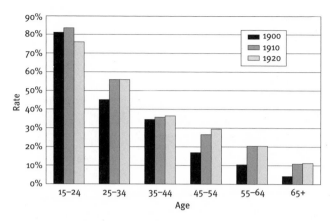

Source: 1910, 1920, and 1930 Integrated Public Use Microdata Services, Social History Research Laboratory, University of Minnesota.

and depressed conditions of the 1890s. Even the World War I–era boost to farm prices failed to improve prospects for white tenant farmers hoping to enter the ranks of farm owners. The overall tenancy rate remained flat and increased in three of the six age cohorts.

For black farmers, however, agriculture in Middle Tennessee offered much fewer opportunities for owning land; 76.5 percent of Middle Tennessee's black farmers labored under some form of tenancy arrangement in 1900. Ten years later 74.4 percent did so. Despite the slight decline, the relationship between age and tenancy that characterized white farmers' situation did not exist among black farmers (see Figure 3.2). Across all ages, most black farmers cultivated land they did not own. Black tenancy rates did tend to decrease with age, but the decline was extremely small. For Middle Tennessee's black farmers the prospects for rising into the ranks of farm owners were bleak.

Black tenants also tended to farm smaller plots and poorer land than did their white Middle Tennessee counterparts. The sharecropping system under which most black tenants farmed gave landlords incentive to limit the size of tenant plots to promote intensive land use. Small plots also ensured that sharecroppers could provide a ready reserve of wage labor for the landlords' fields. Typical of this practice of assigning sharecroppers small plots was the arrangement by which G. S. Campbell, a large landowner near Hopkinsville, Kentucky, northwest of Nashville, operated his farms. Campbell leased his less productive land to black sharecroppers, who raised

Figure 3.2. Tenancy Rates of Black Tennessee Farmers, by Age, 1900–1920

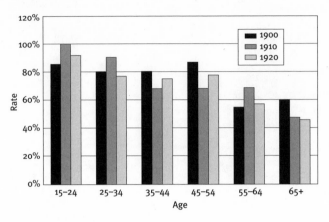

Source: See Figure 3.1.

corn and tobacco, making sure that these "croppers [were] given small acreages . . . so that they [were] available as wage hands to assist on the [landlord's] wheat crop."[22]

By what means did young black and white men rise to the ranks of farm owners? The fortunate simply inherited land. Inheritance has always been central to the intergenerational transfer of land in agricultural societies, and Middle Tennessee's partible inheritance traditions were no exception.[23] Indeed, tenancy often served as a precursor to inheritance. A significant portion of Middle Tennessee tenants farmed land owned by relatives, usually parents. Such tenancy arrangements provided younger farmers with a means of earning a living from the family farm and allowed them to start a family while learning farm management and preserving their parents' ownership and livelihood. No comprehensive figures exist for the years before 1930, but by that year fully one-fifth of all Tennessee tenant farmers were related to their landlords. This figure was even higher in the western Highland Rim, where one-quarter were related to landlords.[24]

However widespread inheritance as a means of land acquisition was in the nineteenth century, it was not so in the twentieth. One elderly farmer contrasted the difficulties that young men entering farming faced in 1901 with his own experience as a youth. "When I began to farm," he recalled, "the farmers owned land and the sons worked, and they were given part of the land, or were helped to buy a farm close by; and it was an easy matter for the farmer's son to start out for himself and get a farm. . . . [W]hen a man got to be twenty-one or twenty-two years old he married a farmer's daughter, and he was set up on a farm." By 1901, however, farms were neither as large nor as prosperous. He explained, "[While] there are a good many farmers who are making good money . . . their sons cannot always be kept on the farm. A young man comes up and the father is not able to give him a number of acres of land and a couple of mules as he used to do, and [the son] does not like the idea of starting out with nothing."[25]

Being related to one's landlord offered no guarantee of preferential treatment, however. Some men denied their sons patrimony, which led to family conflict over the use of scarce farm resources. One Bedford County farm boy complained that his father would neither invest in work stock nor let his older brothers make their own crop on any of the family's land. After a fight with the father "over some work," his oldest brother left the farm at age sixteen. The farm boy himself left when he turned eighteen to take a "good job" with a farmer in the next county. Organs for rural reform such as the *Southern Agriculturalist,* a Nashville-based farm journal, criticized farm parents who did not understand that "the farm is for the boy, not the boy for the farm." The journal advised farm sons to be self-interested. "If the boy cannot stay on the farm and get what is coming to him, let him go somewhere else," it asserted in 1920. The need for such exhortations suggests that a growing number of small Middle Tennessee landowners were unable to spare land for their sons.[26]

Fragmentary evidence suggests that by the 1920s only a favored few Middle Tennesseans inherited land. Data from a mid-1920s survey of forty farm owners in Overton County, in the eastern Highland Rim, reveal that fewer than one-fifth of farm owners (seven farmers) became so through inheritance. The typical means of becoming an owner was by purchasing land by working oneself up from a tenant or a farm laborer. Three-fifths of the farm owners (twenty-four farmers) in the Overton County survey moved from the ranks of tenants or farm laborers to owners; twelve of those moved from tenant to owner, six from farm laborer to tenant to owner, and six directly from farm laborer to owner. The remaining one-fifth (nine farmers) moved from other, unspecified occupations to farm ownership.[27] These figures suggest that the majority of young men entering farming had to buy their land if they were to rise into the ranks of the landowning.

Acquiring the means to purchase a farm, however, was becoming more difficult because of a growing imbalance between land availability and population. Rural Middle Tennesseans were a prodigiously fecund people, and like southerners throughout the region, they begat large families.[28] The size of Middle Tennessee farm families is best indicated by the total marital fertility rates, or the average number of children married women bore over the course of their reproductive years. Although rural Middle Tennessee fertility rates were slightly below those of the entire rural South, they were still high by national standards. By 1910 married farm-dwelling white women in Middle Tennessee had given birth to an average of 6.6 children, and married black farm women had given birth to an average of 6.0. While southern fertility steadily declined over time, it remained persistently higher than nonsouthern levels.[29]

Declining mortality rates, especially among children, compounded the growing rural population pressures. Reliable estimates on nineteenth-century mortality are sketchy and incomplete, but the leading students of child mortality conclude that nationally, among whites, child mortality rates began to decline sometime in the 1890s in both urban and rural regions of the nation. Blacks, however, saw little decrease in child mortality.[30]

Data for Tennessee in the 1920s, however, show greater decreases in mortality rates, especially for blacks, as the traditional killers of rural children such as typhoid fever, dysentery, and other enteric diseases declined sharply. Among rural Tennessee whites under two years of age, the number of deaths from diarrhea and enteritis fell from 40.8 per hundred thousand in 1917 to 32.5 per hundred thousand in 1928. Among rural black children under two, the death rate for the same class of diseases fell from 48.9 to 23.3 per hundred thousand. Overall infant mortality rates for Tennessee whites (children under one year of age) fell from 84.5 to 67.5 per hundred thousand during the years 1917–28. Black infant mortality decreased as well, from 185.2 to 101.8 per hundred thousand during the same period, although the rate was over twice as high as the white figure.[31] As more rural children survived past infancy, farm families were able to reach their desired number of children with fewer births. The net effect was the same: strong population pressures upon the agricultural economy.

Rural Middle Tennessee was nearly as populated as the cotton-dominated Black Belt of the Lower South and slightly less so than the Georgia and Carolinas Piedmont. By 1890 the region supported a population density of thirty-five persons per square mile, which increased to thirty-eight persons per square mile by 1900, where it remained through 1930. Overall population growth followed a similar course. Middle Tennessee's 1890 population (exclusive of Davidson County, home of Nashville) stood at 617,881. Population grew dramatically in the 1890s, increasing by 9.4 percent. Only heavy outmigration from the countryside, as we will see in Chapter 5, helped keep Middle Tennessee's overall population steady after 1900, increasing less than 1 percent in 1900–1910 and 1910–20 before declining nearly 2 percent in the 1920s in the face of a heavy exodus of rural people.[32]

The overall stability in Middle Tennessee's population, however, masked growing demographic pressures on farmland. Rural Middle Tennessee's

Table 3.2. Number of Middle Tennessee Farms, by Geographical Region, 1890–1930

Section	1890	1900	1910	1920	1930
Central Basin	35,192	41,725	44,693	47,454	44,306
Northern Highland Rim	11,675	16,034	18,051	19,440	19,582
Eastern Highland Rim	10,824	14,239	14,922	16,016	15,889
Western Highland Rim	9,174	11,904	12,701	13,036	11,489
Cumberland Plateau	2,480	3,193	3,278	3,518	3,335
Total	69,345	87,095	93,645	99,464	94,601
(% change)		(26.7)	(7.5)	(6.2)	(−4.9)

Source: See Table 3.1.
Note: Nashville and Davidson Counties are excluded from figures.

high fertility, declining mortality, and limited job opportunities off the farm meant that increasing numbers of young men sought to earn their livelihood as farmers. Despite high levels of outmigration, the number of farms increased sharply from 1890 to 1900 — 26.7 percent — and continued to increase, though at lower rates in the 1900s and 1910s. The number of farms did not decline until the late 1920s, when the region's agricultural economy had all but collapsed (see Table 3.2).

More Middle Tennessee families working more farms placed strong upward pressures upon agricultural land values. When the region's land values are deflated by an index of farm commodity prices and converted into real dollars, farmland prices show a steady increase, as shown in Figure 3.3. The average value of an acre of Middle Tennessee farmland in real dollars (1914 = 100), weighted by the area of each county, rose from $16.83 in 1890 to $28.26 in 1930. In other words, the price of Middle Tennessee farmland increased faster than the price of the products the land produced. Rising land prices reflected Middle Tennessee's burgeoning population and the high demand for farmland, a situation common to underdeveloped agricultural economies with few off-farm opportunities.[33]

Rising land values were selective in their effect upon Middle Tennessee farmers. Landowning farmers benefited from the general increase in land prices; higher land values meant an increase in their wealth. For young farmers striving to break into the ranks of the landowning, however, the rise in farmland values raised the cost of that ascent. Those who did become landowners tended to possess smaller, less productive farms.[34] "It becomes harder and harder for the young farmer without capital to grow into the farm-owning class," and "the agricultural ladder is getting longer

Figure 3.3. Middle Tennessee Farmland Values, 1890–1930 (in 1914 dollars)

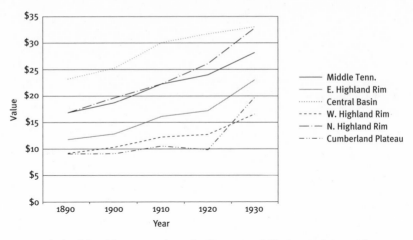

Source: Calculated from Thomas Pressley and William H. Scofield, *Farm Real Estate Values* (Seattle: University of Washington Press, 1965), and George F. Warren and Frank A. Pearson, *Prices* (New York: John Wiley & Son, 1933), 24–27.

and harder to climb," complained a Middle Tennessee farm journal.[35] Fewer young men were able to buy land, and those who were able to buy farms had to work harder and longer to do so. No matter how highly farmers may have valued self-sufficiency or high levels of household production, and no matter how adverse to market production, they could not escape this most fundamental market transaction: the purchase of land. The disruption of the intergenerational transfer of land and the upward pressure on Middle Tennessee farm values resonated throughout the Middle Tennessee agricultural economy, affecting land owners and tenants, established farmers and those coming of age and just entering farming.

The effects of a growing rural population were not lost on Middle Tennessee farmers, either. "The great trouble is there are too many people farming," declared one Middle Tennessee farmer. The *Southern Agriculturalist* proclaimed that "there are more people at work on the farm of this country now than should be." Quoting approvingly from Herbert Quick's *Real Trouble with the Farmers*, a popular tract on the 1920s farm crisis, the newspaper also argued that the "chronic disease" of Middle Tennessee agriculture was "the steady increase of land values that is all the time forcing more farmers in to the tenant class."[36] More and more Middle Tennessee farmers found themselves farming fewer and fewer acres, trying to support families on less and less land. In 1890, there were 14 acres of farmland for each

Figure 3.4. Distribution of Middle Tennessee Farms, by Size, 1890, 1910, and 1930

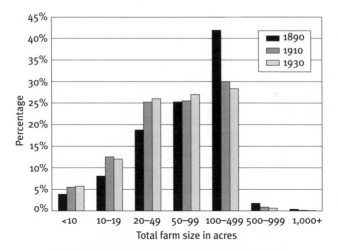

Total farm size in acres

Source: Inter-University Consortium for Political and Social Research, *Historical, Demographic, Economic, and Social Data: The United States, 1790–1970* (Computer file) (Ann Arbor, Mich.: Inter-University Consortium for Political and Social Research, 2001).

Middle Tennessean; in 1930 there were only 11.8. These years saw a sharp increase in the number of small farms and a decline in larger farms capable of supporting a family, as shown in Figure 3.4. In 1890, only 31 percent of Middle Tennessee farms counted fewer than fifty acres of improved and unimproved land. By 1930, that figure had grown to 44 percent. The number of farms that counted at least 100 acres fell from 42 percent to 28 percent during the same forty-year period.[37]

Farmers wanting to expand their production without buying additional land could increase the amount of land they cultivated by renting extra acreage. J. B. Williams, from Putnam County, in the eastern Highland Rim, recalled that his parents owned ten or twelve acres and rented additional land "to do their farming with."[38] The increasing value of farmland translated into higher rents, however, so renting additional land was not always feasible. In addition, since land in cash-poor Middle Tennessee typically rented for shares of the crop, a farmer interested in renting had to find another owner willing to lease only a few acres. Hence, combining ownership and tenancy was confined primarily to areas adjacent to Nashville, where cash tenancy predominated. Furthermore, the fragmentation of a farmer's cultivated plots posed a number of disadvantages, including extra time spent traveling to dispersed fields and the difficulties in protecting the land from free-roaming livestock.[39]

More commonly, Middle Tennessee's small farmers cultivated the land they had more intensively. Ester Boserup, in her influential critique of Malthusian thought, *The Conditions of Agricultural Growth*, identifies intensification as one of the responses to rising rural population pressure. The Malthusian view assumes that population growth is a direct function of levels of agricultural production at any particular time. Or, simply put, the amount of food available determines the population size. Improvements in agriculture may lead to greater food production and allow greater population growth, but these developments are exogenous, that is, they are independent and unrelated to population growth. Boserup, an economist studying the rapid population increase in the post–World War II developing world, argued that population growth itself spurs improvements in agricultural production. Farmers, facing population pressures and a growing demand for food, would intensify their production and improve their agricultural techniques, largely through more frequent cropping, less frequent fallowing of farmland, and the adoption of new tools.[40]

In the nineteenth century, before mounting population pressures induced changes in land use, Middle Tennessee farmers, particularly those in the mountainous regions east of Nashville, had engaged in forest fallowing, a land-extensive practice that had largely disappeared in Europe and North America. When the fertility of agricultural land declined as a result of intensive cropping, it was put to "rest" and allowed to revert back to forest. Farmers cleared the secondary hardwood growth in fields that had lain fallow by burning the underbrush and girdling the remaining trees. After a few years, the dead trees were felled and burned. The multiple burnings released nutrients into thin, overworked soils. When a field's fertility faltered, it was put back into fallow and the cycle began again. Typically, farmers kept over two-thirds of their farmland in fallow.[41]

Population pressures disrupted the forest fallow cycle after the 1890s. As Middle Tennessee farmers brought more land under the plow, they cultivated their farms more intensively and placed less land in fallow. From 1890 to 1920, the ratio of uncultivated to cultivated land declined from 1.12 to 0.81. The sharpest declines occurred in the mountainous Cumberland Plateau and Highland Rim, where forest fallowing had been most widely practiced and where population pressures were strongest. A 1920 *Southern Agriculturalist* editorial decried the changes in Middle Tennessee agriculture that were forcing farmers to "put more labor on each acre" but not allowing them to get ahead. The editorialist keenly understood the essence

An eroded Tennessee farm in the 1930s (Tennessee Dept. of Conservation
Photographs, RG 82, Tennessee State Library and Archives, Nashville)

of agricultural productivity in pointing out that the "'intensive theory' of
smaller, more highly cultivated farms" was a dead end because "the largest
production per man rather than the largest production per acre is the goal
to be aimed at."[42]

Shortened fallow periods and the expansion of agriculture onto marginal
lands put great stress on Middle Tennessee agriculture. Not only were farm
families—tenants and owners—trying to scratch out a living from smaller
farms, but those farms increasingly consisted of poorer, less productive
land. From 1890 to 1920, cultivated farmland in Middle Tennessee increased 16.3 percent from 4.1 to 4.7 million acres.[43] The region's irregular
and hilly topography meant that poor, relatively unproductive land—steep
and difficult to farm, deficient in nutrients, and poorly draining—was inter-
mixed with fertile, productive land. Eroded ridges, or "knobs," known for
their poor soil dotted the otherwise fertile Central Basin. In the western
Highland Rim, fertile bottomlands bordered steep, eroded slopes and broken ridges. Scratching a crop out of these "barrens" was difficult; one investigator for the state planning office in the 1930s described the farms here as
"half-hearted attempts at agriculture," the land better suited for forest than
farms—a characterization that certainly held true twenty years earlier. A

similar situation prevailed in the eastern Highland Rim. Coffee, Cannon, Moore, and northern Franklin Counties comprised the "flatlands," a region of thin, weak soils where even the scrub oak and hickory trees grew poorly, rarely reaching more than fifty feet in height.[44]

Government planners were not the only ones who appreciated the difficulties in making a crop from these marginal lands. One Pickett County farmer recalled that "there was thousands of acres [in Pickett County] that ought to never have been cleaned up. It ought to have been left as forest." Cultivating these lands was a short-term proposition; "the first few years you got the best off it [but then] it would wash in gullies."[45] There were "hundreds and even thousands of acres of waste land" in West Tennessee's Weakley County. Gullies "ten, fifteen, twenty feet deep" were a common sight, and "often great patches of an acre or more are absolutely gone."[46] Throughout Middle Tennessee, farmers brought poor land under the plow, and it was there, as one observer noted in the 1920s, that poverty was "found in the greatest abundance."[47]

Traditional farming practices did little to preserve soil fertility. A turn-of-the-century observer decried the "deplorable indifference" of Middle Tennessee farmers to soil erosion. Traveling through the Middle Tennessee's wheat-growing districts, he saw everywhere the telltale gullies developing in the wheat fields that bore "incontestable witness to the very large amount of equally precious soil that had been removed by the hard April rains." Such soil-preserving practices as applying straw to slopes on hilly fields, contour plowing, terracing, and deep plowing were rarely employed. Even the simplest methods of responsible soil conservation "are not known to everybody," he wrote, and he predicted that farmers' sons would either "fight the wolf from the door, or flee from the worn out land to the city."[48]

Smaller farms and poorer land meant a decline in what Middle Tennessee families could produce from their farms. For example, the typical Middle Tennessee farmer planted 18.8 acres of corn and harvested 476 bushels in 1889. In 1930 he planted only 13.6 acres of corn and harvested a mere 310 bushels. Per-acre yields declined as well. Middle Tennessee farmers harvested an average of 25.0 bushels of corn per acre in 1889, whereas in 1929 they harvested an average of only 22.8.[49]

Declining farm production placed sharp economic pressures on Middle Tennessee farm households. One elderly Tennessee farmer expressed these difficulties clearly when he contrasted conditions in the mid-1930s with those of his youth in the 1890s. "The farms can't keep up the big families like they used to," he recalled. "Not near so many folks can live on the farms and work the land and make a living as a generation ago. The young folks have nothing to look for ahead on a farm now as I did when I was a young man, plenty of land then."[50]

Middle Tennessee farmers faced a dilemma as they entered the twentieth century. For young men entering agriculture without the benefit of inheritance, obtaining land grew increasingly more difficult. In addition, landowning farmers and tenants found themselves farming smaller and smaller plots, having to support their families on less and less. The pressures that were undermining traditional agriculture gave rise to an impulse to innovate.

CHAPTER 4

Turning to Urban Markets

Although Middle Tennessee's growing population did place sharp pressures upon its small-scale, general farming regime, it did not dictate the region's agricultural destiny. Farmers responded to the demographic and economic stresses undermining Middle Tennessee agriculture by working harder and turning to new crops and new markets. Nashville's commercial and industrial development may have been limited, but it did provide new or expanded opportunities for Middle Tennesseans to remain in agriculture while earning additional income through producing for urban markets or off-farm work.

Middle Tennessee farm families increased fruit, vegetable, poultry, and dairy production for the Nashville market; they turned increasingly to livestock production for Nashville's stockyards and meatpackers; and they turned to logging the old-growth hardwood forests of the Highland Rim and Cumberland Plateau for Nashville's lumber mills and wood-products factories. Consequently, farm families had to work harder and longer throughout the year. As men logged the forests, women became the poultry, vegetable, and cream producers. Farm families combined any number of these activities to augment declining returns from farming. Typical was Oma Hubbard's father, who, in addition to working their family's small farm in the 1910s, "done anything that there was to be done that he could do to make a living for his family because it was a big family. . . . [He] made crossties, cut hickory, any kind of work [he] could get to." Getting by was more than ever a family affair that called forth greater effort from each member of the household.[1]

After 1900 new markets created by Nashville's urbanization helped smaller, marginal farmers stay on the land. However, the viability of these income-producing efforts collapsed in the 1920s. By the 1920s Nashville's integration into national fruit and produce markets undermined the demand for locally grown produce. Rising standards in the city's stockyards, which favored well-heeled producers of high-quality, corn-fed animals, eliminated the demand for free-range livestock, and the timber industry declined sharply in the 1920s as Middle Tennessee's once bountiful old-growth hardwood forests were finally exhausted. Only poultry and cream production remained a viable activity for small producers. Consequently, thousands of Middle Tennessee men and women were leaving the country-side, many of them following the fruit, vegetables, poultry, milk, livestock, and timber they once carried into Nashville.

Contemporary observers noted that the growth of Nashville and other southern cities and towns offered expanding markets for local farm prod-ucts. Speaking before a convention of Tennessee farmers in 1913, W. W. Finley, president of the Southern Railroad, stated that throughout the South "thriving manufacturing and commercial cities and towns are growing up, giving the Southeastern farmer the advantage of a home market." Finley predicted that Tennessee fruit and vegetable farming, dairying, and live-stock production would "grow in importance with the continued develop-ment of local markets and the increasing demand of Northeastern cities for fruits, vegetables, dairy products, and meats."[2]

Middle Tennessee farms rarely specialized in fruit or vegetable produc-tion; market gardening was a commercial extension of the region's house-hold economy and, in particular, an extension of the farm wives' kitchen gardens. The cultivation of these crops required relatively little land, and labor demands for vegetable and fruit crops, while high, were usually most pressing during slack periods on the farm. Thus, otherwise idle labor and machinery could be put to work to bring in much-needed cash.[3]

Three major obstacles faced Middle Tennessee farm families in their new endeavor, however: poor roads, limited markets, and increasing competi-tion in Nashville, the preeminent Middle Tennessee market. Bringing fruit and vegetables to market over Middle Tennessee's roads before the 1920s to even nearby markets could be difficult. Before the good-roads movement of the 1920s, rural Middle Tennessee roads were generally impassable most of the year.[4] Those of Bedford County in the Central Basin were typical of the poor state of Middle Tennessee's unimproved dirt roads. They were de-scribed as "execrable . . . simply disgraceful"; when muddy, "the wheels of a buggy could sink so deep in the stiff, tenacious mud and sloughs that a single horse is incapable of pulling it out."[5] A 1915 highway survey found that only 12 percent of Tennessee's roads could be considered "improved roads," that is, properly graded and paved with gravel or macadam. These few stretches of improved roads were concentrated in urban counties like

Nashville's Davidson County. Produce dealers in Nashville frequently lamented the "spells of wet weather" that made "country roads impassable again" and disrupted local trade.[6]

Poor roads only compounded the lack of local markets for fruits and vegetables. Few of the many villages and small towns that dotted Middle Tennessee were large enough to offer substantial markets, and the presence of extensive gardens and milk cows in these towns made them weak markets for locally grown produce. The larger Middle Tennessee towns of Murfreesboro, Columbia, and Clarksville, however, offered some opportunity for fruit and vegetable sales, and the few coal-mining towns of the eastern Highland Rim offered good local markets. Oma Hubbard's family, for example, sold berries and vegetables, especially potatoes, in the nearby town of Clifty in the 1910s.[7]

Nashville, then, was the place to sell produce. The farmers who sold their produce in Nashville hauled it to the curb market at the city's public square on Wednesdays and Saturdays from April to October, offering it for sale either directly to consumers or to the numerous wholesale dealers located nearby. Independent retail grocerymen and itinerant produce hucksters, who peddled in the city's working-class neighborhoods, bought most of it. Ellis Jones's father, a tenant farmer near the city, sold vegetables, especially potatoes, from the "big garden" his family tended, as well as his own cured hams. Jones noted that for his father selling his produce this way "was a sideline occupation but it paid pretty good." As an adjunct to general farming, market gardening could provide critical extra income.[8]

The competition in Nashville, however, put Middle Tennessee producers at an increasing disadvantage. Lacking any storage facilities or marketing organization, Middle Tennessee growers sold their produce at the peak of production rather than the peak of prices. The result was that Nashville would be awash with whatever fruit or vegetable happened to be in season, and the prices farmers received were invariably low. For example, nearly all Tennessee strawberries came to market in May, and most potatoes came to market in July.[9] In the early 1920s Middle Tennessee farmers also had to compete with Florida and California truck producers, whose extensive marketing cooperatives offered a well-organized system of grading, packing, and shipping that delivered high-quality, low-cost produce in quantities that appealed to Nashville's bulk buyers. Out-of-state produce came to dominate the Nashville market in the 1920s, sidelining the city market and its local farmers.

Nashville's expanding multistore, self-service grocery concerns were the chief buyers of this produce. These firms operated on what contemporaries called the "grocery-cafeteria" plan or "help yourself system." The high volume of these multistore concerns allowed them to bypass local jobbers and wholesalers, purchase large quantities directly from growers, and thus undersell independent grocers. The innovator in Nashville was H. G. Hill, head of the city's leading self-service grocery concern. Before World War I Hill regularly contracted for entire railroad car lots of produce to supply his twenty-store grocery empire. By basing his retail prices on carload cost and operating on a cash-only basis, Hill's firm could "sell . . . at the same prices the average [independent] grocer has to pay for his goods."[10] In 1918 Hill's success in Nashville attracted the Piggly Wiggly chain, which expanded into Nashville from its home city of Memphis. By 1923 Nashville grocerymen boasted that the 4,000 carloads of fruits and vegetables shipped into the city each year ensured that "Nashville gets its quota of fresh fruits and vegetables from every section of the country."[11]

As multi-unit self-service stores came to dominate the city's grocery industry, local growers found themselves cut out of the grocery marketing system and relegated to serving an ever-smaller market of independent grocery dealers. By the 1930s Tennessee-grown fruit, with the sole exception of strawberries, was rarely found in the city's markets. Even in the case of apples, a crop for which Tennessee producers were famous, Nashville's grocers ordered from out-of-state some 400 carloads, or 280,000 bushels, a year, a situation one local groceryman likened to "carrying coals to Newcastle."[12]

Tennessee-grown vegetables fared only slightly better than Tennessee-grown fruits. With Middle Tennessee farmers poorly organized, uniform grading and packaging was practically nonexistent. Nashville's grocery jobbers complained that local farmers would hide inferior produce in the bottoms of boxes and barrels. As a result, locally grown vegetables suffered a "bad name" for quality and fetched lower prices than the imported variety. One observer noted that ten pounds of California tomatoes, uniform in size and color, neatly packed, and wrapped in tissue paper, sold for about the same price as fifty pounds of poorly packaged, irregularly shaped Tennessee-grown tomatoes. The state agriculture commissioner complained that "generally [Tennessee produce growers] are marketing their products at a disadvantage by selling in small quantities, [showing] indifference in grading, and [exhibiting a] want of uniformity of product."[13] A state planner observed that the arrival of produce-laden refrigerator cars from California into the Nashville market continued "unabated." The end of the public square's role as Nashville's main produce market came in 1923 with the construction of a "new produce center," with ample cold storage, at the Harrison Street railroad terminals north of the city's downtown, where railroads could unload their produce directly into the wholesalers' warehouses.[14]

Smaller farmers who were trying to supplement their income with market gardening found the competition from out-of-state growers too difficult to surmount. Indeed, Middle Tennessee's fruit and vegetable farmers suffered a similar fate as the state's manufacturers, as discussed in Chapter 2, of being out-marketed and out-produced by out-of-state competitors.[15]

There was one notable farm product that remained immune to these competitive pressures: moonshine. Middle Tennessee farmers had long used stills to convert their surplus grain into a high-value, low-bulk commodity. Moonshiners enjoyed a market for their spirits in Nashville after Tennessee enacted statewide prohibition in 1909, and demand only expanded with the passage of the Eighteenth Amendment and national prohibition. For farmers close to Nashville willing to accept the risks, the business could be lucrative. Moonshining was centered in the Highland Rim counties that abutted the western and northern borders of Davidson County. These counties were close to Nashville, and the Highland Rim's hilly terrain was well suited to concealing stills from prohibition agents. A raid on Sumner County yielded "forty-two sources of 'white mule'" (i.e., stills). Cheatham County developed such a thriving "moon-shine district" that the moonshiners outstripped the local grain supply. One local merchant's son recalled of his father's country store that "a large part of his business was in sales of sugar and meal used in whiskey making."[16]

Moonshiners responded to urban tastes as well, making beer in addition to the traditional corn liquor. This was the case with a farmer in the community of Pleasant Shade in Sumner County, who was discovered by federal agents not only to have the standard moonshine apparatus—a seventy-five-gallon still—but a brewery, too, equipped with four fermenters and an inventory of four hundred gallons of beer in his barn.[17]

Moonshine found its way into Nashville along the same routes as Middle Tennessee's agricultural produce. Farmers like Monroe Massey of Dickerson Pike brought in bootleg liquor along with their other goods to the city's curb market in the public square. While Massey had the unfortunate luck to have been caught with his small stock of eight pints, his business was an example of the public square's vigorous liquor trade. Other times, farmers simply drove in from the country and made their deliveries directly to thirsty Nashvillians.[18]

Middle Tennessee farm families enjoyed more success with poultry and dairy production because the merchants handling the trade overcame the marketing problems that beset the region's fruit and vegetable growers.

Merchants began investing in the Middle Tennessee poultry trade in the early 1900s, particularly in the eastern Highland Rim. Important poultry markets developed in the eastern Rim towns of Algood and Cookeville soon after the arrival of the Nashville-based Tennessee Central Railroad. Local merchants such as Cookeville's R. Perry Morgan, an early pioneer of the trade, built warehouses near rail lines and purchased chickens, turkeys, and eggs from nearby farmers. Morgan's Cookeville business was so successful that he opened warehouses in Livingston and Algood and sent buyers into the counties along the Upper Cumberland River and its tributaries. The Tennessee Central Railroad, seeing the potential for increased freight traffic, encouraged the trade by sponsoring a poultry association after 1914 in its Highland Rim and Cumberland Plateau territories. In one ten-week period in 1922, Putnam County shipped sixty-two railroad cars of live birds and twenty-eight cars of eggs.[19]

When corn and wheat prices fell sharply in the 1920s, poultry became more important to Middle Tennessee farmers and county agricultural extension agents played a key role in promoting the industry. In Murray, Kentucky, just northwest of Nashville, the extension agent worked with the local farm bureau secretary to contract with "five or six regular poultry buyers." The buyers would then "send out the word to the farmers' wives" and collect the birds and ship them by the carload. A "poultry shipping and feeding plant" in Morristown, Tennessee, shipped northward 1,800–2,000 broilers a day.

As significant urban poultry markets developed in Tennessee, agricultural extension agents, home demonstration agents, and local farm bureau leaders promoted raising "standardized, high quality poultry products" by advocating the adoption of "purebred" hens. In 1924, extension agents working with home demonstration agents in Bradley, Cumberland, Marion, McMinn, Putnam, Roane, and White Counties distributed over 30,000 Rhode Island Red and Barred Plymouth Rock fertilized eggs to farm wives and local poultry clubs in an effort to "replace mongrel flocks with purebred chickens." Proponents of standardization in Putnam County, the center of the state's poultry industry, noted that the "scrub hens . . . are losing out fast by the standardization route."[20] By 1929 Middle Tennessee farms averaged $23 each in sales of chickens, ranging from a low of $13 per farm in the Cumberland Plateau to a high of $29 in the eastern Highland Rim.[21]

Farm women held the primary responsibility for raising chickens, and when the industry expanded in the 1920s, they took a leading role. Female home demonstration agents organized women's poultry associations to promote poultry production, sometimes with remarkably successful re-

Women turned to poultry to augment farm incomes (Tennessee Dept. of Conservation Photographs, RG 82, Tennessee State Library and Archives, Nashville).

sults. In 1921, Rutherford County agent Harriet Wendle organized local women into an "egg circle" to improve egg production, teaching them how to get their chickens to produce infertile eggs and to raise appearance and cleanliness standards of their product. Soon thereafter, the leaders of the egg circle resolved to make "a real business of their cooperative marketing project." They secured a charter and issued stock, which they sold to local poultry breeders, bankers, and merchants. The $1,400 initial capital investment allowed the now-named Rutherford County Poultry Association to build a plant and hire a male manager. In 1926 the association sold about $40,000 in poultry and eggs.[22]

Dairy production operated as an extension of the household economy and, like poultry production, served as an important means of earning cash income. Dairying was also an extension of a woman's role in the farm economy. "Butter and egg money" was a woman's preserve, the work of wives and daughters on the farm. Throughout Middle Tennessee, making butter was the chief means of converting cow's milk into a salable product. Mrs. Alvie O. Smith of Giles County noted in 1920 that she began selling butter "several years ago" to the Pleasant Valley Ladies' Aid Society. She prepared her product carefully, using a brick mold and wax paper wrapping before shipping it to Nashville.[23]

After World War I, the rise of commercial creameries in and around Nashville created a strong market for fresh cream. By 1920 six commercial creameries had established themselves in the counties surrounding the city. These creameries responded to changing urban tastes by manufacturing butter that urban consumers perceived as "much superior to the general run of country butter."[24]

Creameries often dealt both in dairy and in poultry products, reflecting the fact that farm wives traditionally were responsible for care of both chickens and dairy cows. For example, the Rutherford County Creamery in Murfreesboro, southeast of Nashville, which produced some two million pounds of butter annually under the Magnolia label, also dealt in fresh eggs and poultry. In 1925 Swift & Company took advantage of this growing market by opening a large poultry processing plant and creamery and by advertising that "cream producers may send their cream [and] poultry raisers [may] exchange their eggs and poultry for cash."[25]

By the 1920s Middle Tennessee farm women were separating the cream from their cow's milk and selling it to commercial processors. Women controlled cream production, and like poultry raising, it could provide an important source of income. Cream separator manufacturers geared their advertisements to women, showing women operating their machines. The advertisements for the "Sharpless Suction Feed Separator," for example, stated bluntly, "[L]et the women buy the separator—they have to clean it and in many cases turn it twice a day."[26] Robbie Sanford, who was raised on a farm twenty-five miles south of Nashville, recalled that her mother "bought me a piano with what you would call back in those days butter and egg money . . . first it was butter, then they came around with separators and we sold the cream."[27]

Farm women also brought in much-needed family income by selling other items in Nashville, including medicinal roots such as ginseng and yellowroot, chestnuts, goose feathers, beeswax, wool, and tallow. In areas on the periphery of Nashville's hinterland where cash was scarce, like in the eastern Highland Rim and Cumberland Plateau, these goods would be bartered. Farmers and their wives traded with storekeepers, but barter "prices" were listed in local newspapers for goods that had a market in Nashville. One eastern Highland Rim farmer recalled that his mother would trade goose feathers at forty-five cents to the pound with a local storekeeper for clothing and "come back with the awfulest stuff you ever seen."[28]

Nashville's active market for livestock, including hogs, cattle, and sheep, and growing meat-processing industry created another means for Middle

Let the Women Buy the Separator—
They Have to Clean it and in
Many Cases Turn it Twice a Day

Cream separators were marketed toward women
in the 1920s (*Southern Agriculturalist*).

Tennessee farmers to augment their incomes. Occasionally farmers close to the city sold their own cured meat in town along with their produce. For farmers farther from Nashville, hogs and cattle came by hoof or rail to the city's Union Stockyards. Hogs were "the real cash crop of the Tennessee farmer." In 1920 the Nashville Union stockyards posted receipts of 614,523 hogs.[29] Beef cattle production was much more limited. When the Tennessee Department of Agriculture offered advice to farmers, it invariably was to "raise more hogs."[30] In addition, since most Middle Tennessee counties' fence laws protected the open range for livestock, small farmers and tenants were particularly attracted to hog raising. Free-range hogs, which fed on the mast of the forest until fattened on corn or silage just before being brought to market, cost very little to raise. They were an inexpensive source of meat for farm families and a ready source of cash when sold.

Nashville's meat processors, like Middle Tennessee's fruit and vegetable growers, faced competition even in their own trading hinterland as the large midwestern packing houses moved into Nashville. In 1917, for example, Armour & Company opened a branch in Nashville and later extensively expanded to include cured and fresh meats. The firm could announce to its Nashville and Middle Tennessee clientele that its beef and pork "come in direct in refrigerator cars from the packing house of Armour & Co. in Kansas City." By 1925 Swift & Company had also moved into the Nashville market selling fresh western and midwestern meat (although continuing to rely on local poultry and dairy products, as discussed above).[31]

Competition in the meat industry brought complaints from livestock dealers that the poor quality of free-range stock coming to Nashville was limiting the market's growth. They lamented that "we lack only the pure-bred" livestock necessary to make Nashville the "Mid-Market of the South." The *Nashville Tennessean* reported that "cheap hogs were a drag on the [Nashville] market, but good corn fed stuff went along at all times, and the demand was for this latter class of hogs only." Market observers reported that "only strictly choice corn fed hogs" were in demand at Nashville's stockyards and that "all mast fed, peanut fed and doubtful hogs are being discriminated against."[32]

In the early 1920s, Middle Tennessee's larger pork producers complained of the problems caused by lax fence laws and free-range hogs. P. E. Alven, a Maury County farmer, despaired that too many farmers "are trying to make a living on a few hogs on the free range" and called for legislation establishing a three- or four-strand barbed-wired fence as a legal fence so "progressive farmers could afford to fence their land."[33] One Franklin County farmer complained of a "very poor man [who] managed to get a hold of a farm adjoining my own." This new farmer brought with him "about a dozen shoats," which were "all of the razorback type of hogs, with rail-splitting noses." These rail-splitters were "into every man's fields . . . constantly destroying various crops." Because these free-range razorbacks "spoiled the looks" of the local buyer's carload, he lost half a cent per pound on the entire lot once they were shipped to market. From Houston County came the report that forest fires there "are mostly set for the purpose of having early pasture for the stock running at large." Farmer G. H. Miller complained that "the free range system" was the "curse of agriculture."[34]

In the 1920s Tennessee Department of Agriculture officials, in concert with the expanding agricultural extension service, mounted a campaign to raise the quality of farmers' herds through the introduction of "pure-breds" and by "driv[ing] the [free-range] scrub from the farm." A prominent Nashville-based agricultural paper advised farmers to "kill the scrub sire." To make a profit in hog raising, it asserted, farmers would have to "get good hogs . . . [and] raise them largely on pasture crops, feed them a balanced ration, [and] give them sanitary quarters to live in." Agricultural reformers criticized the open range as an impediment to the modernization of the state's agriculture, and they worked to promote state and county ordinances that required farmers to fence their stock. By the end of the decade, most Middle Tennessee counties, with the exception of a few in the eastern

Highland Rim and Cumberland Plateau, had closed the open range. These efforts were justified as a means of eliminating the "razorback influence" on Tennessee hogs and the "heretic" variety of free-range cattle. The campaign also cited the need to protect reforested land from free-range cattle and to keep newly constructed motor highways free from roaming herds.[35] Petty hog producers who depended upon the open range saw the market for their stock dry up at the same time that fence laws made it more difficult and expensive to raise livestock. Fence laws also did away with an important source of inexpensive, home-grown meat.

Logging timber from Middle Tennessee's extensive hardwood forests comprised the most important off-farm work for the region's farmers. The men that logged the virgin hardwood forests along the Upper Cumberland River and its tributaries in the eastern Highland Rim and Cumberland Plateau supplied the timber that lay behind Nashville's emergence as the nation's leading hardwood lumber market in the 1890s. The western Highland Rim, the other center of Middle Tennessee timbering, specialized in railroad ties for markets in Nashville and towns farther up the Tennessee River, such as Paducah, Kentucky.

The lack of an extensive rail network and the dependence on the Cumberland River to move timber meant that the logging industry in Middle Tennessee up through the 1920s was dominated by small, locally controlled operators. In this regard logging operations differed from those in the nearby Appalachian Mountains, where large, northern-owned timber companies moved into the area in the 1890s and purchased timber rights on a gargantuan scale, employing large gangs of full-time lumbermen to clearcut vast tracts of land. These companies hauled the profits out with the wood, leaving a population as impoverished as the denuded landscape.[36] In contrast, one scholar has even gone so far as to characterize logging along the Upper Cumberland River as a "folk industry" that permitted farmers to control their own "economic destiny."[37] Local control allowed farmers to retain a larger share of the return on their ownership of the timber and on the labor expended to log it. Just as important, however, local control allowed Middle Tennessee farmers to integrate logging into their diversified farming regime.

Timbering was well suited to the rhythms of the agricultural calendar. Farmers worked the forest during slack times on the farm in midsummer and in the winter. Along the Upper Cumberland River and its tributaries, farmers felled trees and hauled them to nearby creeks or rivers. The logs were collected, branded on the ends with special branding hammers, and lashed together into rafts to await the "tides," the periodic late-winter and spring rushes of high water that swelled the creeks and carried the log rafts

These Tennessee farmers also worked as tie hackers,
ca. 1915 (Looking Back at Tennessee Collection,
Tennessee State Library and Archives, Nashville).

to the Cumberland River. Once on the Cumberland, the logs would be sold
to log buyers, combined into even larger rafts, and piloted down river to
lumber markets in Nashville by crews of three to five raftsmen.[38]

The logging operations along the western Highland Rim that produced
railroad crossties complemented the rhythms of the agricultural calendar
as well. As one farmer recounted, "I never missed a crop, but winters and
leisure time I done a lot of [tie] hacking." Farmers culled the best trees from
their own land, or, more typically, would purchase a tract of timber from a
landowner for either a fixed price or a share of the timber, usually one-third
of it. "Tie hacking" was laborious and time consuming. Working in crews
of six or more, loggers would fell the trees and drag the logs out of the forest with horses or mules. Then the logs would be "scaffolded up" on thick,
squared timbers to prevent the tie hackers' axes from hitting the ground.

Loggers then split and hacked, by hand, the logs square with broad axes. Usually two crossties could be hewn from large logs, although single log ties—called pole ties—came to be preferred by the railroads.[39]

The earnings from logging provided an important and reliable cash income for Middle Tennessee farmers, especially those in the more isolated sections of the eastern and western Highland Rim and the Cumberland Plateau. For many Middle Tennessee farmers, especially those farming marginal farms, logging was their *only* reliable source of cash income. J. B. Williams recalled that his father, a farmer trying to scratch a living out of twelve acres of Putnam County farmland in the early years of the century, "went after" self-sufficiency, raising mostly corn. When it came to earning cash, however, "timber was number one and farming was next." The elder Williams, his son recounted, "worked in a lumber mill some, off and on, getting trees [but] they didn't have much mills up there," so he "had quite a lot of getting into the woods and get[ing] the logs out."[40] Another farmer recalled that "we would take a load of timber to town and bring back a sack of corn and a bale of hay and have a little change left over in our pocket."[41]

Timbering was also an important part of tenant farmers' efforts to acquire the means to purchase a farm. The relationship of logging to the purchase of farmland was noted in the mid-1920s by the authors of a survey of farming in Overton County, who observed that "it is difficult for the average tenant on farms in this county to accumulate enough to buy a farm, unless they engage in some outside occupation, such as logging, [saw] mill work, [or] hauling timber."[42]

Participants in a folk industry or not, Middle Tennessee loggers were quite capable of denuding the region's virgin forests without the aid of northern capitalists. As was the case for the Great Lakes lumber industry, Nashville's hardwood-lumber industry declined because by the 1920s, virtually all of the old-growth forests were cut, and logging as a means of livelihood for Middle Tennessee farmers went into a steep decline.[43] The Nashville *Banner* boasted in 1910 that Nashville stood at the center of "immense forests of hardwood lumber" and that one needed "no prophetic vision to foretell the great advantages Nashville possess[ed] in hardwood manufacturing and the lumber market," but the truth behind these optimistic booster claims was that most of the best timber within the city's hinterland would be gone by 1930.[44]

Statewide, the peak year for lumber production came in 1909, when Tennessee produced 1.2 billion board feet of lumber. During the years 1880–1930, the total area of woodland on Tennessee farms declined by 52 percent, or some 5.8 million acres. In Middle Tennessee the heaviest decreases occurred in the western side of the Cumberland Plateau, the main source of supply for Nashville's lumber mills from the 1890s through the 1920s.[45]

As logging cut the size of the forests within Nashville's hinterland, the tracts of old-growth forest that supplied the best hardwood timber became especially scarce. One observer in Overton County in the 1920s noted that the county's formerly expansive stands of virgin timber were "rapidly being depleted."[46] By 1931 only thirty-eight of Tennessee's ninety-five counties had any old-growth forest remaining. Of the 6.2 million acres of woodland in these thirty-eight counties, only 401,000, or 6.5 percent, were old growth. While fifteen of these counties were in Middle Tennessee, only 188,000 acres, or 6.2 percent, of the three million acres of woodland in these counties could be considered old growth. By 1930 Middle Tennessee's remaining old-growth forests were a mere fragment of the vast stands of oak, hickory, poplar, walnut, cedar, and ash that had stretched across the Central Basin, Highland Rim, and Cumberland Plateau just fifty years earlier.[47]

Deforestation was not new to Middle Tennessee, however. It began first in the late nineteenth century in the Central Basin in the counties closest to Nashville. The cedar forests surrounding Nashville were so heavily logged that as early as 1874 the once-abundant tracts of red cedar in Davidson, Rutherford, Sumner, and Williamson Counties were, according to J. B. Killebrew, the secretary of the Tennessee Bureau of Agriculture, "nearly exhausted." Meanwhile, overcutting in those areas where cedar remained plentiful, such as Bedford, Marshall, Maury, and Wilson Counties, was "rapidly exterminating the forests." Ash, used for tool handles and wagon-wheel spokes, was another important species that had been abundant in the Central Basin and throughout the Highland Rim but was now, according to Killebrew, "growing scarce except in places remote from facilities or transportation."[48]

By the mid-1920s logging declined as a major prop supporting the Middle Tennessee farm economy. The rafting of logs down the Cumberland to Nashville ceased altogether in 1931 as the deepening depression decimated the demand for lumber and wood products. While rail and motor-truck competition played a role in the decline of rafting, the primary cause was overcutting along the Cumberland River and its extensive system of tributaries. Overcutting also sent the western Highland Rim's crosstie industry into decline in the 1920s. Demand for crossties also declined as railroad construction slowed. In addition, the widespread adoption of creosote by railroads extended the life of crossties and allowed the use of nearly any type of wood, rather than the cedar and white oak that had put the western

Highland Rim at a competitive advantage. Tie-hackers also suffered as railroads began insisting upon exact and uniform specifications for crossties, favoring owners of steam and gasoline-powered mills over the independent tie-hackers.[49]

Family farming, which had been the cornerstone of a highly diversified and independent agriculture in the late nineteenth century, no longer offered much promise for young people by the 1920s. Increasing pressures upon the land and rising values made the ascent to farm ownership more difficult. Middle Tennessee farmers had fed the city, and its timbermen had logged the wood to build it. Middle Tennessee farmers' attempts to bolster their livelihoods through market linkages to Nashville had prolonged Middle Tennessee's farm economy only temporarily. By the early 1920s Nashville's integration into national produce and meat markets had undercut Middle Tennessee's petty fruit, vegetable, and livestock producers, while deforestation undercut the timber industry.

The traditional path up the agricultural ladder from tenant to owner no longer guaranteed the security or the standard of living it had thirty years earlier. Instead, the ladder had become, as one scholar of southern economic development has noted, "a treadmill."[50] The final response of young Middle Tennesseans was simply to leave the countryside.

CHAPTER 5

Leaving the Countryside

As prospects for continuing Middle Tennessee's general farming regime grew bleaker after 1900, a growing portion of the region's population, particularly the young, migrated from the countryside. Moving was not a new experience for rural Middle Tennesseans; it was a well-established strategy by which farm families overcame hard times and coped with economic change. These rural mobility patterns involved long- and short-distance moves. Thousands of Middle Tennesseans resettled in western and southwestern states in the last two decades of the nineteenth century. More important and frequent were the varieties of short-distance, often temporary, migration strategies that rural families employed to bolster the family economy. Farm owners and tenants changed farms, children were sent to live and labor with other families, and young people entered into seasonal and circular migration patterns before starting their own households. After 1900 a new wave of Middle Tennesseans moved out of agriculture altogether as they migrated to Nashville, other southern cities, and cities beyond the South.

The changing destinations of the dominant migration streams flowing out of rural Middle Tennessee and their changing demographic composition reveal the nature and extent of changes in agriculture sweeping Middle Tennessee in the early twentieth century. The volume of migration from rural Middle Tennessee increased as the region grew more urban-oriented and as migration-selectivity patterns changed; blacks became more mobile than whites and women more than men. Above all, migration in Middle Tennessee was a movement dominated by young adults.

Middle Tennessee's progressive reformers, concerned with the health of rural society, responded with alarm to the migration taking place in the 1910s and 1920s. They sought to stem the exodus by bolstering rural communities with improved schools and modern roads. However, progressives misunderstood the causes of the movement out of rural areas. Better schools and roads did nothing to address the problems facing Middle Tennessee farmers and served only to quicken the pace of migration. School and road reform likely hastened outmigration by better preparing young people for urban employment and by integrating isolated sections of Middle Tennessee into the regional economy.

Moving was a central feature of life in southern agriculture, and especially so in Middle Tennessee. A Chattanooga-based farm journal reported in the early 1880s that "about one half, or more, of our farmers live in such a way as to produce the impression that they are mere denizens, sojourners, campers."[1] Many of these "sojourners" were preparing to move west. Before the state attracted more permanent white settlers in search of better and cheaper land westward-moving herdsmen in search of open range on which their hogs and cattle could graze were the first to reach Tennessee. Most black and white Middle Tennesseans were themselves children or grand-children of migrants who had moved west—voluntarily or involuntarily—from North Carolina or Virginia before the Civil War.[2]

The lore surrounding the movement west to Tennessee constituted an active part of local memory. One Tennessee farm woman, born in 1873, re-called of her community that "most of the people around here, their grand-sirs was the Tarheel kind." Idella Woods recalled her parents' separate west-ward treks to Tennessee just before the Civil War. Her mother moved from Virginia, and her father came from North Carolina. The migration from North Carolina and Virginia to Tennessee continued until the end of the nineteenth century, although at much reduced levels.[3]

The descendants of westward migrants, late nineteenth-century Middle Tennesseans did not hesitate to continue the movement west to Texas, Ar-kansas, Missouri, and Oklahoma in search of cheaper and more plentiful land upon which to farm. James Morgan wrote his brother in Nashville in 1870, "I am determined to go west where land is cheap." Morgan wrote that his brother Tom sought to leave the farm behind and also "has concluded now to go to Texas. . . . [H]e talks of going into the grocery business."[4] A correspondent in Bedford County reported that "visions of new wealth in new countries have decoyed many of the best citizens from the county" and thus "there has been more emigration from the county than immigration to it." Another correspondent reported that the desire to migrate west was strong in isolated Cumberland County, where "many would go [west] if they could sell their lands."[5]

Black Tennesseans' "pioneering spirit," as Carter Woodson described it, sent them west as well. Most famous was the well-organized movement of the "exodusters," who left Nashville in 1879 for Kansas.[6] Texas, Okla-homa, Arkansas, and the Mississippi Delta continued to draw black Tennesseans searching for lower farm rents, higher wages, and the opportunity to become landowners away from the oppression of the older southern states. Indeed, for some black Tennesseans the West did not stop at California; in the winter of 1900–1901, there was an organized movement of some 700 black men who left Nashville to work on the sugar plantations of Hawaii.[7]

The southwestern states continued to draw large numbers of black migrants in the 1890s and early 1900s. Ray Stannard Baker noted in 1908 that planters and landlords in "the rich alluvial lands of Mississippi and the newer regions of Arkansas and Texas" were "able to pay more wages and give the tenants better terms [and thus] lure away Negroes of the East."[8]

In the 1900s Oklahoma attracted the last wave of black and white migrants to the Southwest. Oklahoma appealed to many Middle Tennesseans, even though the chief crop there was cotton, a somewhat unfamiliar crop to the majority of tobacco and general farmers from the region. One Middle Tennessee migrant to "indian territory" wrote to his hometown newspaper extolling Oklahoma's cheaper sharecropper rents: just a quarter of the cotton crop and an eighth of the corn crop rather than the prevailing Middle Tennessee rate of one-half of all crops. Another migrant to Oklahoma tailored his advice specifically to those who found the ascent to landownership too expensive in Middle Tennessee. He advised those who owned their farms to stay but advised tenants renting steep hillsides and "paying half of what you make" to head west.[9]

As large as the trek westward has loomed in the history of nineteenth-century America, it comprised only a small part of Middle Tennessee rural mobility patterns. Most Middle Tennessee migrants moved short distances, a central strategy for those farm families trying to earn a living off the farm. Generally these patterns were seasonal or circular—migrants, whose initial intentions often were not a permanent change of residence, moved short-distances for limited durations.

Tenant farmers moved most frequently. Tenants and sharecroppers engaged in year-to-year contracts, and changing farms could yield any number of improvements: lower rents, the chance to farm more productive land, access to healthier workstock and better implements (if not already owned), living in a nicer farm house, or working for a less demanding landlord.

Moving and poverty were inextricably linked. Fleta Cole, a white Middle Tennessee sharecropper's daughter, recalled that her family "was allus poor —shifting from one farm to another."[10] Ella Paschall recounted how there "aint but one time since we married when we was noways settled." Soon after they married she and her husband sharecropped for a good, honest landlord, and "crops were extry good for two years straight." The couple "saved up a hundred or two to spare" and bought a small mortgaged farm in the early 1920s.[11]

Paschall's experience shows that by the 1920s, owning a farm offered no guarantee of prosperity or security. She and her family held on to their farm for only a few years. "Everything hit up but good luck," she recalled. One of their children took ill, running up large medical bills. Then problems hit the farm itself. "Half of the stock on the place come down with some sort of misery or other [and] most of them were dead cold before we could start paying [our debts] on them." Disease decimated her chicken flock, and "we lost the farm [and] we was worse off than we'd been." Having slid back down to the "sorry living" of sharecropping, Ella Paschall and her family moved again, hoping soon to save enough money to leave sharecropping and at least rent for cash rather than on shares.[12]

Knowing that tenant families moved frequently reveals little about their destinations. For all their shifting from farm to farm, they tended to circulate within a limited area. Since tenancy and sharecropping were based on credit relationships as well as rental agreements, a tenant's reputation for farming skill and hard work, not to mention tractability, particularly if one were black, was important in getting the best tenancy and share arrangements. Since credit markets were local, for the poorest tenants—those owning neither tools nor workstock—a reputation for skill and hard work could be their only capital asset. Hence, many tenant farmers tended to stay in the same general vicinity where they were well known among landlords. The converse was true as well. Tenant farmers, who for one reason or another wanted to escape a reputation for intractability, laziness, or ineptitude or, in the case of blacks, for challenging established patterns of racial subservience, had an incentive to move farther away, to where they were not known.[13]

The locally specific nature of many agricultural skills worked to limit long-distance tenant mobility as well. Raising dark-fire tobacco of the Black Patch in the northern section of Middle Tennessee and the peanut culture of Humphreys County, for example, involved highly specialized techniques and tools. Farmers experienced in working these crops could change farms often, but their investment in skills and tools meant that they were likely to stay in the areas where these crops were grown. By the same token, landlords who hired tenants or sharecroppers were reluctant to employ anyone unfamiliar with local conditions and crops. Even in the much more pervasive general-farming areas of Middle Tennessee, knowledge of local soil and weather patterns was essential to successful farming, and this prerequisite served to limit the geographical scope of movement by otherwise highly mobile tenant farmers.[14]

An analysis of the World War I draft registration records of men aged twenty-one to thirty-one in two rural Middle Tennessee counties — Robertson and DeKalb — reveal these patterns of short-distance rural mobility. These records, unlike census returns or vital records, indicate the place of birth of registrants, allowing one to track short-distance, intrastate and intracounty moves. Quite typical of counties throughout rural Middle Tennessee, Robertson County, which was immediately adjacent to Nashville in the northern Highland Rim, supported an extensive tobacco and general farming regime, and the more remote DeKalb County, located in the eastern edge of the Central Basin, also supported general farming.[15]

In both Robertson and DeKalb Counties the registration records show that the overwhelming portion of young men were natives of the county in which they resided. In Robertson County 75 percent of the sample had been born in the county, while in Dekalb County 89 percent of the sample were county natives. The few non-natives in these counties migrated from adjacent Middle Tennessee counties or nearby places in Kentucky.[16]

On the surface, these figures suggest extremely low levels of rural population mobility. Few of the draft registrants moved into either Robertson or DeKalb County from somewhere else, and those who had moved from only a short distance away. A closer examination, however, reveals a more complex pattern of mobility within each of these counties. A large portion of those born in each county no longer resided in the community of their birth. In Robertson County 40 percent of the county natives had moved at least once in their lifetimes, while in DeKalb County 53 percent of county natives had done so. Farmers were more likely than nonfarmers to be intracounty movers. In Robertson County 57 percent of the sample worked as farmers or farm laborers, but 75 percent of intracounty movers were so employed. In DeKalb County, where virtually no employment outside agriculture existed, the two figures were much closer: 84 percent of the registrants worked in agriculture and 90 percent of intracounty migrants worked as farmers or farm laborers. Unfortunately, the registration records do not indicate a farmer's tenure status. Undoubtedly, however, tenants were more mobile than owners, and farm laborers were the most mobile of all.[17]

The perspective of John Graves, a scion of a Middle Tennessee landholding family, provides another view on these frequent but geographically constricted patterns of mobility that prevailed in Middle Tennessee. In his view, the most skilled tenants tended to stay on one farm. These tenants "knew how to manage farming operations and needed only limited supervision [by the landlord]." It was common for "this type of family to stay a decade or longer at one place." More mobile were sharecroppers who "knew how to produce and manage the enterprise" but "usually stayed around three years on a farm before moving to another farm in the same community." The most transient were the poorest sharecroppers, who "moved annually from one community to another," escaping debts and poor reputations or desperately seeking a better arrangement. While Graves's judgments about the personal characteristics of tenants should be viewed with skepticism, his overall assessment of the frequency and destinations of tenant moves is accurate and supports the findings from the World War I draft registration records.[18]

These rural mobility patterns contradict the argument that farm tenancy, particularly sharecropping, tied tenants to one landlord through coercive measures such as debt peonage.[19] Indeed, moving was an essential element in the tenant household's economic strategy and the tenant families who stayed on one farm tended to do so not because of coercive measures but because they were doing relatively well.

Not all moving was done as a complete family. Middle Tennessee farm households depended upon the labor of children. Laboring on the family farm was most typical, but it was also common for poor families to send children away to labor on other farms or in nearby towns. For families working marginal farms, the need to be relieved of the expenses of feeding and clothing their children outweighed the value of their farm labor. Daughters, in particular, were prone to being sent away from the home to work. The reluctance to put daughters behind the plow or to put them tending row crops made their labor less valuable in the fields than that of sons.[20] To be relieved of feeding and clothing one, two, or three children could make an important difference in a family's economic well-being. Also, the demand for domestic labor made daughters easily employed on other farms or in nearby small towns. Santifee Paschall "har'd out" one son and three daughters to local families. One daughter worked as a domestic servant; another helped nurse an injured woman. The youngest daughter accompanied her brother to a local farm, where he worked, presumably, as a farmhand. This twelve-year-old daughter was "staying out there and walking to school" with the farmer's own daughter. In exchange, "she's making her board and keep," Santifee Paschall noted. "I miss all the chil'ren," she further recounted, "but by their working we manage by nippity tuck to git along." Miss them she might, but the imperatives of the family economy meant that mobility was an essential strategy for family survival.[21]

The disruption of a family by death or divorce also meant moving for children. Finits Evits, one of ten children, was hired out to a Kentucky tobacco farmer after his mother's death left him an orphan. His labor on six acres of tobacco was to be exchanged for living expenses during the four-month school term. But such moving did not always yield the promised reward.

In Evits's case, the farmer he hired out to failed to uphold his part of the bargain and did not supply him with the proper clothes to attend school. The divorce of parents could lead to a similar situation. Lillie Glasgow and her three siblings were apportioned among various relatives in Williamson County when their parents divorced.[22]

While tenants moved and children left home to labor, outmigration from rural Middle Tennessee owed more to patterns of circular migration closely tied to the life cycle and family formation. As entering Middle Tennessee's farming regime grew more expensive and more difficult, young men left their homes to work as agricultural laborers or work short stints in "public works" before returning to the countryside, getting married, starting families, and farming on their own as either owners or tenants. These short periods of migration could keep Middle Tennessee's young men in agriculture, tying them closely to the crop cycle. These mobility patterns became woven into the folk life of the Cumberland Plateau region, where the custom of a young man being "set free" by his father was a rite of passage. Being set free, Ward Curtis recalled, meant that "you were a man of your own head; [one's father] wan't your boss no more." It also meant a son was free to find his fortune elsewhere.[23]

Many of these young men worked in Middle Tennessee's logging and lumber concerns. Erie Woods worked in sawmills making barrels for three years. He then settled down to farming, making two crops. Only then, in 1904, did he get married.[24] But circular migration patterns could also take young Middle Tennessee men far from home. Some of them would head west to Texas, Oklahoma, and Kansas, following the annual harvest northward as the wheat ripened. Most of these young migrants would return to their homes in the South, but many "remain[ed] as wage hands the following year" working as hired farm help. Other young men headed north to Illinois and Indiana, harvesting corn as it ripened, and then returning to Tennessee.[25]

Many young men went to labor closer to home, in the few coal mines of the Cumberland Plateau for a time before going into farming. Mines extracting coal of varying quality developed in the 1880s in White County, and in the early 1900s newer mines spread across the Cumberland Plateau, with Cumberland, Fentress, White, and Grundy Counties developing the largest mining industries. Like timbering, working the mines was woven into the patterns of rural life. Younger men went off to the mines for a period while their families tended the crops. Ray Bob Lewis, a White County miner from 1918 to 1924, recalled that many of his fellow miners "lived in the country and worked in the mines," returning to their homes in the countryside only periodically.[26] But the coal industry in Middle Tennessee could offer only limited employment. Tennessee's eastern Highland Rim and Cumberland Plateau mines extracted low-quality coal and were poorly capitalized. Despite the hopes of investors and local boosters, the region never developed an extensive mining industry on the scale of nearby eastern Kentucky. By the 1920s most of the mines had closed or were in decline; a few, such as the Davidson-Wilder mines, held out until the early years of the Depression. The mine at Clifty, one of the largest on the Plateau, illustrates the temporary, transitory nature of mining. It employed 300–400 men at its peak and shut down in 1924. Clifty, which had been a thriving town before World War I, practically disappeared when the mining company sold the houses in the defunct mining village for about $30 to people who came into town, dismantled their newly purchased houses, and rebuilt them in the countryside.[27]

Illustrative of these seasonal and circular migration patterns is the case of Finits Evits, who we last saw when he was hired out as an orphan. When Evits was old enough to set out on his own in the 1910s, he first "hired out to farmers by the year." Not satisfied, he "didn't stay more than a year at a place" but still managed to save some money, which he put into making an ultimately unsuccessful crop with his older brother in Stewart County, Kentucky. The crop's failure drained Evits of his savings, and he set out moving again. This time he moved south to the Tennessee River bottoms, west of Nashville, and hired himself out as a timber worker hacking crossties. Eventually, he saved enough to marry and settle down to farm as a tenant and tie hacker.[28] Starting a family did not mean an end to Evits's moving. He balanced farming in Middle Tennessee with two stints in Paducah, Kentucky, working as a laborer in lumber yards and a plumbing outfit. By his own account, he earned good wages in Paducah, but he "always wanted to farm" and "went back to the farm" in Middle Tennessee as soon as he could.[29] During World War I, Evits did "very well." Strong crop prices allowed him to buy two mules, and he set his sights on buying a farm. However, he "lost out" during the postwar agricultural depression. His troubles were compounded by an illness that prevented him from harvesting his tobacco crop. Evits lost his mules and had to sell his unharvested crop to his landlord at a sharp loss.[30]

As young men like Evits found it increasingly difficult to establish themselves as farmers, more and more sought to leave the countryside permanently. The extent of the movement out of rural Middle Tennessee can be measured by the net outmigration from the region, or the change in its population due solely to population mobility. Although net-migration estimates offer no account of the frequency of moves or indicate the variety

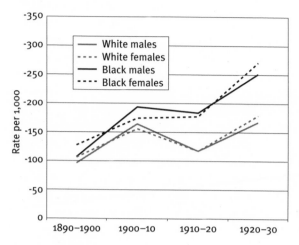

Figure 5.1. Estimated Net Migration Rates of U.S.-Born Population from Rural Middle Tennessee, by Sex and Race, 1890–1930

Source: See Appendix.

of destinations that migrants chose, they are well suited to assessing long-term migration trends among entire populations. The forward survival-rate method used in this study also allows for an assessment of migration selectivity by yielding net-migration estimates by sex, race, and age.[31]

Net migration estimates show the demographic consequences of the crisis in Middle Tennessee agriculture. Net outmigration increased sharply from a low of 56,159 in 1890–1900 to 96,319 in 1900–1910. Net migration from the region fell to −76,200 in 1910–20 before there was a full-fledged exodus in the 1920s. In 1920–30 rural Middle Tennessee experienced a total net migration of −110,896, twice the figure of the 1890s. As shown in Figure 5.1, the erratic but steadily rising rate of net migration shows the increasing propensity of rural Middle Tennesseans to leave the region. Net migration rates for the entire population of rural Middle Tennessee rose from −91 per thousand in 1890–1900 to −142 in 1900–1910. In the following decade, the net migration rate fell to −112 before it swelled to −162 per thousand in 1920–30.

These decennial estimates do not allow for a measure of the short-term fluctuations in population mobility. The decline in net migration in 1910–20 obscures the onset in 1916 of the Great Migration of black southerners northward. In all likelihood, migration increased in 1916 in concert with this well-documented event, then declined with the postwar recession of 1920–21, before resuming with renewed vigor for the remainder of the 1920s.[32]

The exodus of black southerners during and after World War I points to an important aspect of Middle Tennessee migration: it was a highly selective process. Not all rural Middle Tennesseans showed the same willingness to leave the region, and the subpopulations that showed the greatest propensity to leave Middle Tennessee reveal the pressures mounting upon the region's agriculture. Black Middle Tennesseans were much more likely to leave rural Middle Tennessee than whites. Fewer opportunities for blacks in the region's agriculture compounded by racial oppression lay behind higher rates of outmigration. For example, in 1890–1900 the rate of black outmigration per thousand (males and females combined) stood a full thirteen percentage points above the rate for whites. The onset of the Great Migration can be seen in the widening gap between black and white migration rates after 1910. The difference in rates rose to twenty points in 1900–1910, fifty-three points in 1910–20, and seventy-five points in 1920–30.

The sharp divergence between black and white migration rates after 1910 is indicative of the strong northward pull upon black southerners that began during the World War I and continued into the 1920s. The strength of that pull can be understood by examining the distribution of Tennessee-born *interstate* migrants. As Table 5.1 shows, before 1910 most Tennessee-born blacks who had moved out of the state were located in the predominantly agricultural states of Arkansas, Louisiana, Oklahoma, and Texas, which comprise the U.S. Census Bureau's West South Central region. The second most popular destinations were Alabama, Kentucky, and Mississippi, in the census's East South Central region. Both sets of destinations indicate strong rural-rural migration patterns. After 1910 the destinations of black interstate migrants shifted overwhelmingly to the industrial states of the Midwest. By 1920 the east north central states of Ohio, Indiana, Illinois, Michigan, and Wisconsin were the leading places of residence of Tennessee-born blacks. The portion of Tennessee-born blacks living in the older, rural destinations had fallen sharply.

Tennessee-born whites had a greater stake in agriculture, so the pull of industrial jobs in the north, while increasingly powerful after 1910, was much weaker than that on black Tennesseans. When white Tennesseans migrated from the state, they tended to either head to other agricultural states in the West and Southwest or move short distances to border states. As Table 5.2 shows, the west south central states were the leading interstate destination for the period 1890–1930. While predominantly rural-rural, these migration streams contained important rural-urban elements

Table 5.1. Tennessee-Born Blacks Residing in Other States, by Census Region, 1890–1930

Census Region	1890	1900	1910	1920	1930
New England	0.1%	0.2%	0.2%	0.2%	0.2%
Middle Atlantic	0.6	1.3	1.6	3.5	4.7
East North Central	11.0	15.9	19.6	34.9	46.1
West North Central	14.7	13.2	12.6	13.4	12.3
South Atlantic	2.8	3.8	4.3	5.1	5.1
East South Central[a]	28.7	28.3	25.9	18.8	15.5
West South Central	40.8	35.6	33.5	21.4	13.7
Mountain	0.8	1.1	1.2	1.2	0.7
Pacific	0.5	0.6	1.2	1.5	1.7
Total	100	100	100	100	100
(N)	86,381	103,374	123,899	147,103	175,852

Source: U.S. Population Census, 1890–1930.
Note: Census Regions are comprised of the following states: New England: Conn., Maine, Mass., N.H., R.I., Vt.; Middle Atlantic: N.J., N.Y., Pa.; E. N. Central: Ill., Ind., Ohio, Mich., Wisc.; W. N. Central: Iowa, Kans., Minn., Mo., Nebr., N.D., S.D.; South Atlantic: Del., D.C., Fla., Ga., Md., N.C., S.C., Va., W.Va.; E. S. Central: Ala., Ky., Miss., Tenn.; W. S. Central: Ark., La., Okla., Tex.; Mountain: Ariz., Colo., Idaho, Mont., Nev., N.M., Utah, Wyo.; Pacific: Calif., Ore., Wash.
[a] The Tennessee figure is not included in the regional total.

as well. The Oklahoma oil industry, for example, attracted many Tennesseans after 1910. White migration to the east north central states increased after 1910, but not to the extent that black migration did.

Black Middle Tennesseans' higher migration rates led to sharp proportional and absolute declines in rural Middle Tennessee's black population. Twenty-two percent of rural Middle Tennessee's population was black in 1890, and that figure progressively declined to only 12.6 percent in 1930 as the total population of black residents in the region fell 38 percent. Rural Middle Tennessee's white population, despite its high rates of outmigration, increased by over 100,000, a 22.7 percent increase over the years 1890–1930. In addition, a rise in employment opportunities for females in Nashville and more distant cities in the 1920s helped draw women from the countryside. By the 1920s the migration stream out of rural Middle Tennessee had become female-dominated. Indeed, in 1920–30, black women showed the greatest rate of migration from rural Middle Tennessee.

The age structure of net migration reveals the tendency of young adults to leave the region as farming became less attractive as a livelihood. Demographers have long observed that young adults make up the most mobile segment of populations in industrializing societies, and in this regard

Table 5.2. Tennessee-Born Whites Residing in Other States, by Census Region, 1890–1930

Census Region	1890	1900	1910	1920	1930
New England	0.1%	0.2%	0.2%	0.3%	0.3%
Middle Atlantic	0.6	0.9	1.0	1.5	2.1
East North Central	9.0	8.4	6.9	10.0	16.8
West North Central	20.1	17.9	12.8	10.3	8.3
South Atlantic	5.2	7.2	7.2	11.6	13.8
East South Central[a]	18.0	20.3	18.1	19.4	19.6
West South Central	42.3	39.8	45.0	37.7	29.1
Mountain	1.6	2.0	3.2	3.5	3.0
Pacific	3.2	3.4	5.0	5.8	7.0
Total	100	100	100	100	100
(N)	410,253	415,920	546,686	601,340	702,835

Source: See Table 5.1.
Note: See Table 5.1.
[a] The Tennessee figure is not included in the regional total.

Middle Tennessee was no exception.[33] As Figures 5.2 through 5.5 show, the age structure of net migration was skewed toward the twenty-five to thirty-four and thirty-five to forty-four age groups in each of the decades between 1890–1930 among blacks and whites, as well as males and females. Young adult men were most vulnerable to the pressures of rising Middle Tennessee farmland values. By the 1920s young women were also moving out of the countryside into cities to work before marrying and starting families, replicating the circular migration patterns of men.

The age structure of white migration shows most clearly the dominance of young adults in rural Middle Tennessee's seasonal and circular migration patterns. In all decades, the net migration was greatest among white males and females in the twenty-five to thirty-four age group and then fell sharply among older age groups. Migration rates were much lower among children and the thirty-five to forty-four age group, suggesting that it was rare for entire white families to leave rural Middle Tennessee.

Black migration, on the other hand, encompassed a much broader age spectrum than white migration. Black migration rates peaked at three age groups: under fifteen, twenty-five to thirty-four, and thirty-five to forty-four. The high migration rates of children, young adults, and those approaching middle age imply a movement of families. Unlike white rural Middle Tennesseans, who were using migration of individual family members as a strategy to cope with declining opportunities in agriculture, black rural

Figure 5.2. Age Structure of Net Migration of U.S.-Born
Population from Rural Middle Tennessee, by Sex and
Race, 1890–1900

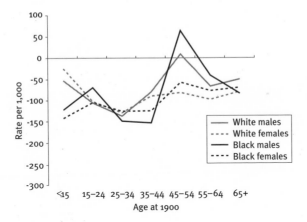

Source: See Appendix.

Middle Tennesseans gathered their families and left agriculture, turning their backs on farming, Middle Tennessee, and the South.[34]

Rural people were well aware of this exodus of young adults from the countryside. One elderly farm woman noted that in her community there were "plenty of children, plenty of old people" but the "young folks" had "gone everywhere and anywhere to get away from farming life." So many young adults had left that life in her community was noticeably quieter and people were more law abiding. "With most of the young hot blood [gone]," she observed, "there's mighty little trouble with the law" and personal conflicts "scarcely ever comes down to the point of where blood's spilt these days." A survey of farm life in Overton County in the late 1920s found that most of the "younger people" either had left or were planning to leave. A similar investigation of Bledsoe County found that young adults were leaving in droves and "as a rule, they not only left their community, but their county and often their state."[35] The exodus of these young people in the 1920s depleted rural Middle Tennessee of its most productive population, leaving the very young and the old to predominate.

The exodus from Middle Tennessee's farms provoked alarm from Tennessee's progressive reformers. Migration from agriculture, Tennessee's rural progressives argued, threatened the "foundation on which all other industries and professions rest, and on which all depend for sustenance and support." They predicted that if the migration from agriculture continued, enough farmers could "drift away from the farms until production could

Figure 5.3. Age Structure of Net Migration of U.S.-Born Population from Rural Middle Tennessee, by Sex and Race, 1900–1910

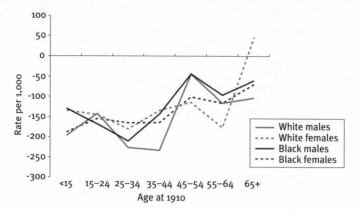

Source: See Appendix.

not meet consumption demands." The *Nashville Tennessean*, citing the 1920 census report that found slightly more than half of the nation's population living in urban places (2,500 or more), forecast that "the day was not far distant when the United States would no longer be able to feed itself."[36]

These predictions of food shortages in the cities, while often bandied about, were, of course, an alarmist fiction. Such dire statements were offered more to boost the morale of embattled farmers than as warnings of the future of the nation's food supply. Progressives concerned themselves not with the ability of farmers to feed the nation but with the health of a rural society they saw being drained of its most "progressive farmers" and slipping into a steep decline. This formulation put the problems of rural society strictly, and simplistically, into numerical terms. To progressives, outmigration, more so than high tenancy, persistent poverty, low farm incomes, or any of the other formidable economic problems farmers faced, posed the most pressing threat to the countryside. Tennessee commissioner of agriculture Thomas F. Peck framed the issue starkly in the early 1920s: "The hope of the country depends on checking the drift to the cities from the farms."[37]

This is not to say that Tennessee's progressives were unconcerned with the economic problems farmers faced in the 1910s and early 1920s. They constantly complained of the disparities between the earnings of the "producers" and the prices paid for food and other farm products by the consumer. They acknowledged that "for the past several years, those engaged in agriculture have been receiving less for their capital and labor invested than

Figure 5.4. Age Structure of Net Migration of U.S.-Born Population from Rural Middle Tennessee, by Sex and Race, 1910–1920

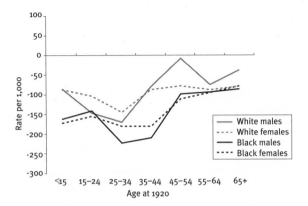

Source: See Appendix.

any other class of our citizenship." Middle Tennessee progressives strenuously promoted their solutions to the region's farm problems with their usual tirades against the tariff, balanced with prescriptions for crop diversification and cooperative purchasing and marketing organizations.[38]

However, for all the energy Middle Tennessee progressives expended on promoting solutions to the farmers' economic woes, when it came to the problem of migration, they slighted economic explanations for the exodus. Tennessee progressives, drawing heavily on the national awareness of rural problems raised by Theodore Roosevelt's Country Life Commission, by the early 1910s agreed that migration grew out of a social and cultural crisis undermining rural communities.[39] They pointed to poor schools, weak churches, and limited opportunities for social interaction as the crux of the crisis spurring farm families to pour into cities and towns. A 1911 rural school report epitomized this view, arguing that "many of the institutions peculiar to the country life are on the decline: that the country church is weakening, the glamour is being lifted from the old-time country home, rural population is declining, and there is a manifest decay of country life."[40]

When progressives did turn their attention to the economic problems facing farmers, they preached a gospel of development and cooperative marketing that sought to make Middle Tennessee's small family farms more like the businesses that were thriving in the region's cities and towns. Nonetheless, progressives believed that outmigration was a problem of

Figure 5.5. Age Structure of Net Migration of U.S.-Born Population from Rural Middle Tennessee, by Sex and Race, 1920–1930

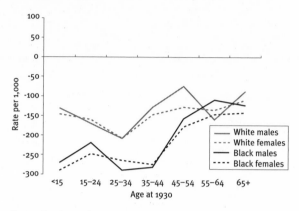

Source: See Appendix.

communities and culture because this view fit with the leading rural reforms that progressives were advocating in the 1910s and 1920s. Thus, the problem of outmigration from agriculture was folded into a larger view: that many of the countryside's problems stemmed from a rural culture that was backward and resistant to change.[41]

Rebuild and strengthen rural communities, progressives argued, and not only would the drift from the farms be stemmed, but it would be reversed as more vital rural communities "induce[d] good people to move to the country and make homes."[42] But how to accomplish this? To the reform-minded progressives of the 1910s and 1920s in state government and to the urban and small-town middle class, the key to revitalizing the countryside and stemming outmigration was to make the countryside more like the cities and towns that attracted rural dwellers. Modernize the countryside by extending the services that urbanites enjoyed, and its people would stay, progressives argued. The economic problems of Middle Tennessee agriculture would be solved by sponsoring cooperative marketing plans that would put the farmer's operation on a more sound business footing.

Tennessee progressives turned to the two leading rural reform measures of the day: the creation of a state system of consolidated public schools and the construction of a state system of hard-surfaced roads and highways. Improving schools and roads, long championed by reformers and supported by broad constituencies, was, according to rural progressives, the key to bolstering rural communities and stemming the outflow of population.

In regard to poor schools, one observer asserted, "Farmers, if they secured educational advantages for their children, had to move to the towns or villages." Rural progressive reformer W. B. Stokely, noting the heavy migration from Tennessee farms between 1900 and 1910, argued that these former rural-dwellers "went to the cities and towns . . . in search of better school facilities and greater social opportunities."[43] A 1911 report on the state's rural schools concluded similarly that "whatever other hypotheses may be advanced as the cause of the influx of population to the cities, it is certainly true that a large number of desirable inhabitants of the country are leaving their homes in order to secure proper education advantages for their children."[44]

Poor schools continued to be blamed for migration in the early 1920s. Tennessee commissioner of agriculture T. F. Peck acknowledged farmers' economic problems: "[W]e all know the handicaps under which farmers are laboring because of high taxes and the high cost of farm equipment coupled with the generally prevailing low prices of farm products." But, he argued, "there is another reason generally overlooked—a reason more far-reaching in its influences than all the other handicaps—and that is the lack of up-to-date facilities of education for the boys and girls of the rural districts. This latter condition has been the cause of more drift from the farm than all other causes combined."[45]

Progressives' vision of improved schools meant closing the small, scattered, one-teacher community schools that dotted the countryside and consolidating them into larger, multiteacher, multicommunity schools. Larger schools with better-paid, more professional teachers would offer an education comparable to that of the towns, keeping farm families from moving. Such schools would also be free of excessive, and presumably unprogressive, local community control.

Consolidation proposals were strongly opposed by many rural Middle Tennesseans. Opponents saw their local schools as bulwarks of community and feared that consolidation would reduce local control over teachers and curricula and increase taxes. Farm parents complained that "the distance is too great to send the children" and that the students "get very little benefit from the public school." Another rural parent complained that local school boards "tax us for a [teacher's] salary and pension." To many rural Tennesseans, the education offered by the modern consolidated school held dubious value, and could even be dangerous. "It is sad that we poor parents must sacrifice our money, our children's time, their morality with their soul included, for so little worth while [sic] in return," opined one opponent.[46]

Even among progressives, the consolidated school had its detractors. The Nashville-based *Southern Agriculturalist*, a leading mouthpiece of progressive reform, carried on a debate over the merits of school consolidation in 1920. One regular contributor to the paper voiced rural people's chief objections to education reform, arguing that consolidated schools would work to dissolve the local ties that developed around community schools. With small community schools, "every family feels a proprietary interest in the neighborhood school. The touch is intimate between the school and the home. Everyone knows the teacher, and she is a part of the community." When local schools are consolidated and the "school is taken out of the immediate neighborhood and set farther away in less familiar surroundings, this [community] link weakens materially." Consolidated schools would thus create "the sense of alien partnership." Although larger schools allowed the hiring of more, better-trained teachers, she continued, those teachers would become "also much more a part of the educational machine and much less a part of the intimate, sympathetic life of the community." Regardless of these objections, however, the paper's editors came down firmly on the side of consolidated country schools "as the road out of our educational difficulties."[47]

Despite opposition, in 1913 Tennessee's legislature passed a comprehensive education reform program that included consolidating community schools and providing transportation for the students. Since consolidation occurred at the county level, it proceeded steadily after World War I and into the 1920s. In 1914 Tennessee's 5,147 one-teacher schools comprised 70 percent of all elementary schools. Eight years later, the number of one-teacher schools had plummeted by one-third and accounted for only half of the state's elementary schools.[48] In 1921 state legislation replaced the separate high school and local elementary school district boards with one county board of education. These new countywide boards, largely controlled by "progressive men," eventually overwhelmed the remaining local resistance to consolidation and rural education reform.[49]

Rural school reform meant that children increasingly attended better schools for longer school terms. In the 1920s, the number of local one-teacher schools declined by a third across the state, while consolidated schools with three or more teachers doubled in number. The ninety-five-day school term that prevailed in Tennessee's rural elementary schools in 1902 rose steadily to an average of 156 days in 1930.[50]

White rural women eagerly took advantage of these new educational opportunities. Women tended to stay in school longer than men in rural Middle Tennessee. A 1920 survey of farm families in Williamson and Montgomery counties in Middle Tennessee found a sharp divergence in male and female education levels. Among farm-owning white families, wives were much more likely to have attended some high school than their hus-

The one-room schoolhouse, Crossville, Tenn., 1935 (Library of Congress)

bands. Nearly a third of these farm wives in Montgomery and Williamson Counties possessed more than an eighth-grade education, while the
portion of farm husbands who had gone beyond the eighth grade stood at
around one-fifth for Williamson County and one-seventh for Montgomery
County.[51]

The declining country church and a lack of social outlets for farmers compounded the effect of poor schools, progressives argued, weakening the
bonds of rural communities and loosening their ties to the farm. The opinion that "country churches belong to one of three classes—the sick[,] the
dying, and the dead" was widely held among reformers. Poorly attended
churches lacking strong leadership led to rural communities that were
"dead spiritually, rotten morally, and [most important] with[out] . . . progressive farmers." By the same token, "the social side of farm life" also required progressive reformers' attention. Farmers were "no longer willing
to be isolated for months from the rest of the world," they claimed, suggesting that loneliness helped fuel the move to the city. A 1927 social survey of
one Middle Tennessee county attributed the heavy outmigration of young
adults from the county to "insufficient recreational activities."[52]

Improved roads, the other reform issue on which Tennessee progressives
focused, was believed to be a key to rural modernization and revitalization.

Roads, progressives promised, would encourage economic development by "shorten[ing] the distance to market, to the school, to the railway station, and the country store." But progressives played down the economic benefits of roads and instead stressed their role as a catalyst for education reform. Indeed, they argued, good roads were essential for school consolidation. Better roads would allow rural students to travel farther to the larger consolidated schools, and thus eliminate the need for the more numerous one-room schools. Consolidated schools promised less outmigration. In 1913 a speaker before the reform-minded Middle Tennessee Farmer's Institute promised the farmers there that if they supported the movement for better roads, they could "do away with the one-room school house, have better schools and keep [their] children at home."[53]

Progressives also promised that improved roads would integrate rural Middle Tennesseans into the wider urban region, giving them an incentive to stay in the countryside. As T. F. Peck noted in a 1921 speech before a gathering of Middle Tennessee farmers, poor roads had isolated farmers and deprived rural people "of the advantages of what we term advanced civilization." Building more roads and integrating them into a state system of highways, Peck argued, would "remove the cause for so many leaving the farm for the towns . . . by providing those living in the country [with] educational, church, and social advantages equal to the towns." With the rural population thus assured of "good roads and good schools," he concluded, "we will have no trouble in inducing people to live in the country."[54]

Tennessee's progressives largely achieved the school and road-building reforms advocated in the 1910s and 1920s. They failed, however, to reverse the migration from the farms and repopulate the countryside. Indeed, it is likely their reform measures actually worked to promote migration. Better schools meant rising levels of education along with increasing material aspirations that could not be met in the countryside. Rural young people were increasingly better suited for urban jobs. To many of them, a modern road was simply a better road out of the countryside. Young farm women, in particular, acquired the education to became more employable in places like Nashville, where there was a great demand for women with basic literacy skills to fill the city's expanding clerical and sales sector. It is no coincidence that the confluence of education and highway reforms in the 1920s led to the highest rates of outmigration from rural Middle Tennessee.

School reformers, who acknowledged the relationship between better education and outmigration, blamed teachers and curricula for instilling aspirations in students that attracted them to city life. As early as 1911 the Tennessee Department of Public Instruction claimed that "the entire trend of [rural children's] education has been away from the farm and into the

Paved highways facilitated tenant mobility, as this Tennessee tenant farmer shows in the 1930s (Library of Congress).

city." It recommended that "a rural coloring must be given to the whole rural school process . . . to create a tendency among young people reared in the country and educated in the country school, to remain on the farm."[55] Seventeen years later, the author of an article in a state agricultural journal made the same accusation, complaining that schools were "actually encouraging" young people to move to the cities.[56]

Similarly, even as progressives championed the construction of modern rural highways, they denounced Middle Tennessee farmers' logical desire to take advantage of the new roads luring them away from their farms. Typical of this reaction was an editorial in *Tennessee Agriculture* that blamed the economic troubles of farmers on the extravagance of automobile ownership. Not only were automobiles "expensive luxuries" to buy and maintain, they were expensive "in time taken away from work that should be done on the farm." Lambasting the rising material expectations that poured into rural communities after roads were built, the author criticized farmers "for buying things [they] could wait for" and "easing up on work and trying some easier way to get by."[57]

Indeed, while roads did bring to previously isolated sections of Middle Tennessee more of the "advantages of . . . advanced civilization," to farmers the most important part of this civilization was the automobile, and they embraced this innovation enthusiastically. A 1927 survey of a county east of Nashville reported that "automobiles are rapidly taking the place of buggies in many communities."[58] Farmers purchased automobiles before virtually any other modern agricultural implement or household convenience, including indoor plumbing or electric lights. The portion of all Tennessee farm households owning an automobile rose from 8.9 percent in 1920 to 34.2 percent in 1930. Although farm owners were more likely to own an automobile—41.7 percent did so in 1930—tenant farmers also scraped the money together to buy automobiles; in 1930 one-quarter (25.4 percent) of tenant households owned a car. Farmers bought cars while they still plowed their fields with mules; the portion of farms owning tractors rose from 0.7 to only 2.7 percent in the 1920s. Ownership of motor trucks followed a similar pattern; only 3.5 percent of farm families owned one in 1930, up from 0.5 percent in 1920.[59]

The spread of roads and the rise of automobile ownership indicated a general integration of even the most remote section of Middle Tennessee into the wider regional economy, and an increasing diffusion of new, urban values about work and consumption in the countryside. In turn, young people became increasingly dissatisfied with the hardships of farm life. Older rural dwellers commented on the younger generation's aversion to the hard work of farming, complaining that young people "can't seem to abide by the hard scuffling ways you have to do to get by on a farm."[60] Pioneering folklorist Olive Dame Campbell's observations of the spread of new consumerist values to the southern highlands were even more true for Middle Tennessee. She noted the rapidity of change, observing that while "granny may still wear her sunbonnet and ride her side saddle, her granddaughter not uncommonly has bobbed hair and carmine lips." The creekbed road and "canvas-topped wagon" were quickly being replaced by "the hard-surfaced highway" and the "omnipresent Ford." To progressives' dismay, their efforts to diffuse modern, urban values, making the countryside more like the city, had unintended consequences.[61]

Middle Tennessee progressives had sought to stem migration from the countryside by bolstering communities with road and school reforms. That they failed is largely due to their confusion in identifying the decline of rural communities as a cause of migration rather than a result. The underlying social and economic trends that were making the acquisition of land, and then earning an adequate living from that land, more difficult sent young adults moving. New cultural values took root in an environment where material progress moved slowly.

In the 1920s the movement from the region's farms became a flood tide as the economic foundations of agriculture continued to weaken and the material expectations of many young people rose with their awareness of the "miscalled goods of civilization [that were] borne in every jolt wagon that works its way" into the country. Critics like Southern Agrarian Andrew Lytle called upon rural people to "throw out the radio and take the fiddle down from the wall" and turn their back upon the present. Unfortunately, by then southerners had long been reserving their Saturday evenings for tuning their radios to WSM's Grand Ole Opry. Lytle's call was a poetic rebuke of the modern, but it offered nothing to Middle Tennesseans trying to scrape a livelihood from the farm and only highlighted the rural life's lack of appeal.[62]

CHAPTER 6

Going to Nashville

Nashville exerted an increasingly powerful draw upon thousands of rural people. Each decade between 1890 and 1930 saw ever larger numbers of migrants pouring into the city. But Nashville was only one of many destinations for migrating rural Middle Tennesseans. The city's moderate size limited its ability to attract and absorb all those leaving the region. Nashville would be no instant city; indeed, its position relative to other southern cities in its ability to draw people from the countryside slipped as nearby rivals— Atlanta, Birmingham, and Memphis—each surpassed it in the urban hierarchy of the South after 1900.

At its most basic level, migration is the product of the spatial differentiation in earnings; migrants move from low-wage rural areas to higher-wage cities. Migration, in this view, is essentially an investment whose costs are outweighed by expected, future returns in the migration destination. Economists have argued that low wages and meager agricultural earnings in the South and better paying industrial employment in the North explain the movement of blacks out of the region. Studies of migration to southern cities and towns similarly stress the earnings differential between city and countryside, or between developed and underdeveloped counties in the region.[1] The *Nashville Tennessean* understood the very real economic motive underlying migration, asserting that "the hegira from the farms . . . follows from the natural desire of the human being to better his living conditions." African American Samuel Dean, a Bedford County sharecropper's son, put it more bluntly as he recounted his migration history to a Works Progress Administration interviewer: he was "[l]ookin' for better all the time."[2]

Migration to Nashville grew out of the push of economic, social, and even familial crises in the countryside and the pull of urban jobs. Initially, rural Middle Tennesseans came to Nashville to bring produce to the city's markets, livestock to its stockyards, or timber to its lumber mills. Soon, rural men and women were working for short stints there and then returning home to the countryside. An increased demand for labor during World

War I played a crucial role in this development. By the 1920s, as agriculture faltered and Nashville's demands for workers increased, people were moving in droves. By then, migrants had blazed many paths from countryside to city and what had been temporary, circular migration patterns to Nashville grew increasingly permanent and linear. Women, in particular, saw urban migration as a means of achieving a measure of independence not possible in the countryside, or as a way of escaping oppressive family or social relationships. In the 1920s migration to Nashville for both young men and young women had become routine.

Many rural migrants first encountered Nashville when they rafted timber, drove livestock, or hauled produce into the city.[3] Their short-term circular movements between city and hinterland brought the countryside in closer communication with the city and cleared the paths through which more permanent migrants would follow. The men that steered the rafts of hardwood timber down the Cumberland River returned to their homes with news of the city. Rowland Everette, who piloted four to six timber-rafts down the Cumberland River each year in the 1910s and 1920s, noted that the prospect of going to Nashville was a powerful draw when he organized rafting crews: Rafting "was dangerous all right, but we was wantin' to go to Nashville." Rowland recalled that "usually we took a new man or two—someone who had never been to Nashville . . . he's wantin' to go see the town."[4]

These frequent but brief trips to Nashville also served as important conduits for information about urban opportunities. Rural migrants living in Nashville would meet friends and family from the countryside by "going down there [to the stockyards] to meet them when they know they're going to bring in stock." The same was true of the public square's produce market, where country people would learn about the availability of work in Nashville and rural migrants in the city would ask about life back in the countryside.[5]

The attractions of these trips to Nashville were much more than the pay raftsmen, drovers, and other workers would earn for their labors. Indeed, it seems that many quickly recirculated their earnings back into the Nashville economy. Of his fellow timber rafters, Everette Rowland recalled, "most of them would buy whiskey, [and] a lot of them would get drunk before coming back [to the countryside], some of them would get in jail."[6] Livestock drovers were not to be outdone in rowdiness. When Claude Bickford's father, who drove cattle regularly from his farm in Van Buren County to the city's stockyards in the 1910s and 1920s, and his crew finished their business, they turned their sights on Nashville's entertainment. "They just tore up Nashville," so Bickford's father told him. One night after some heavy drinking, the drovers went to the cinema to see a Western. Jordenia Johnson, who had never seen a motion picture, fled the theater during a stampede scene, yelling, "Hup! Hup! Hup! Don't just sit there you damned fools, they'll run over you."[7] Fred Boyd, who was in the moonshine business, learned his way around town by "delivering the finished [product] to the buyers in Nashville in my father's truck." He decided to move his family there in the late 1920s.[8]

Shopping trips and family visits also brought rural people into the city regularly. Daisy Perry rode horseback to downtown Nashville from her farm in northern Davidson County for her monthly shopping trips in the late 1910s. In the early 1920s, Camilla Caldwell and her family traveled regularly from their home in Hartsville, Kentucky, to shop in Nashville. "I'd really pull my daddy's leg to bring me to Nashville because I'd want a particular kind of clothes or sweater," she recalled. Both women later moved to Nashville permanently.[9] "I was supposed to be on a visit," another young farmer's daughter recounted of her first trip to Nashville in the late 1920s when she was nineteen, "but all the time I was looking for work, no certain kind, but any kind." She returned back home with the offer of a clerical position "at a very low salary."[10]

Middle Tennessee's developing infrastructure also provided conduits for information about conditions in Nashville. When the Tennessee Central Railroad penetrated the eastern section of Nashville's hinterland in 1902, it brought that entire region into closer communication with the city. J. B. Williams recalled that "when they put that Tennessee Central through there they ran a passenger train there once a day, two or three times a week, and that's how they would get their word then [about work in Nashville]." According to Williams, returning migrants would say, "[Y]ou come to Nashville and make a lot of money. . . . [Y]ou could take these youngin's to Nashville and . . . everyone of them would get a job in the cotton mill. You'd have plenty of money."[11]

The heated atmosphere of wartime mobilization and the heavy demands for unskilled labor it created spurred a rapid movement of rural people into the city. Williams's parents, for example, learned "about how DuPont put in a big powder plant" near Nashville. With the plant and other war industries gearing up, his parents saw "so many things happening around a city, so they thought they could get a bigger job by coming on here to the city. It was a pulling power that [Nashville] had." In 1916 Williams's grandfather moved his family to Nashville, and his father and his young family followed soon thereafter.[12] Not all wartime migrants remained in Nashville after the war, but those who returned to the countryside brought with them a knowledge of Nashville and the opportunities for work that the city offered.

Nashville's business leaders anticipated that the war effort would be a boon for the city's economy, which had been sluggish at the outbreak of the war. The *Nashville Tennessean* proclaimed triumphantly, "IT IS THE BIGGEST ORDER AMERICAN BUSINESS EVER RECEIVED," adding that "Middle Tennessee and Nashville is [*sic*] upon the threshold of unbounded prosperity."[13]

War contracts may have stimulated production in Nashville's factories, but the heavy migration of rural people did not begin until the spring of 1918, when DuPont Engineering Company began construction of a government munitions plant on 5,000 acres of land at Hadley's Bend on the outskirts of the city. By early fall the Old Hickory powder plant employed some 34,000 in the powder factory and an additional 12,000 in construction. At least 30,000 of these workers lived in hastily built company housing adjacent to the plant. The latter figure included some 5,375 black workers living in a segregated "colored camp" and 662 Mexican workers living in the "Mexican village."[14]

The powder plant's labor needs quickly outstripped the available local supply. In February, DuPont opened a recruitment office to hire construction workers. By April, the firm was sending labor agents out to scour Tennessee and other parts of the South, recruiting workers for construction crews and plant operations. Agents drew from a $100,000 "floating fund" to loan migrants transportation money, which was later deducted from the workers' wages. In August alone, labor agents recruited 6,544 workers to the plant. The company paper reported that the "shortage of labor is being rapidly overcome by the daily arrival of large numbers of workmen from various sections of the country. Every train brings a load of workmen."[15] Right up to the armistice, men and women continued to stream into Old Hickory in search of unskilled production and construction jobs.

Old Hickory's production workers were overwhelmingly southern migrants. LuCretia Owen, a welfare worker employed by DuPont, noted in her diary that while "the majority of heads of departments come from the northeastern states, . . . the laborers come from the South Central states." Her observation is confirmed by a report in the company paper on labor recruitment. In one week in August 1918, labor scouts recruited some 2,200 workers from eight southern states to work as laborers in plant construction and in production. The leading states of origin were Tennessee and Oklahoma, with 450 workers from each; 400 came from Arkansas, 300 from Missouri, 200 each from Kentucky and Louisiana, and 100 each from Mississippi and Texas.[16]

The rush to recruit labor brought to the gates of Old Hickory many poor rural families with little or no money and desperate for work. One destitute family of five arrived with the "understanding that they could get a house." Company officials housed this and others like them in temporary "squatter housing," hastily constructed apartments lacking heat or stoves.[17] And once Old Hickory started employing large numbers of women as production workers in October 1918, the plant became flooded with female applicants. Many women arrived at the behest of labor scouts. One train alone brought in over 200 "recruits" to the women's employment office. Large numbers of women also learned of jobs at Old Hickory through newspaper advertisements or word of mouth and simply showed up at the plant. Two young girls who "ran away from their homes and hitch-hiked to Nashville and on to the plant" arrived hungry and broke. Another woman, "under the guise of patriotism," left her husband of ten years and two children to work at Old Hickory. LuCretia Owen counted teenage orphans, former showgirls, and farmers' daughters trying to help support widowed mothers among the women working at Old Hickory.[18]

The poverty of the workers arriving at Old Hickory often mirrored that of the southern countryside. So many destitute women were arriving at the plant that the quartermaster department had to set aside dormitory rooms for transient women "stranded without any funds." Large numbers of women workers arriving at the plant lacked proper clothing. At first, welfare workers employed by the plant solicited donations of clothing from other women workers, but the need quickly outpaced donations. Old Hickory's welfare department eventually established accounts with Nashville stores "for the purpose of buying the necessary clothes for girls who reach the reservation [i.e., company housing] destitute." Large numbers of men and women at Old Hickory did not have proper shoes, either. The prevalence of inadequate footwear was not only a sign of the poverty of the recently arrived workers; it also posed a safety hazard. Plant officials estimated that "poor shoes" accounted for one-third of the accidents at the plant, as workers slipped or injured their feet stepping on sharp objects.[19]

Large numbers of the laborers at Old Hickory arrived ill or undernourished. Pellagra was not uncommon among the workforce. It was reported that many of the women workers arrived at the plant "underweight." Old Hickory's management used the plant's cafeteria—"good food served by the duPont [sic] Company at cost"—as a recruiting tool, boasting of meals that certainly surpassed in quality and quantity those served at most southern farm tables. "No sandwich and cold lunch plate satisfies the powder plant woman. Roast Beef and 'extras' are what her appetite demands," reported the plant newspaper, noting that "the crowded cafeterias and mess-halls speak for the appetites" of the workers. One wonders how frequently such fare made it to Old Hickory's mess-halls, however. An item in the same issue of the company paper reported that wartime rationing had led to "food regulations [being] more strict than ever" and that workers should expect shorter rations of sugar, meat, and butter.[20]

At war's end, the boom in Nashville's factories went bust as contracts were abruptly canceled and layoffs swept the city and Old Hickory. After demobilization, production ceased at the plant, the workers were released, and the "wartime population [was] driven away, was lost sight of and forgotten." Old Hickory became a "ghost city."[21] The men and women let go from Old Hickory were reluctant to return to the farms from which many of them had come, even though DuPont paid for their return transportation. "The girls released are not content to return to their homes. They have been fired with the easy way of making money and they flood the employment offices at Nashville, overrun the hotels and Y.W.C.A. searching for jobs," noted LuCretia Owen in her diary in early December. Two weeks later she similarly observed that "our offices are flooded with girls wanting to get jobs in the village [near the plant] or Nashville."[22] An extreme case was that of Beryl Gazin, who began working at Old Hickory because "her mother didn't need her at home any longer" and who had heard that "girls here could have a good time . . . [and] make a lot of money and live away from home." When Gazin lost her job and LuCretia Owen ordered her to leave the women workers' dormitory, "she flew into a violent rage, snatched the order from my hand and struck at me, ran out the door and started toward the bachelor's quarters where her brother lives." When she was later apprehended by two plant officers and asked "whether she preferred the house of detention to a trip home[,] she chose jail." Her incarceration was brief, and upon her release, she went to Nashville.[23]

Even though many workers left Nashville after demobilization, the war effort did influence subsequent migration trends. Just as Nashville's market linkages and infrastructure fostered a circular movement to the city that laid the foundations for a more permanent migration, the heavy migration during the war paved the way for a steady stream into the city in the 1920s. Indeed, the pace of migration to Nashville during the war had been so dramatic that the city's leaders feared it would begin anew when the Old Hickory plant was converted to peacetime manufacturing. In 1920 Nashville's leaders cautioned against renewed migration: "Laborers from other cities are warned not to make a rush to Nashville expecting to find a bonanza here[;] as they did in 1918[,] each manufacturer will provide his own labor, and it will be natural for them to employ as many Nashville men as possible [and] labor from local circles. In any case 'foreign' labor is distinctly not wanted at the present time."[24] In 1923 DuPont laid plans to begin producing rayon at Old Hickory, and the local business leaders warned that

Table 6.1. Estimated Net Migration of U.S.-Born Population to Nashville, Tennessee, 1890–1930

Decade	Total	Rate (per 1,000)
1890–1900	1,687	23
1900–1910	3,975	41
1910–20	5,092	47
1920–30	16,501	122

Source: U.S. Population Census, 1890–1930.
Note: See the Appendix for explanation of forward-survival-rate method employed in calculation of estimates.

"those wishing employment at the big plant should not come to Nashville until the work is actually begun." They feared that "the news of the plant's being located in Nashville would cause an influx of labor similar to that when the work began at the powder plant."[25] By the late 1920s, the plant employed some 5,000 workers, a sizable number but only a fraction of wartime levels.[26]

The effect of World War I on migration to Nashville is reflected in total net migration and the rate of net migration to the city, as shown in Table 6.1 and Figure 6.1, respectively.[27] While net migration to Nashville during the three decades between 1890–1920 rose steadily, increasing from 1,687 in 1890–1900 to 5,092 in 1910–20, it more than tripled to 16,501 during 1920–30. Net migration rates followed a similar course, rising steadily from 23 per thousand in 1890–1900 to 47 per thousand in 1910–20, and soaring to a rate of 122 per thousand in 1920–30. The *Nashville Tennessean* observed in the 1920s that "since the war ended . . . the movement from the country to the city has not ceased." Indeed the high rate of net migration to Nashville in the 1920s started in 1918, one year after the American entry into World War I, declined during the postwar depression, and resumed in the 1920s.[28]

Migration to Nashville, like the movement out of rural Middle Tennessee, was a selective process. Blacks and whites showed markedly different propensities to migrate to the city. As Figure 6.1 shows, although the rates of black male and female net migration increased every decade, they tended to trail white rates. Both black and white women, however, showed higher migration rates than their male counterparts. In every decade except 1890–1900, white women showed the highest migration rates to Nashville while black women showed the second highest rates.

Figure 6.1. Estimated Net Migration Rates of U.S.-Born Population
to Nashville, Tennessee, by Sex and Race, 1890–1930

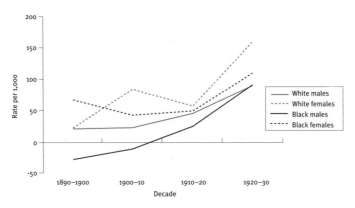

Source: See Appendix.

There were two reasons for the preponderance of female migrants. The first was that Nashville's labor market offered ample employment for both black and white women. By the 1920s Nashville's growing female clerical and sales sectors were drawing large numbers of white women to the city, while domestic work provided employment for black women.[29] The second was that since Nashville's manufacturing sector offered relatively fewer prospects for men, many were migrating to other places, particularly northern industrial cities.

That the city was enmeshed within larger patterns of migration that tended to draw some men to other destinations can be seen in the age structure of net migration rates shown in Figures 6.2 through 6.5. They demonstrate that Nashville exerted a relatively weaker pull on young men than on young women. In each decade between 1890 and 1930, black and white men tended to show lower inmigration rates than women in the younger age groups, fifteen to twenty-four and twenty-five to thirty-four. Nashville's pull on older migrants was weak; for every decade until the 1920s, the thirty-five to forty-four age group shows a negative figure, indicating net outmigration. Migration to Nashville remained a phenomenon dominated by young adults.

Did outmigration or low levels of inmigration of working adults mean that Nashville was serving as one step on a ladder leading rural migrants to larger cities in the North? A definitive answer cannot be given, but evidence from a one-seventh percent sample ($N = 1{,}710$) drawn from the records of the Selective Service records in 1917 is suggestive that for some, step migration was the case. Twenty-one- to thirty-one-year-old men were required

Figure 6.2. Age Structure of Net Migration of U.S.-Born Population to Nashville, Tennessee, by Sex and Race, 1890–1900

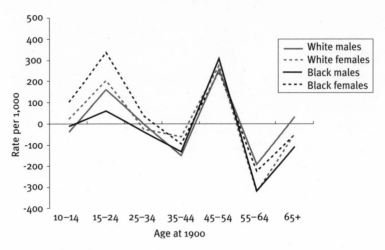

Figure 6.3. Age Structure of Net Migration of U.S.-Born Population to Nashville, Tennessee, by Sex and Race, 1900–1910

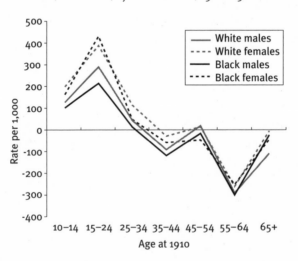

Figure 6.4. Age Structure of Net Migration of U.S.-Born Population to Nashville, Tennessee, by Sex and Race, 1910–1920

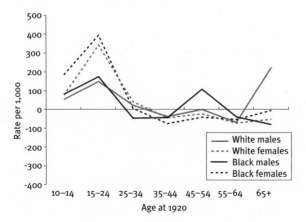

Source: See Appendix.

Figure 6.5. Age Structure of Net Migration of U.S.-Born Population to Nashville, Tennessee, by Sex and Race, 1920–1930

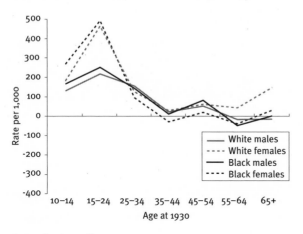

Source: See Appendix.

Table 6.2. Gross Migration of U.S.-Born Males, Ages Twenty-One to Thirty-One, to Nashville, Tennessee, 1917

Race	Migrants		Natives		Sum	
	%	N	%	N	%	N
White	64.6	707	35.4	387	100	1,094
Black	66.9	382	33.1	189	100	571
Total	65.4	1,089	34.6	576	100	1,665

Source: One in seven sample of the 5 June 1917 draft registration, World War I Selective Service Registration Records, RG 163, National Archives and Records Administration, East Point, Georgia.

to register for the draft on 5 June 1917; all those who had turned twenty-one after the first registration were required to register in the late spring and summer of 1918.[30] Draft registrants were required to indicate the name and address of their current employer. A small portion (4 percent) of the sampled Nashville registrants listed employment in other places. These registrants seem to have been caught in transit on draft registration day. They were young men in the process of moving north, where they had jobs waiting for them, or perhaps they were migrants back in Nashville to visit.

These itinerant registrants, however, offer a snapshot of outmigrating Nashvillians' destinations. In 1917 most went north. Two-thirds went to midwestern states, almost exclusively to industrial cities such as Chicago and Detroit. Another 23.2 percent went to northeastern states. Only 10 percent headed to places in the South, including other destinations in Tennessee. One-half (50.7) of these outmigrants had migrated to the city before the draft registration, and 49.3 percent had been born in Nashville. Black and white Nashville natives comprised only one-third of the U.S.-born cases in the total sample (see Table 6.2). Yet they comprised half of those heading north. A significant portion of these northward-bound migrants had been born in the rural South, and thus they fit the step migration pattern identified by historians of the Great Migration northward.[31]

By 1917 the majority of young adult men living in Nashville were migrants to the city. The 1917 draft sample, as shown in Table 6.2, reveals that two-thirds of both black and white U.S.-born men between the age of twenty-one and thirty-one were migrants; 66.9 percent of black men, and 64.6 percent of white men. A 100 percent sample from the subsequent 1918 draft registration of twenty-one-year-old males ($N = 1,008$) confirms the high portion of migrants in the city's population; 62 percent of twenty-one-year-old, U.S.-born men were migrants in 1918. The 1918 draft registration required registrants to state their fathers' place of birth, allowing a glimpse at intergenerational migration patterns. Among Nashville natives in the 1918 sample of twenty-one-year-old males, only 44 percent had fathers born in the city. Another 45.7 percent of registrants had fathers who were native-born migrants to Nashville, while 11.4 percent had fathers who were foreign-born immigrants.[32] Thus, in 1918 male migrants to Nashville and the male offspring of migrants to Nashville comprised the vast portion of the city's young adult male population.

The high levels of gross migration indicated by the draft records are supported by two separate surveys of low-income families in Nashville conducted in 1934. Among the heads of black families surveyed, 81.9 percent were migrants to the city; the figure for whites was slightly lower, at 79.3 percent.[33]

The draft cards have nothing to say about the migration of women, and available contemporary social surveys do not offer a clear picture of the proportion of migrants in Nashville's general female population. Since net migration rates among women exceeded those of men, however, one would expect a higher degree of gross migration.

The 1917 draft data indicate that short-distance movers predominated among Nashville's migrants. Three-fourths (74.4 percent) of the migrants had moved from some other place in Tennessee, and one-half (51.6 percent) had migrated from one of the forty-one rural counties this study has identified as lying in Nashville's Middle Tennessee hinterland. Very few migrants hailed from other states. Only 16.4 percent of migrant men in the 1917 sample had been born in other southern states, and a mere 6.1 percent of Nashville's migrants were born outside the South.

Wartime mobilization modified, but did not reorient, these short-distance migration patterns. A comparison of male migrant origins in the 1917 and 1918 draft registration data show that the percentage of Tennessee-born migrants to the city declined from 77.5 to 71.9 percent. The percentage of migrants from beyond the South declined as well, from 6.1 to 5.1 percent. The number of migrants from southern states other than Tennessee, however, increased from 16.4 percent to 23 percent. Thus, under the pressure-cooker of wartime mobilization, Nashville's migration patterns drew only slightly more heavily upon other southern states while still attracting most of its migrants from the Middle Tennessee hinterland, as indicated in Map 6.1.

Survey data show that female migration to Nashville followed a similar pattern of short-distance moves. One survey found that two-thirds of the women migrants in the sample had been born in places within a seventy-

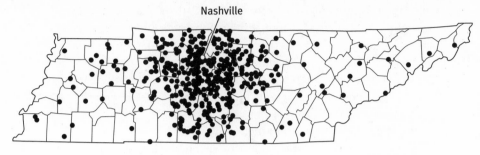

Nashville

● = Two Migrants

Map 6.1. Place of Birth of Tennessee-Born Male Migrants to Nashville, 1917

five-mile radius of the city. A similar survey found that 88 percent of female migrants in the city's semicharity homes had migrated from other places in Tennessee.[34]

Nashville's migrants came overwhelmingly from rural places. Most originated from the open country or tiny hamlets; few hailed from even the small urban places that dotted Middle Tennessee and the South. In the 1917 sample of male migrants, 53.5 percent were born in rural areas or in towns and villages with populations of less than 200; 20.6 percent of migrants were born in places with populations between 200 and 2,500; and 19.0 percent were born in towns with populations between 2,500 and 10,000. Only 7.1 percent of the sample migrated from places with populations of 10,000 or more. The origins of female migrants were strikingly similar; according to data from the survey of women migrants living in semicharity homes for working women, 57 percent were from open country, another 22 percent were from towns with populations of fewer than 2,000, and only 9 percent were from larger towns or cities with populations greater than 5,000. Thus, migrants to Nashville tended to be young adults from rural places within Nashville's Middle Tennessee hinterland. There was a heavy outmigration stream from the city as well, much of it directed to the North by the late 1910s. Among those migrants that stayed in Nashville, women outnumbered men and whites outnumbered blacks.[35]

Migration to Nashville was rarely a one-way process; the city's rural migrants moved between city and countryside frequently. While no adequate statistical measure of the frequency of moves is available, the repeated movement between city and countryside is clearly evident from oral histories, contemporary social surveys, and social welfare case records.

Many of Nashville's migrants intended their stays to be only temporary and longed to return to the country. Some longed for "the freedom that you had in the country [where] you didn't have to go to work and work for somebody else every day [and] you did your own work."[36] A. C. Jones, who worked in Nashville as a streetcar motorman in the 1920s and 1930s, felt that "nothing beats farm life if you're able to own a good [farm]." He recalled with fondness the "log-rollings and barn-raisings they used to have at home in Smith County," and he noted that "people in town never have good times like that." Jones saw life in Nashville as distinctly inferior, even decadent and immoral. The boys who rode his streetcar to school were "slicked up and pasty faced youngsters" who "carry on with the feisty little girls and run off at the mouth till you get ashamed to hear them." Jones's prescription for these boys was "to do some plowing and I mean plenty of plowing!" As for Nashville's theaters and cinemas, they were "just tearing down the morality of the people . . . [and were] keeping young folks from church."[37]

Men tended to make the decision to migrate on the basis of wages and work by incorporating migration to Nashville into broader employment goals, be they in the city or countryside. For example, migrants like Jones thought that they could always go back to the farm. Many migrants intended their stays in Nashville to last only as long as it took to earn enough to return to the countryside, where they could establish themselves as farmers. In this way, migration to Nashville was just an extension of the patterns of mobility that had long predominated in rural Middle Tennessee.

Illustrative of this pattern of circular migration is the experience of Daisy Perry's husband. During World War I, he left his home in the small farming community of Neptune, northeast of Nashville, to work in the Old Hickory powder plant. He had just wed and made the move because "he thought he could find a better job." After the war, however, he returned to the countryside to farm as a tenant before "buying some acreages of his own . . . just off the Clarksville Highway" north of Nashville, where he farmed successfully throughout the 1920s.[38]

Not all migrants were successful in parlaying temporary migration to Nashville into a step up the agricultural ladder. When A. C. Jones was in his twenties, he worked on his father's farm, with wintertime stints in his uncle's store. In the 1910s he moved to Carthage to operate the local telephone exchange, but he saw that "there wasn't much future in the phone business in Carthage, not to make anything out of, I mean." Thinking he could "make some money" in Nashville, he went there to work in 1920. Jones stayed until 1922 and then returned to Smith County to lay in two crops on his family's farm. But for all his love of country life, he could not earn a living, and he returned to Nashville in 1924. Jones continued to dream of a return to Smith County to "spend the rest of my days there." Even though by the 1930s he owned a house and lot in Smith County, he continued working as a streetcar motorman, awaiting his pension before returning.[39]

When Fred Boyd migrated to Nashville from Cheatham County in 1929, he intended "to stay there and save enough to live one year while we made our first crop back on the farm." But Boyd had a family, and "the saving was quite slow." Soon more children came, and "before we could accumulate our 'stake' the first child was in school and we didn't want to change his school." Boyd and his family stayed in Nashville. He worked at the Jarman Shoe Company, "because of their reputation for good pay," for forty-two years. Like A. C. Jones, only upon his retirement in 1971 did Boyd and his wife return to Cheatham County.[40]

Some migrants held tenaciously to the dream of building a career in agriculture, moving back and forth between city and country in a desperate attempt to earn a living in farming. Ben Jones, born in 1878 in Hickman County, farmed there until the 1910s, when he somehow lost his farm. By 1917 he was working in Nashville as a day laborer, trying to scrape together enough money to resume farming again. At least twice in the 1920s, Jones returned to his home in Hickman County, but each time he failed at farming. By 1929 he was back in Nashville working again, but he returned to the countryside in 1930 as a sharecropper, only to lose his crop to drought. He suffered through the Depression in the slums of north Nashville, working only intermittently.[41]

Many migrants went to Nashville to leave agriculture permanently, even if they professed admiration of rural life. Samuel Dean, the black sharecropper's son we saw earlier, thought that "country life is the best life they is." Nonetheless, he left the wheat-farming region of Bedford County where he was raised as soon as he reached adulthood. He moved first to the nearby town of Shelbyville, where he began "public work" in an ice factory sometime in the late 1890s. He moved to Nashville sometime in the 1900s after mortgaging his small Shelbyville home to settle a divorce, and worked in a feed mill. Around 1910 he headed to St. Louis and worked in meatpacking houses but then returned to Nashville. During World War I Dean headed north to Akron, Ohio, but again returned to Nashville after a few years.[42]

The difficulties in earning a living on the farm prompted Ellis Jones to migrate to Nashville. A white tenant farmer's son, he moved to Nashville as a young man in the mid-1920s. "I didn't follow my daddy's footsteps at all . . . didn't like it [i.e., farm life]," Jones recalled. Farming as a tenant did not offer him a decent standard of living in the 1920s. To Jones, "it seem like the farm occupation [was] getting so costly and so sophisticated that the average feller cannot do it, so he's seeking . . . some other way of making a living." Jones saw that a successful future in farming required more resources than he could ever muster: "If you're going to be on the farm and make money you've got to diversify. You don't want a hundred acres, you want a thousand acres, [but] it's so expensive that you can't own that much land."[43]

Rural Tennessee women had entirely different motives for leaving the countryside. Men tended to view migration in the context of larger career goals, no matter if they stayed in a city like Nashville or returned to the countryside to resume farming. While women also were motivated by work and career, the decision to migrate was strongly shaped by their social, familial, and economic relationships.

Many of Nashville's female migrants moved to the city not by individual choice but as part of a family economic strategy. J. B. Williams's grandfather brought his family, which included four grown daughters and two sons, to Nashville in 1916 to work at the Morgan & Hamilton textile mills. Williams's grandfather was a produce dealer of apparently little success, and he was always looking for ways to employ his children. Previously the family had lived in Kentucky and had even gone as far as South Carolina to work in mills there. With each move, Williams's grandfather "was going where his children could get the best work" to support the family.[44]

A similar strategy brought Louise Williams (no relation to J. B. Williams) to Nashville in 1925. Williams was the oldest of nine children. Her father farmed as a tenant in Cheatham County, "never coming out even at the end of the year." In 1924 he took ill and was unable to work. He reasoned that if he moved the family to Nashville, "the younger children could get something to do in Nashville to keep food on the table."[45] Louise initially remained behind in Cheatham County when the rest of the family moved to Nashville. Having just graduated from high school in 1925, she stayed to teach in one of the county grammar schools. She still contributed to the family income by sending her paycheck, after paying for room and board, to her parents in Nashville. However, Louise's mother needed her help with the other children and "wrote such blue letters that I promised her that I would come home [to Nashville] at the end of the school term and try to find work."[46]

Life in the countryside had fundamentally different meanings for men and women. For men, rural life meant the independence to "work their own farm."[47] For women, rural life offered few avenues for such independence. Rural communities could be stifling, even oppressive, in ways directly related to women's roles in the agricultural economy and to their relationship to their families and communities. As Idella Woods glumly characterized her choices growing up in rural Middle Tennessee, "They wasn't anything for a girl to do in them days but git married."[48] As Nashville's offices and factories developed a demand for women workers, more and more rural women moved to the city.

Curiosity, wanderlust, and a desire for independence motivated women to migrate to Nashville. One woman told an interviewer, "I didn't have to [migrate to Nashville], and I like the country, but I wanted to get experience in different things . . . to get out and do new things."[49] Another migrant girl stated flatly, "I wanted to have freedom and make my own way in the world."[50] Indeed, some women showed an almost impulsive desire to migrate to Nashville. Mary Brown simply hopped on a Cumberland riverboat from her home in Shop Springs with some friends and steamed into Nashville. She met some other girls in Nashville "and decided to stay and work."[51] Roberta Vick had been living with her grandmother when she "left to find work" in Nashville.[52] Nellie Preville left home after she saw an advertisement "wanting girls to travel selling shirts on commission" for a clothing firm. Together with two other girls, two men, and a manager she "took in many of the Southern towns," ending up in Nashville.[53] Julia Brown (no relation to Mary) left home in 1928, traveling through East Tennessee selling magazine subscriptions before she went to Nashville.[54] Billie Nell Banks hitchhiked to Nashville from outside Knoxville.[55]

Some women fled rural poverty. A young farmer's daughter living in Nashville, the fourth of nine children, noted that on the farm "my wishes were not all satisfied and I was denied many things." Her unmet wants were made all the more unbearable by a more fortunate cousin whose "boastfulness of her better fortune made my realization of [my family's poverty] doubly hard."[56] When another young migrant woman in Nashville was asked if she wanted to return to the countryside, she replied, "I could never go back now."[57]

Women who did migrate to Nashville by themselves continued to keep in close contact with their families in the countryside, and this reduced the risk of financial, emotional, and social isolation inherent in long-distance moves. One young salesclerk stated, "I do go back often [to my family's home in the country], almost every week." Another young female migrant reported that "a lot of girls from the farm go back home every weekend and spend their vacations at home."[58] Many women sent money back home to help with the family finances, too. A young woman who migrated to Nashville in the late 1920s—the daughter of a "plain ordinary farmer"—remitted as much of her paycheck back home as she could afford. "I am doing all I can to help the folks at home, especially my younger sister who is in [her] second year [of] high school. I want her to have a better opportunity than I had," she said.[59] Another migrant woman reported that she worked nearly twelve-hour days at a commercial laundry to send money back to her family in the countryside.[60]

While many women migrated to further their family's economic fortunes, many others went to Nashville to escape their families. For all the romanticized visions of country life that prevailed at the time, rural women held no illusions about life on the family farm. Consequently, many of the young women who poured into Nashville in the 1920s headed straight to the city's Young Women's Christian Association, whose records provide a glimpse of the troubled family lives migrant women left behind.

Lela McClaren is a case in point. One of seven children living on a farm near Eagleville, Tennessee, she was eighteen when she migrated to Nashville in 1931. She reported to a YWCA official that "her father has been extremely strict with her" and this was "one of the reasons for her leaving home."[61] Fourteen-year-old Lillie Shropshire came to Nashville in the late 1920s after her mother died, leaving her with only a stepfather, with whom she did not get along. She "just wanted come to down here" to live with her sister, who had earlier migrated to Nashville with her husband.[62] Robbie Sanford recalled that "there were no opportunities for making money [in her rural community]." She "just plain had a fight with [her] father and left" his Williamson County farm for Nashville in the early 1920s. When asked why she chose Nashville, Sanford responded matter-of-factly, "where else was I to go?"[63]

The stigma of pregnancy out of wedlock also sent women to Nashville, where they could stay in homes for unwed mothers. Grace Brimm was sent to Nashville's Florence Crittenden Home for unwed mothers in 1929 by her sister after Grace's lover refused to marry her.[64] Other women sought out the clandestine abortion clinics doctors operated out of the city's hotel rooms. One such physician was arrested for performing a "criminal operation" upon a girl from the Middle Tennessee town of Lewisburg who had apparently come to Nashville solely for that purpose.[65] Another woman was reported to have attempted to perform an abortion upon herself, landing herself in the hospital.[66]

Nashville also offered an escape for rural women who were married to abusive husbands. Maude English and her three teenage children came to Nashville to escape her husband, who drank excessively.[67] Another migrant woman told an investigator: "To be quite frank, I came [to Nashville] to get away from my husband. He would get drunk and come and try to make trouble for me and my baby. I had a baby which I had to support . . . and I had to get work [and] I didn't want to stay in [my hometown], so I came here to my sister's."[68] In Hattie Teal's case, while she was bedridden with illness in the late 1920s, her husband sexually abused her eleven-year-old daughter. "When the child finally told her of this," a YWCA social worker reported, Teal "went to their minister about it asking his advice. He had stated that the woman must be loosing [sic] her mind as the husb[and] was a good church member and incapable of doing such a thing." Teal's only option was to head to Nashville, which she did in 1929. In Nashville Teal sought "to find work where she could keep her daughter with her as the child [was] extremely shy and afraid of men."[69]

An unfortunately similar situation entrapped Valera Pollack. She hitch-hiked to Nashville after she had "trouble with her stepfather" in October of 1931. Her stepfather had "been drinking for some time and was abusive." Indeed, it was discovered that he had "first tried to assault Valera when she was 8 year[s] of age." When young Valera told her grandmother about the initial incident, she told her to "throw something at him should he attempt it again." Pollack had been married, but only "lived with [her husband] a year" since "he would not work nor would he have a home of his own." By November, Valera had written the director of the Nashville YWCA asking if "there is a law that could make Floyd [her husband] take care of me and provide for me for he is . . . working and has bought him a car."[70]

There is a long sociological tradition of viewing rural-urban migration as leading to social disorganization and the disruption of families in the urban environment. However, as the cases like Valera Pollack's show, troubled families were common to the countryside as well. Women's dependent position in the rural family meant that they often bore the brunt of violence, alcoholism, and abuse. Leaving such situations was an important factor in the migration of women to Nashville.

Migration to Nashville grew out of the complex interactions of the push of economic, social, and familial crises in the countryside and the pull of urban jobs. Circular and seasonal migration patterns tied to the rural life cycle drew people to the city. Linkages between Nashville and its rural hin-terland attracted migrants to the city for short visits, which fostered the flow of information about urban conditions and further promoted migra-tion. Women, in particular, migrated to Nashville with the expectation of earning a living, and their decisions to leave the countryside were motivated by dissatisfaction with the constraints of rural life and the desire to escape oppressive family and social relationships.

CHAPTER 7

Men's Work

Once in Nashville, rural migrants had to find work. Male migrants tended to enter the city's labor force at the bottom of the occupational hierarchy. However, strict racial segregation in Nashville's labor market meant that race transcended migration status in determining employment. Only within each racial group did the way migrants found work and the level at which they entered the city's occupational hierarchy strongly influence Nashville's class structure. Similarly, organized labor followed the color line, limiting employment opportunities for black men. When the city's workers made a concerted effort to organize during World War I, white rural migrants followed suit, but only to the extent that unions advanced their interests. When the tide turned against labor after the war, the city's migrants abandoned the labor movement.

The employment data supplied by the 1917 draft registration records provide a means for understanding quantitatively the role of race and migration status in shaping Nashville's male working class. The limitations of the data should be noted; the 1917 draft registration provides only a snapshot of the city's population of twenty-one- to thirty-one-year-old males. No conclusions about migrant working women can be drawn from this data, and the lack of education data in the records hampers a full assessment of the factors affecting employment. Furthermore, the sample includes only young adults and identifies only individuals at an early stage in their careers.

The unique strengths of the data are important, however. The draft data are the only systematic source that allows for a detailed examination of the short-distance and intrastate migrants that comprised the bulk of Nashville's population. By categorizing the occupations of migrants and natives in the sample into a four-part occupational hierarchy, the draft data offer the best quantitative evidence on the interaction between migration, race, and occupational structure at a critical point of time in Nashville's development.[1]

As shown in Table 7.1, migrants were slightly more likely than city natives

Table 7.1. Occupational Rank of Nashville Males, Ages Twenty-One to Thirty-One, by Migration Status, 1917

Occupational Rank	Migrants	Natives
High white collar and professional	4.6%	3.5%
Low white collar	25.1	30.5
Skilled	22.7	25.5
Semi-/unskilled	47.6	40.4
Total	100.0	99.9[a]
(N)	(1,048)	(537)

Source: One in seven sample of the 5 June 1917 draft registration, World War I Selective Service Registration Records, RG 163, National Archives and Records Administration, East Point, Georgia.
[a] Total does not equal 100 due to rounding.

to be employed in semiskilled or unskilled jobs, such as factory operatives or laborers. They were only slightly less likely than natives to work in skilled manual occupations, such as the construction trades or other skilled manufacturing trades. Migrants were also less likely than natives to work in low-white-collar positions, such as clerks or salesmen. On the other hand, migrants were slightly more likely than natives to be represented among professional and high-white-collar workers, such as company officials, university-trained engineers, and doctors. However, since migrants outnumbered natives in the sample by two to one, migrants comprised the majority of workers in all categories.

Appreciating the racial segmentation of Nashville's labor market is essential to understanding what work migrant men found. The color line was explicitly drawn, assiduously maintained, and operated on all levels of employment. Thus, the profile of Nashville's working class changes dramatically when the draft registration data are broken down by race. Few of Nashville's black workers, either native or migrant, worked in anything above unskilled labor. Despite being home to many important black institutions—such as Tennessee Agricultural and Industrial Normal School, Fisk University, and Meharry Medical College, as well as the publishing house of the National Baptist Church—Nashville had an attenuated African American white-collar and professional class. Among all black men in the sample—migrants and natives—only 1.7 percent worked in high-white-collar or professional occupations, in contrast to the 5.6 percent of whites in the sample so employed. The disparity between the number of black and the number of white low-white-collar workers was even more striking; 3.0 percent of blacks worked in white-collar occupations, compared to 39.3 percent of whites. Black representation in the skilled trades was equally low. Only 10.6 percent of black Nashvillians held skilled manual jobs; in contrast, 30.4 percent of white workers labored in the skilled trades.

The preponderance of Nashville's black workers were clustered at the very bottom of the occupational hierarchy. A full 84.8 percent of the black men in the sample worked as semiskilled or unskilled workers, compared to the one-quarter (24.7 percent) of whites in similar employment. Even within this lowest occupational category, black Nashvillians worked in the jobs that required the least skill and paid the lowest wages; in addition, workers in these jobs faced the highest levels of cyclical and seasonal unemployment. "Laborer" was the most common occupation listed by black draft registrants; 36.0 percent of working registrants described themselves as so employed. Only 3.3 percent of white workers described their occupation as laborer. Black laborers were, according to a 1904 investigation, hired "by the job" and could expect to face frequent periods of unemployment.[2] An investigator in the early 1920s noted that "practically all of the unskilled [casual day] labor of Nashville is done by Negroes [and] in all of the writer's observations, not a single white man was found doing this type of work."[3]

Discrimination in the craft and trade unions was one factor limiting black employment in the skilled trades. Although unions affiliated with the American Federation of Labor were required to maintain nondiscriminatory membership policies, these were rarely enforced in the South.[4] A local Nashville observer confirmed this fact, reporting that "in reality . . . negroes are frequently excluded [from union locals] by the 'black ball.'"[5] A turn-of-the-century writer to a local paper complained that "in this city, to my personal knowledge, there are a score or more of skilled Negro mechanics who are subject to enforced idleness by reason of the colorphobia which dominates the trade unions."[6]

Most union locals simply barred black workmen. The local of the Brotherhood of Carpenters and Joiners barred black carpenters, and white union carpenters would not work on jobs with black carpenters. The Stone Masons' Union followed a similar policy, and white masons also refused to work on jobs alongside black masons.[7] However, the racially restrictive policies of the city's white-dominated unions were not always so clear cut. Nashville's unions balanced racial exclusion with a limited degree of integration when it was in their economic interest. In trades where skilled black men were numerous enough to mount a competitive threat, break strikes, or undercut wages, white-dominated unions admitted black workmen, albeit in subordinate positions and on a limited basis. Nashville's Bricklayers' and Plasterers' Unions both admitted black workmen by 1904. The Bricklayers' Union admitted a limited number of black workmen on an equal basis, and by the 1920s black bricklayers composed about one-fifth of union membership. Black plasterers made up an even larger proportion of the Plasterers' Union, comprising two-fifths of the membership. The plasterers, however, accepted black tradesmen on a subordinate basis, barring them from working as better-paid ornamental plasterers.[8]

In some situations white-only unions tolerated black locals, but only as long as work tasks also remained strictly segregated. A "colored carpenters' union" was organized in 1918 at the behest of the white local. This union seems to have had few members and a very short life.[9] Excluded from the white union, black stone masons also formed their own union. However, work tasks were strictly segregated. Black masons specialized in what Nashville masons referred to as hard-stone, or country stone, masonry, while white stone masons specialized in the higher-skilled, better paying and less arduous soft-stone and ornamental work.

How this pattern of racial and task segregation operated in practice can be seen in the construction of two notable Nashville landmarks: Union Station in 1898–1900 and Hume-Fogg High School in 1910–11. Both buildings were designed in styles that made ample use of Middle Tennessee stone on the building's exterior — Union Station in Romanesque revival and Hume-Fogg High School in a Gothic style complete with decorative crenelation. Black masons laid the foundations and did the rougher hard-stone work. White masons came in after them and completed the more elaborate ornamental and soft-stone work.[10]

In trades where black workers comprised the majority of workmen, they formed their own autonomous locals. By 1904 there were black locals of the Hod Carriers' Union and the Barbers' Union.[11] Both were affiliated with Nashville's central labor organization, the Trades and Labor Council. In addition, by 1904 there was a "colored laborers" union, an earlier, also short-lived manifestation of a local for black carpenters, and a union for black stationary firemen.[12] In 1918 a newly organized railway Helpers' and Laborers' Union joined the Nashville's Trades and Labor Council, and after World War I it became an all-black affiliate of the Brotherhood Maintenance of Way Employees. Black railroad workers also organized a car cleaners' union.[13]

Black unions, however, tended to be short-lived and weak. The Hod Carriers' Union seems to have expired after the death of its early leader, Richard Kittrell, in 1908.[14] A new local with a membership of ninety was installed in June of 1917. But the new union was unable to guarantee its members a standard wage. After the wartime boom, the union even lost the power to guarantee its members work, as the white-dominated Bricklayers' Union ceased to recognize the hod carriers' jurisdiction and began to hire nonunion laborers to haul brick and mortar.[15] By the late 1920s, the union had only thirty members. The Hod Carriers' and the Firemen's Unions and the black railway union largely provided members with a social outlet and insurance. Only the partially integrated Plasterers' and Bricklayers' Unions and the segregated Hard-Stone Masons' Union could actually deliver wage and employment benefits to black tradesmen.[16]

Exclusion from Nashville's trade unions meant exclusion from many of the most lucrative job opportunities for skilled black workingmen. C. W. McKissack, a black Nashville bricklayer excluded from the local, wrote to the U.S. commissioner of labor in 1918, complaining of employment discrimination in the construction of the Old Hickory powder plant. "I have been informed," McKissack wrote, "that none but Union Brick-Layers are employed [in the construction of the plant] and a band of our people well experienced in this business have been denied on the part of the brick-layers Union of this city a charter and for that reason we have been unable to work in the construction of the plant."[17]

A trenchant example of how profoundly racial discrimination divided the city's organized workers can been seen in the annual Labor Day festivities. Each year the Trades and Labor Council sponsored an elaborate Labor Day celebration for the city's workers, complete with a parade and festival. After the parade, white unionists celebrated at segregated Glendale Park, while the "colored celebration" was held on the other side of town at black-only Greenwood Park.[18]

Although discriminatory practices were pervasive in the building trades, they paled in comparison to the nearly complete exclusion of blacks from the city's manufacturing industries. In 1925, for example, Nashville's Standard Furniture Company employed 170 workers, only 15 of whom were black. The city's hosiery and textile factories excluded black workers from production jobs. The May Hosiery Mill, with 229 workers, employed its 21 black female employees as cleaning women. The Werthan Bag Company, a cotton and burlap bag manufacturer, employed only 26 black male laborers out of a workforce of 333; the Warrioto Cotton Mill employed 22 black men and women out of a workforce of 317. And it is highly unlikely that the black workers at the Werthan and Warrioto mills were employed in production jobs.[19] A canvass of the city's employers by Fisk University sociologist George Edmund Haynes indicated that in the building trades, black workmen had "little or no difficulty from the side of employers. Negroes who are union men and *above average* workmen in skill will get work." Haynes found, however, that among Nashville's manufacturers, "there is still a decided attitude of employers against using Negroes" in the city's factories.[20]

Black manufacturing employment was concentrated in Nashville's phosphate fertilizer industry. The city's three leading fertilizer manufacturers—Tennessee Chemical, Reed Fertilizer, and Federal Chemical—hired black workmen almost exclusively for the hot, dirty, noisome work. From the 1917 sample of draft registrants, all but 2 of the 23 men working in Nashville's fertilizer factories were black and one of the two white employees was a white-collar clerk.[21]

Some black workmen worked in the city's smaller foundries. However, just as in the building trades, tasks were divided along racial lines, with the lower-skilled work going to blacks. Jakes Foundry employed black foundry workers, but, as one observer noted, "the white men do all the foundry work for jobbers and also the foundry work for the Tennessee Central Railroad." The firm's black employees did only the "rougher foundry work."[22]

The local traction company and the city's three railroads hired large numbers of black workmen, but only as unskilled laborers. In response to a survey of hiring practices in 1927, the Nashville Railway & Light Company replied that black workmen were hired as "laborers only."[23] Positions as clerks, linemen, and streetcar conductors were for whites only, a reality that is confirmed in the 1917 Selective Service data.

These patterns of racial segregation are especially visible in the occupational distribution of the city's largest employers, its three major railroads, the Tennessee Central; the Nashville, Chattanooga & St. Louis (NC&StL); and the Louisville & Nashville (L&N). All three lines operated not only large rail yards in the city but also extensive shops for the maintenance of locomotives and rolling stock. The 1917 draft registration data show that the railroads employed few black workingmen at anything above a general laborer. Of the sixty-two black railroad workers in the 1917 sample, only one held a white-collar occupation, that of a rate clerk, and only six were engaged in the skilled trades. Only three black workers were employed as firemen or boilermen. The remainder, 88.7 percent of black railroad workers, were semiskilled and unskilled laborers, typically general laborers, car cleaners, and freight haulers. Skilled positions on locomotives and in the railroad shops and terminals were for whites alone.

The means by which black men, especially migrants, found work reinforced these patterns of racial segmentation. "Ganging places," informal labor markets that sprang up at various points across the city where black casual labor was hired, channeled black workers into unskilled jobs. Quasi-officially sanctioned by police, who tolerated their presence, the two most important of these ganging places were located at opposite sides of Nashville's city center. The oldest, dating back at least to the 1890s, operated along the city's waterfront at First Avenue and Broad Street. The other stood at the opposite, western end of the downtown district at Tenth Avenue and

Table 7.2. Occupational Rank of White Nashville Males, Ages Twenty-One to Thirty-One, by Migration Status, 1917

Occupational Rank	Migrants	Natives
High white collar and professional	6.3%	4.1%
Low white collar	37.9	41.9
Skilled	29.7	31.8
Semi-/unskilled	26.0	22.2
Total	99.9[a]	100
(N)	(680)	(365)

Source: See Table 7.1.

[a] Total does not equal 100 due to rounding.

Church Street near the railroad yards. Men would gather before daybreak to await the arrival of employers seeking general laborers. At the riverfront location, one observer estimated that 200 men each day "stop daily hunting for work." The city's wholesale houses, truckers, and draymen drew heavily from these markets, hiring men to help with the heavy work of loading and hauling. House servants, gardeners, and other general laborers were also hired at these informal labor markets. Hourly wages were standard, and workers who accepted lower wages faced ostracism, or perhaps worse, by others in the group.[24]

For the black working class in Nashville, both native and migrant, strict barriers existed to employment in the trades and manufacturing. The industrial jobs that drew black workers northward during and after World War I simply did not exist in Nashville.[25] Thus, migrant men entering Nashville were sorted into one of two nearly separate, race-based labor markets. With racial segmentation in the workforce so profound and pervasive, occupational differences between migrants and natives only become meaningful within racial groups. These differences illustrate not only how migrants fared compared to city natives, but also where different groups of migrants entered the urban economy. In essence, the question becomes not only "how did migrants fare compared to natives?" but also "which migrants fared better than others?" As Table 7.2 shows, white migrants were somewhat more likely to hold high-white-collar/professional occupations than Nashville natives. Compared to migrants, native Nashvillians, however, were slightly overrepresented in the two middle occupational categories—low-white-collar and skilled manual occupations—while they were slightly underrepresented in the lowest category. Overall, the differences in employment between white migrants and natives were slight.

Table 7.3. Occupational Rank of Black Nashville Males, Ages Twenty-One to Thirty-One, by Migration Status, 1917

Occupational Rank	Migrants	Natives
High white collar and professional	1.4%	2.3%
Low white collar	1.4	6.4
Skilled	9.8	12.2
Semi-/unskilled	87.5	79.1
Total	100.1[a]	100.0
(N)	(367)	(172)

Source: See Table 7.1.

[a] Total does not equal 100 due to rounding.

The occupational distribution of black migrants and natives differed significantly from whites. Compared to black natives, black migrants were underrepresented among high-white-collar and professional workers. Table 7.3 shows that 1.4 percent of black migrants were employed in the highest occupational category while 2.3 percent of black natives were so employed. A similar situation existed among black low-white-collar workers; while only 1.4 of migrants worked in such jobs, 6.4 percent of black natives did so. Like white migrants, however, black migrants were underrepresented among the skilled manual workers. The overwhelming portion of black workers, both native and migrant, labored at jobs classified at the bottom of the occupational hierarchy, but migrants were more likely than natives to labor in such occupations: 87.5 percent of migrants labored at semiskilled and unskilled occupations while only 79.1 percent of natives did so.

Migration distance and class structure were closely related—but in different ways for whites and blacks. Among whites, migrants from beyond the South tended to work in the best paid, high status, white collar and professional occupations. A full 16.4 percent of non-southern-born migrants worked in the highest occupational category. Only 4 percent of Middle Tennessee migrants held such jobs. In other words, while non-southern-born migrants comprised only 9 percent of all migrants, they comprised 23.3 percent of all high-white-collar and professional workers in the migrant sample. Migration streams from beyond Middle Tennessee and the South brought to Nashville highly trained professionals—physicians, engineers, ministers, university professors, and the like—who sought work in a national labor market.

Nashville's white laboring class, on the other hand, was drawn overwhelmingly from Middle Tennessee. As Table 7.4 shows, the occupational

Table 7.4. Occupational Rank of White Nashville Male Migrants, Ages Twenty-One to Thirty-One, by Region of Birth, 1917

	Region of Birth			
Occupational Rank	Middle Tenn.	Other Tenn.	Other South	Non-South
High white collar and professional	4.0%	6.8%	9.4%	16.4%
Low white collar	34.4	41.1	41.9	49.2
Skilled manual	32.1	27.4	25.6	24.6
Semi-/unskilled	29.5	24.7	23.1	9.8
Total	100.0	100.0	100.0	100.0
(N)	(427)	(73)	(117)	(61)

Source: See Table 7.1.

distribution of white Middle-Tennessee-born migrants was more heavily skewed toward manual occupations than was that of migrants born in other places. One-third of Middle Tennessee–born migrants worked as skilled manual workers, compared to only 27.4 percent of migrants from other places in Tennessee. Migrants from other parts of the South and migrants from beyond the region each contributed about one-quarter of their numbers to Nashville's skilled working class.

A large number of Nashville's white semiskilled and unskilled workers were born in Middle Tennessee and the South. Nearly 30 percent of Middle Tennessee–born migrants, 25 percent of other Tennessee-born migrants, and 23.1 percent of migrants born in other southern states worked as semiskilled and unskilled workers. Only 9.8 percent of nonsouthern migrants did so.

Very few blacks migrated long-distance, and their occupations were skewed heavily toward unskilled labor. Nashville's black middle and upper classes tended to be native to the city. Well-to-do blacks were closely tied to black-controlled institutions, particularly churches, religious organizations, schools, and universities, and to services provided exclusively to the black community. Not surprisingly, six physicians and three ministers comprise the entire top occupational category for black Nashvillians in the 1917 sample (see Table 7.5). Of the six physicians, three were natives and three were migrants; of the ministers, two were natives and three were migrants.

It was among the black low-white-collar workers, particularly those engaged in business occupations, that the disparity between the number of migrants and natives was greatest. Only 11 out of a sample of 570 black

Table 7.5. Occupational Rank of Black Nashville Male Migrants, Ages Twenty-One to Thirty-One, by Region of Birth, 1917

Occupational Rank	Region of Birth			
	Middle Tenn.	Other Tenn.	Other South	Non-South
High white collar and professional	0.7%	3.3%	4.0%	0.0%
Low white collar	1.4	0.0	2.0	0.0
Skilled manual	9.9	10.0	8.0	25.0
Semi-/unskilled	88.0	86.7	86.0	75.0
Total	100.0	100.0	100.0	100.0
(N)	(283)	(30)	(50)	(4)

Source: See Table 7.1.

Nashvillians were employed as clerks or salesmen, and of these, 8 were native to the city. These figures suggest that being native to Nashville was a distinct advantage for black men in acquiring low-white-collar positions. In all likelihood, the few low-white-collar positions available to black men went to those from established families in the city. Black migrants could fit into the urban economy only at the bottom.

The population size of a migrant's place of birth also helped to determine his occupational rank. As shown in Table 7.6, white migrants from large cities tended to be high-white-collar and professional workers; just under one-fifth (17.6 percent) of migrants born in large cities—those with a population of 100,000 or greater—worked in positions at the top of the occupational hierarchy, and another 58.8 percent worked in low-white-collar positions. Less than one-quarter of these migrants worked in manual occupations. The city's manual workers, skilled and unskilled, were predominantly from rural areas and small towns. The role of urban birth is certainly complicated by the fact that most urban-urban migrants also tended to be long-distance migrants from beyond the South.

Again, the data for black men show a different pattern, as indicated in Table 7.7. The small number of black-white-collar workers and the very low level of black migration from beyond the South mean that black workers were almost exclusively from rural areas and small towns and few worked in anything but semiskilled or unskilled work.

The difference between migrants' and native's employment patterns suggests that the origins of the migration streams flowing into the city, in conjunction with a strictly segregated labor market, strongly influenced the

Table 7.6. Occupational Rank of White Nashville Male Migrants, Ages Twenty-One to Thirty-One, by Size of Birthplace, 1917

Occupational Rank		Size of Birthplace					
	< 200	200– 999	1,000– 2,499	2,500– 9,999	10,000– 24,999	25,000– 99,999	100,000+
High white collar and professional	4.7%	5.1%	10.4%	4.1%	42.9%	7.1%	17.6%
Low white collar	35.9	42.3	44.8	29.6	42.9	42.9	58.8
Skilled manual	31.2	30.8	22.4	35.7	0.0	21.4	17.6
Semi-/unskilled	28.3	21.8	22.4	30.6	14.3	28.6	5.9
Total	100.1[a]	100	100	100	100.1[a]	100	99.9[a]
(N)	(382)	(78)	(67)	(98)	(7)	(14)	(34)

Source: See Table 7.1.

[a] Total does not equal 100 due to rounding.

Table 7.7. Occupational Rank of Black Nashville Male Migrants, Ages Twenty-One to Thirty-One, by Size of Birthplace, 1917

Occupational Rank		Size of Birthplace					
	< 200	200– 999	1,000– 2,499	2,500– 9,999	10,000– 24,999	25,000– 99,999	100,000+
High white collar and professional	1.6%	2.8%	0.0%	1.0%	0.0%	0.0%	0.0%
Low white collar	2.7	0.0	0.0	0.0	0.0	0.0	0.0
Skilled manual	7.7	16.7	8.8	11.1	0.0	9.1	50.0
Semi-/unskilled	88.0	86.0	91.2	87.9	100.0	90.9	50.0
Total	100	100	100	100	100	100	100
(N)	(183)	(36)	(34)	(99)	(2)	(11)	(2)

Source: See Table 7.1.

city's class structure. Among male migrants, whites in the highest occupational category were migrating the farthest distances and coming from large urban places. Low-white-collar workers and blue-collar workers of all skill levels migrated from places much closer to the city. Among the mass of semiskilled and unskilled workers, rural Middle Tennessee–born migrants predominated. Black Nashville's small occupational elite tended to be comprised of city natives, and its large working class was overwhelmingly composed of migrants from rural and small-town Middle Tennessee.

Nashville's men turned to organized labor in the 1910s to further their interests. This was not a development that the city's business leadership sought to promote. A "good, orderly white population . . . constantly recruited from the surrounding countryside" was how Nashville's boosters characterized the city's working class in 1906. Indeed, Nashville's boosters were so intent upon depicting the city's workers as good and orderly to outside investors that a promotional pamphlet made the extravagant claim that "there never has been a strike in Nashville."[26]

Twenty years later, Nashville's business leaders still boasted of a rural-born workforce of the "pure Anglo-Saxon type . . . [that] makes ideal mill hands—loyal, contented, tractable, and quick to learn." Country people, the city's boosters promised potential investors, were immune to the appeals of organized labor, which ensured that "labor disturbances [were] practically unknown."[27]

The docility of the southern workforce was a perennial part of New South boosterism. Rural southerners would adapt easily to industrial life, proponents of the South's industrialization promised, and they would do so while accepting low wages and without posing threats to either the social order or employers' prerogatives.[28] In fact, the city's largely rural-born working class repeatedly failed to live up to its advertised reputation for tractability and contentedness, and Nashville's employers were all too familiar with labor disturbances. Nashville, by and large, was a union town. During World War I, when worker scarcity and government policy seemed to favor labor, and the city was swollen with rural migrants, workers joined union locals in droves. These newly organized, largely male, workers were committed to their unions; the labor unrest at the end of the war was unprecedented in the history of the city as thousands of its workers struck to preserve their wartime gains. Despite the fact that these strikes failed, Nashville's workers stood by their unions as long as labor showed a reasonable chance of prevailing. Their pragmatic attitude toward organized labor mirrored their attitude toward migration; both were to be entered into only when it seemed to be in their interest to do so.

That rural-born southern workers embraced organized labor is not quite the standard interpretation of southern labor history. Historians have followed New South industrialists' lead by portraying the region's rural-born workers as indifferent, indeed hostile, to the appeals of organized labor. "A fierce and petulant individualism" born of the southern workers' "agrarian heritage . . . erected mental barriers to unionism," is the illustrative judgment of an older generation of historians.[29] Recent historians have reached similar conclusions by different means. They argue that southern textile mill workers' failure to embrace labor organization stemmed not from an agrarian individualism but from their "habit of looking to family, kin, neighbors, and on-the-job workmates for mutual self-protection" rather than to outside organizations like labor unions, which they perceived as "foreign," indeed "un-American and atheistic." One study concluded that "mill folk would have [had] to forsake traditional ways for those of modern economic men" for unions to have succeeded in southern textiles.[30]

What is not disputed, though, is organized labor's failure in southern textiles. Despite major organizing drives, unions were largely irrelevant to the experience of southern textile workers. The Knights of Labor in 1886–90, and then the American Federation of Labor–affiliated National Union of Textile Workers in 1898–1902, and its successor the United Textile Workers' Union in 1913–21 met with little more than short-term success in organizing the southern industry.[31]

Drawing on the insights of the new labor history, historians of southern labor have shown that the lack of labor unions did not mean that workers were a tractable and contented group acquiescent to management's authority. Focusing on the textile industry, they have identified the development of an autonomous workers' culture and community that supported a strong tradition of informal collective protest in the mill towns and villages of the region. Despite the failure of trade unions, mill operatives were able to collectively challenge their employers' full authority over the workplace.[32]

Historians' emphasis on the textile industry has led to a lack of appreciation of the places in the South where organized labor actually enjoyed strength, the region's larger cities.[33] With the exception of the United Mine Workers, the unions that prospered in the South were those that thrived in the rest of the nation: the railroad brotherhoods and American Federation of Labor–affiliated trade unions that represented skilled workers in the construction, metal-working, needle, and printing trades.[34]

Thus, Nashville provided a very different environment from that of the South's textile villages and towns. The size and diversity of the city's economy acted as solvents of the intrusive and controlling paternalism that operated in mill towns dominated by one industry. No Nashville employer could exert the textile manufacturers' power over his workers, with his mill-owned housing, and his position as the largest, if not sole, employer. Furthermore, a good deal of Nashville's manufacturing did not take place in integrated factory settings, even in the 1920s. In the city's publishing houses and machine shops, production tended to be shop-oriented and skill-intensive. In these industries, in the construction trades, and in the yards and shops of the city's three railroads, Nashville's trade unionists maintained an important, if not always dominant, presence.

One of those unions was the Typographical Union, which was one of Nashville's oldest institutions, having been founded in the 1850s.[35] The city even hosted the American Federation of Labor's seventeenth annual convention in 1897.[36] On the eve of America's entry into World War I, Nashville's trade unionists operated an active Trades and Labor Council, and counted twenty-eight different AFL-affiliated trade union locals.[37]

Furthermore, Nashville trade unionists were not reluctant to strike. The city's carpenters staged a walkout in 1907. A molder's strike temporarily shut down the Phillips & Buttorff Stove Works in 1912. Indeed, Phillips & Buttorff's Anglo-Saxon workers were so obstreperous the plant managers sought to recruit "quite a number of competent stove molders" through the Industrial Removal Office of the Hebrew Immigrant Aid Society to try to break the strike. The Bookbinders' Union struck the city's printers in late 1913 in a bitter strike that lasted into 1914.[38] Nashville's machinists walked out on strike two days before the American declaration of war on 2 April 1917, seeking to "enforce a living wage" and win union recognition. "Practically every shop in the city [was] affected by the strike order," reported the city's labor paper.[39]

The domestic mobilization for the war effort in 1917–18 gave great impetus to organized labor in Nashville, as it did nationally. The city's trade unions held high hopes for improved working conditions and higher wages, as well as for expanding organized labor's size and influence within their trades. Wartime labor demands pulled thousands of rural migrants into the city. Federal policy toward labor under the War Labor Board, which sought to maintain high and uninterrupted levels of production, encouraged labor organizers. And cost-plus contracts and high wartime profits tempered employers' hostility to organized labor.[40] The result was a great growth in organized labor in Nashville. Existing unions expanded their membership, and new lines of work were organized for the first time.

Labor supplies first grew inadequate in Nashville in the spring of 1918 when DuPont began the construction of a federal munitions plant at Old Hickory. In January 1918 the *Nashville Labor Advocate*, the official organ of the city's unions and the Trades and Labor Council, as well as the Tennessee Federation of Labor, had reported that "in some trades, particularly the building trades, there are workmen out of employment."[41] By the spring, however, work on the DuPont plant at Old Hickory and war orders pouring into the city's factories had tightened Nashville's labor market. By early March, 5,000 workers were employed at Old Hickory. DuPont and its construction contractor, Mason & Hanger, had opened employment offices in the city and were "employing all the labor that can be gotten . . . shipping men into the city from all over this and adjoining states."[42]

The tight labor market spurred union organizing efforts that spring. New members, for example, many of them recent arrivals to the city, poured into the Carpenters' Union "due to the demand for workmen at the government powder plant."[43] By June 1918 the Carpenters' Union reported that its membership had doubled in just one month and that "the demand for union carpenters is [the] greatest in the history of the union."[44] In July the union reported its "largest membership in its history," and that fall, union officials noted that "business is extraordinarily good in the carpenter's line and the members of the [union] are more than getting their share of good times." Other building trades prospered. The Paperhangers' Union reported "wonderful progress in getting new members this spring" and in signing new scale agreements with the leading firms of the city.[45]

Workers and organizers in Nashville took the creation of the National War Labor Board and federal management of the railroads in the spring of 1918 as the green light for organizing those industries where trade unions had only a weak or nonexistent foothold. By March 1918 a drive to organize shop workers in the three railroads in the city was well under way. The Tennessee Central shopmen were reported to be "fully organized." Tradesmen from the shops of the Louisville & Nashville and Nashville, Chattanooga & St. Louis Railroads—boilermakers, blacksmiths, carmen, sheet metal workers, and machinists—met "for the purpose of organizing themselves into a System Federation of railway shop employees." The Machinists' Union increased its membership dramatically as a result of the effort to organize the railroad shop workers. At the beginning of 1918, the machinists counted only 90 members in their ranks, mostly employees of the Tennessee Central Railroad shops and a few "contract shop men." By May the efforts at organizing the L&N and NC&StL brought their membership to over 400.[46] The role of federal intervention was critical. The *Nashville Labor Advocate* understood this, noting that "it is largely through the efforts of the Director General of the Railroads, W[illiam] G[ibbs] McAdoo, that the railroad men have been enabled to organize."[47]

Other organizing drives followed suit. Retail clerks chartered a union with 68 members; leather workers, "Colored Carpenters," and Maintenance of Way workers also chartered locals. The streetcar workers of the Nashville Railway & Light Company organized through the Amalgamated Association of Street and Electric Railway Employees after the company was prevented from enforcing its yellow-dog employment contract. Local waitresses organized under the auspices of the Hotel and Restaurant Employees' Union. The Carpenters' Union also organized boxmakers, hardwood flooring workers, and millwrights at Nashville's wood-products factories.[48]

Organizing efforts continued after the war and into the summer of 1919. New union locals were chartered, and established ones continued to attract new members. The International Brotherhood of Electrical Workers sent two organizers to Nashville in February to make a "survey of the local situation." They reported that the union in Nashville "took on new life during the powder plant era" and that each meeting "has taken in members ever since."[49] The president of the International Bookbinders' Union, Walter N. Reddick, visited Nashville in March as part of a larger trip to "survey the situation of the craft in the South." During Reddick's brief visit, Nashville's Bookbinders' and Bindery Women's Union, No. 83, signed on seventeen new members. Reddick reported that its recent "regular and steady growth" had put the local union "on a better footing that it has been at any time since their memorable fight of 1913–1914." During the spring of 1919, the *Nashville Labor Advocate* boasted that "everybody is organizing here in Nashville" and "never before in the history of Nashville has there been such an intense interest shown in the forming of new unions as at present." Indeed, demands for organizing assistance far outstripped the Nashville Trades and Labor Council's resources. Local labor leaders promised that a "plan is now being evolved to meet the excessive [organizing] demands of the present," but no particular plan was ever implemented.[50]

The speed with which new unions sprang up and old ones grew during the hothouse of wartime conditions calls into question how committed these newly organized workers were to their unions. World War I–era organizing in Nashville could have been simply an evanescent expedient brought on by wartime prosperity, labor shortages, and War Labor Board policies. One measure of Nashville workers' commitment to their unions is how they responded to the period after the war, when employers sought to roll back wartime gains. Demobilization after the armistice brought immediate retrenchment by the city's employers, and Nashville was granted no leave from the wave of intense, sometimes violent strikes that swept the nation in 1919 and 1920.

In early 1919 Nashville's wood-products and leather manufacturers fired the opening salvos in what would be a tumultuous year of conflict between labor and capital. In January the John B. Ransom & Co. locked out the employees at its box factory after recently organized workers refused to accept a five-cent cut in hourly wages. Members of the Boxmakers' Union, No. 1467, organized a committee to inform owner John B. Ransom that "they would not submit to the reduction." Ransom responded quickly, first firing the committee members and then "the more active members [of the union] one at a time." When more employees protested the firings, Ransom locked out the organized workers, "informing them that they were all discharged and all others belonging to the union as well could get off the premises." Ransom steadfastly refused to recognize the union.[51]

That same week, the city's three leading leather manufacturers—the Nashville Saddlery Co., the Early-Cain Co., and Orman-Partee Co.—locked out the nine-month-old Leather Workers' Union. When the firms completed their government contracts, they cut wages from sixty to fifty cents per hour and increased the workday from eight hours, with overtime at time and a half, to ten hours, straight wages. When union members protested the pay cuts, Nashville Saddlery management fired two leading union organizers. The unionized workers still "declined the new rate of pay and ten hours work." The company responded by ordering the men "to get out and stay out" until they would work under the new wages and hours. The two other firms quickly followed suit.[52]

Both lockouts were protracted and bitter affairs. The boxmakers readied themselves for a long fight, confident that "the entire trades-union movement of Nashville, as well as the great Carpenters' Brotherhood and the A.F. of L. are behind the men." They predicted that "it will be a heavy losing proposition for Mr. Ransom to try to break up the union." In mid-February the United Brotherhood of Carpenters sent a "traveling representative," Robert Pettifer, to negotiate on behalf of the locked out boxmakers. Negotiations yielded no settlement, and after three weeks Pettifer left town to attend to business in Memphis.[53]

The pressure against the Ransom Company only increased. In mid-March a strike hit the company's hardwood flooring factory in West Nashville when sixty-five members of the Millmen's Union, No. 3105, who were affiliated with the United Brotherhood of Carpenters, walked out over the issue of union recognition. By then, however, the position of both striking unions had become weak. The boxmakers' strike fund was so low that they held a charity ball to raise money.[54] Three weeks later, the boxmakers and millmen reached a settlement with Ransom in which locked out and striking union men would be allowed to return to their jobs at both plants. No mention was made of the wage, hour, and recognition issues behind the two strikes, and the settlement was a total defeat for the union. Indeed, Ransom failed to rehire a large number of striking workers. The unions were broken. A 1926 survey of the city's unions mentions neither organization, nor was either union mentioned again in the pages of the *Nashville Labor Advocate*.[55]

The Leather Workers' Union showed an equal initial resolve, confident that "all of labor's forces are behind them" and boasting that "the merry war is on to a finish."[56] But their merry war ended much like the boxmakers' and millmen's. Nashville city police harassed pickets in front of the Nashville Saddlery Company, and the leather manufacturer did not have trouble replacing the strikers, and at least one union member, a native of Rockford, Illinois, never honored the strike. Despite intervention by the national union's president, the Leather Workers' Union lost the strike.[57]

Despite these defeats, labor conflicts only increased in the late winter and spring of 1919. The unorganized employees of the Nashville Bridge Company, a manufacturer of steel barges, walked out when management rescinded a promised wage increase. Company manager A. J. Dyer, announcing the cancellation of the wage hike, told his employees that "if any of them were not satisfied with the conditions under which they were working, they could draw their pay and get off the premises." Soon after, about sixty-five workers did just that, organizing under the banner of the Bridge and Structural Iron Workers' Union.[58]

In another case, when the largely female workforce at the city's commercial laundries tried to organize in early June, they were met with a lockout from the Model Laundry. A later attempt to organize the Nashville Laundry met with the same response. There the manager "demanded that the employees who had joined the union turn their union cards over to him before going to work."[59]

The most strident wave of labor conflicts came toward the end of that summer, when a succession of strikes and lockouts swept the city. It began with a strike of organized streetcar drivers in August. The streetcar drivers walked out when the president of the recently organized local, J. H. Gardener, was fired during his regular run on the West End streetcar line. A strike was called in response, and "in an hour's time traffic was completely tied up." Organized motormen's wives became involved by going out into the streets and "urging motormen and conductors to become members of the union." Indeed, the strike was so effective that the next day officials of the Nashville Railway & Light Company agreed to a contract recognizing the union, instituting an arbitration system, and reinstating the fired workers. The success of the union in Nashville inspired Knoxville's streetcar workers to strike in what became an unsuccessful, violence-ridden attempt to gain union recognition.[60]

Nashville's textile workers did not fare as well. A number of operatives had formed a local affiliate of the United Textile Workers' Union the previous spring. After a mass meeting on 2 September 1919, the union organized, by one estimate, "about 700 employees" of the Morgan & Hamilton and Warrioto Mills. The next day, company president Jo B. Morgan Jr.

posted a notice shutting down both plants "on account of the unrest among our help."[61] The textile workers responded by holding another mass meeting at the Ryman Auditorium. David Hanly, legislative chairman of the Tennessee Federation of Labor, quoted Woodrow Wilson's wartime support of "the right of workers to organize and bargain collectively through their chosen representatives" as if it carried the force of law. He told the crowd that while the United States was "politically democratic, it is still industrially despotic."[62]

However, Morgan held fast, refusing to open the plant or rehire union members. The city's Trades and Labor Council supported the fight, taking one dollar from each union member to support the textile workers, but the lockout ended in defeat. A representative of the War Labor Board forged a face-saving but ultimately union-busting compromise, in which all locked out workers could return to their positions. Morgan acknowledged the right of the workers to organize but agreed only to recognize an organization that won the unanimous support of the workforce.[63]

More lockouts and strikes at local factories followed. The Carter Shoe Company locked out its workers when they sought to organize under the Boot and Shoe Workers' Union. Again, the workers invoked President Wilson's public pronouncements on the right of workers to organize, with little apparent success.[64] The 300 tobacco workers at the Weyman & Bruton Company struck at the end of October, seeking a forty-hour work week with overtime, to replace their current sixty-one-hour week. Their pickets, the *Nashville Labor Advocate* reported, "are being intimidated by the usual police guard."[65]

Indeed, police intimidation formed a central part of the Nashville employers' anti-union strategy. When J. B. Lawson, the southern representative of the Amalgamated Association of Street Railway Employees, left Knoxville's streetcar strike for Nashville to assist in an arbitration case, five Nashville police officers abducted him "under threat of death" at the corner of Second Avenue and Union Street, in the heart of the city's downtown. The officers drove him to Springfield, a small town north of the city, "forced him to buy a ticket to Chicago and warned that if he returned to Nashville he would be killed." Lawson later returned to swear out warrants against the men, detectives Gus Kiger, Earl Kiger, Walter Reece, and George Redmond and patrolman C. A. Baskette. A local judge sympathetic to the city's labor movement, Judge J. D. B. DeBow, had to appoint an "attorney general *pro-tempere*" because the district attorney refused to prosecute the case. In the subsequent trial, all five officers were acquitted.[66]

A glimpse of later events indicate just how far employers would go to prevent labor protest. In 1929, county sheriff Gus Kiger met with the Law and

Order Committee of the Nashville Chamber of Commerce. Kiger was asked to "undertake the suppression of the lawlessness existing in and about the foundries of the Phillips and Buttorff Manufacturing Company, Gray & Dudley Company and the Allen Manufacturing Company." Kiger responded that "his office . . . could handle the situation and he would be perfectly willing to undertake it." The meeting concluded with the participants clearly stating Kiger's course of action.

> It was finally understood and agreed that Mr. Kiger and his deputies would undertake the handling of this situation; that at the start he would detail men who were probably unknown to the strikers, who would be in and around the foundries at the time work was discontinued in the afternoon, with the thought that the strikers would take them to be new workmen and would probably try some of their intimidating tactics on these deputies, who would then have first-hand knowledge and would be in a position to handle the situation.

Such undercover work did not come cheap. Douglass Binns of Phillips & Buttorff, Will Allen of Allen Manufacturing, and Sheriff Kiger "were left together to conclude any financial arrangements." The three agreed to "have paid into [the manager of the Chamber of Commerce's] hands . . . some money from time to time, which was to be paid on statements rendered by Sheriff Kiger."[67]

Turmoil in the city's labor relations continued into the spring and summer of 1920. Even after the unionized industrial workers in wood products, textiles, and tobacco had been soundly defeated, the city's skilled craftsmen walked out. In May Nashville's machinists, sheet-metal workers, union bakers, and electricians all called strikes over wages and hours, and in July, linemen at the Nashville Railway & Light Company walked out.[68]

The tide had already turned against organized labor, however. By the spring of 1920, the Open Shop Movement had reached Nashville, and employers were even more emboldened to block organizing drives in the name of the "right to work." The limited federal support for labor was gone as wartime labor and economic regulations that favored organized labor had been hastily dismantled with the war's end. Despite pleas to "the level-headed businessmen of Nashville" to prevent "the ill-advised warfare against organized labor," the city's labor unions suffered stunning defeats.[69] The machinists lost their strike. The Street Carmen's Union was broken when management revoked their existing contract, refused to recognize the union, and fired the organizers, and the subsequent strike descended into violence. Even the venerable Typographical Union struck in May 1921 in an ultimately unsuccessful, eighteen-month effort to implement a previously agreed upon forty-four-hour work week. Smaller unions like the Retail Clerks' Union simply disbanded. As layoffs spread in early 1921, the city's factories began cutting wages, laying off hands, and shutting down production. Organized labor was powerless, and it found itself in its weakest position in Nashville since the 1890s. By 1924, the *Nashville Tennessean* was able to boast that "many Nashville concerns employ no union labor."[70]

What is to be made of this vigorous organization drive and the subsequent wave of strikes that swept across Nashville? The city was not unique in its wartime and postwar experience. Nationally, unions prospered during the war, only to face a bitter retrenchment by employers. Indeed, 1919 was one of the peak years for strike activity in American history. As wartime gains were lost, organized labor entered a period of decline in the 1920s across the nation, and in Nashville.

Nashville's labor movement during and after the war says a great deal about the adaptability of city's migrant working class. Nashville's migrants were not inherently hostile to organized labor. When organized labor seemed to offer a realistic solution to workers' grievances on the job, migrants flocked into unions, and they stuck with them as long as they could. The flurry of organizing activity and the wave of strikes that followed show that Nashville's migrants would stick with the city's labor organizations when they had a chance of succeeding. By 1920, however, with labor in retreat in the city and across the country, success certainly did not seem at hand. When layoffs spread as the postwar depression took hold, many migrants headed back to the countryside. When returning prosperity brought rural migrants back to Nashville, they were wary of the city's greatly weakened organized labor movement. But the migration of the 1920s was demographically different than that of the World War I era; it was a movement dominated by young women, the bulk of whom worked in the city's expanding clerical and sales sector. It is their story that we consider next.

CHAPTER 8

Women's Work

Migrant women comprised the major portion of Nashville's growing female workforce in the years after World War I. The growing demand for clerical and sales workers beckoned many rural Middle Tennessee women to Nashville, where they hoped to enjoy some measure of independence. But achieving that independence was difficult. Nashville's migrant women faced a job market severely segmented by gender and race. Black women, native and migrant, found that few opportunities beyond domestic work were available to them. Significant barriers excluded many white migrant women from the better-paying positions in Nashville's offices and department stores. But even the highest paying positions failed to offer much by way of a career or security.

Reformers and business leaders responded to this influx of rural women in the 1920s with alarm. The "migrant girl" problem was "equally as perplexing as the immigrant" problem, a social worker told members of the Centennial Club, an organization of "civic-minded clubwomen."[1] The *Nashville Tennessean* lamented "America's disappearing girls" and called for efforts to keep the "country [girl] satisfied with her conditions" at home.[2] Mrs. Arch Trawick, the wife of a prominent businessman and a leader in the city's Young Women's Christian Association, stated flatly that "the girl problem is perhaps the greatest social problem of today."[3]

Reformers saw migrant women as powerless before the hazards and temptations of city life. Free from the watchful and protective care of family and community, migrant women were easily tempted by Nashville's "doubtful amusements," which inevitably led to the "dissolution of the moral fibre of young womanhood."[4] Nashville's reformers also perceived the "girl problem" to be a white problem. Black female migrants largely lay outside the interest of the city's white reformers.

Three urban institutions became central to the integration of female rural migrants into the urban social and economic order in the late 1910s and 1920s: church-sponsored boarding homes for working women, employ-

Table 8.1. Percentage of Nashville Women Age Ten and Older Gainfully Employed, 1900–1930

Year	White	Black	Total
1900	17.6	54.9	32.7
1910	20.1	60.1	34.5
1920	27.3	54.0	34.1
1930	25.6	49.2	32.4

Source: U.S. Occupations Census, 1900–1930.

ment agencies, and commercial training schools. Reformers supported these institutions as alternatives to parental and familial control. They protected migrant women from the dangers and temptations of urban life, and in doing so, ordered, routinized, and regularized the process of integrating young female migrants into the city. And, again, these institutions were for whites only.

Migrant women took advantage of these institutions when it was to their personal benefit, which was not always the case. More often, by relying upon their own initiative, friends, and family, migrant women soon found work and began supporting themselves, laying the foundations for new lives in Nashville. While most of Nashville's working women, native and migrant, earned low wages, worked long hours, and faced negligible opportunities for career advancement, migrant women held rising expectations about life in Nashville, and they judged their working lives within the context of the rural life they had left.

Working for wages outside the home was not new to Nashville's women. Large numbers of them had done so during the late nineteenth and early twentieth centuries. As Table 8.1 shows, from 1900 to 1930, the portion of Nashville's working-age women (age ten or older) who were gainfully employed stayed fairly constant at roughly one-third of the city's female population.

The overall stability in participation rates masks demographic trends that transformed the city's female labor force from one that was predominantly black in 1900 to one that was predominantly white by 1930. White women increasingly entered the labor force during the years 1900–1930. The portion of working-age white women employed outside the home rose from 17.6 percent in 1900 to 27.3 percent in the 1920s. On the other hand, most black women—over half—were gainfully employed from 1900 to 1930. As Table 8.2 shows, Nashville's black female workforce in 1900 was nearly three times larger than that of its white workforce. By 1930, a rising propen-

Table 8.2. Occupational Distribution of Nashville Women, by Race, 1900–1930

Occupational Category	1900		1930	
	Whites	Blacks	Whites	Blacks
Manufacturing and mechanical industry	20%	2%	23%	5%
Transportation and communication	0	0	4	0
Trade	12	0	12	1
Clerical	14	0	32	1
Domestic and personal service	33	96	13	88
Professional	20	2	17	5
Total	99[a]	100	101[a]	100
(N)	(2,302)	(7,360)	(12,470)	(9,755)

Source: See Table 8.1.

[a] Total does not equal 100 due to rounding.

sity for white females to enter the workforce, and the heavy pace of their in-migration, made them the majority of female workers by over one-quarter.

The gross statistics on women's participation in the paid labor force also mask a steep decline in female child labor in Nashville during the 1910s and 1920s. The decline, which was part of a larger southern phenomenon, can be attributed to the child labor statues that Tennessee enacted in 1907, 1911, and 1913 and to the overall decline in the use of children in southern textiles by the 1920s.[5] In the 1920s the portion of the female workforce under the age of eighteen declined from 6.9 to 3.7 percent. In 1920, 1,246 women under the age of eighteen worked for wages; by 1930, only 823 did so. The decline in the number of these younger workers was more than compensated by an increase in the percentage of adult women working, especially those in their twenties.

The types of jobs women held in Nashville changed for both white and black women between 1900 and 1930. While manufacturing continued to draw about one-fifth of white women workers, an increasing number of white women took "pink collar" positions in Nashville's expanding clerical and retail sales sectors. As shown in Table 8.2, the portion of white working women employed in clerical jobs rose from just 14 percent in 1900 to nearly one-third in 1930. At the same time, the portion of white women working in domestic and personal service fell sharply from one-third to just 13 percent during the same period.[6] Black women, on the other hand, were excluded from most manufacturing jobs, as well as the newly emerging forms of women's paid labor in the city's offices and stores. Most black working women labored in some form of domestic or personal service. As Table 8.2 shows, the 96 percent of black working women employed in domestic or personal service in 1900 declined only slightly to 88 percent thirty years later.

Traditional avenues of employment for Nashville's black women were also closing. In particular, two occupations that offered working-class black women some degree of freedom from the day-to-day supervision that characterized domestic work, independent seamstress and washerwoman, entered a steep decline. The number of black females employed in the independent needle trades—dressmakers, milliners, seamstresses, and tailors —declined precipitously during the years 1900–1930, from 398 to only 167. The rise of ready-to-wear clothing and accessories spurred the expansion of both factory-based needlework and job opportunities in retail, expansion that opened numerous positions for white women but also sharply curtailed the demand for independent seamstresses and dressmakers, occupations in which skilled black women could earn an independent living.[7]

The number of black independent washerwomen also declined. While taking in laundry was low-paying it at least offered black women a degree of freedom from the from the direct supervision domestic workers were subject to in an employer's home. Since washerwomen typically brought laundry to their own homes, the occupation also allowed women to supervise children and attend to other household tasks. From 1900 to 1930, however, the number of black washerwomen declined from 3,382 to 2,373.

The introduction of home washing machines after World War I was only one factor in the decline of black washerwomen. The rise of large commercial laundries also played an important role. Nashville's commercial laundries understood that black washerwomen represented their chief competition for the business of middle-class housewives, and they sought to turn public opinion against the employ of washerwomen through a racist advertising campaign that associated black women with dirt and disease. McEwen's Laundry advertised itself as "strictly a white man's laundry."[8] Other firms were more explicit. The Nashville Laundry advised potential customers to beware the "risk of contagious diseases that may lurk in the home of the washerwoman." It recommended that to "cut the danger of contagion in the washerwomen's home—send it to the Nashville Laundry."[9] Another advertisement sponsored by four of the city's leading commercial laundries asked, "Which is better—clothes laundered in a big, airy, sanitary laundry by modern harmless methods, or clothes soaked and hung dry in a hovel surrounded by dirt?"[10]

Commercial laundries used racist appeals when
competing with independent black washerwomen
(*Nashville Tennessean*).

Thus, the job market that white migrant women encountered after World
War I offered rapidly growing opportunities for work in the clerical, sales,
and manufacturing sectors of the urban economy. Black women, on the
other hand, found not only that they were excluded from these emerging
occupations but also that traditional sources of employment were no longer
available to them.

For all migrant women—black and white—finding work could be difficult. A 1933 social survey of white, unmarried rural migrant women found
that while it could take up to one month from the day of their arrival in
Nashville to find work, most found work in under three weeks. During the
prosperous 1920s, migrant women certainly found work more easily. But
even in that earlier decade, they needed some way to support themselves
between the time they arrived and when they found steady work.[11]

Family was one source of support. Lillie Shropshire's experience is typical. She migrated from rural Macon County as a teenager in the late 1920s
and moved in with her sister, who already lived in Nashville with her husband. With her sister's help, "I got a job quick as I got here," Lillie recalled
of her job in the General Shoe factory in East Nashville.[12]

But, as we have seen in Chapter 5, many rural women came to Nashville
precisely to escape family. Thus, many migrant women arrived in Nashville
alone, with no family or friends upon whom to rely, or had family unwilling or unable to help them. Typical was the case of "Miss B." She arrived in
Nashville in 1928 alone, without any family in the city to help her. After a
brief and unpleasant stint as a live-in servant, and unable to find other work

that would allow her to live on her own, she moved into one of the city's church-sponsored boarding homes for working women.[13]

Nashville's boarding homes for working women—"semicharity homes," in the local parlance—played an essential role easing women's entry into the labor force and helping them get established in the city. They were called semicharity homes to emphasize the fact that they were not homes for the indigent. They made it their mission to aid and protect young working women from the hazards of city life by providing low-cost housing as well as a restrictive "moral" environment. Because of the low wages, periodic unemployment, long hours, and difficult working conditions migrant women faced, the reformers who supported semicharity homes feared that some unattached migrant women would resort to "immoral" ways of earning a living or otherwise succumb to Nashville's other moral hazards. The mission of all of Nashville's semicharity homes was similar to that articulated by the King's Daughters Home, which sought "to provide a respectable residence and decent living conditions for girls whose wages are too small to permit of their otherwise having them."[14]

By the beginning of the 1930s, Nashville's five semicharity homes for working women, all sponsored by religious organizations, could accommodate about 375 women at any one time. The Girls Christian Home could accommodate just ten to twelve women; the YWCA could house nearly two hundred white women and, in a separate building, twenty-five black women. The other semicharity homes were the Central Church of Christ Home, the Russell Street Church of Christ Home, and the King's Daughters Home. Except for the YMCA, which maintained the segregated branch for black women, Nashville's semicharity homes were white-only.[15]

The establishment of these boarding homes for working women coincided with rise of rural female migration to Nashville in the 1910s and 1920s. The oldest, the YWCA, opened its boardinghouse in 1911. The remainder were founded after World War I, the period of heaviest female migration to Nashville. The King's Daughters Home began operating in 1918, the Girls Christian Home in 1926, the Central Church of Christ Home for Girls in 1927, and the Russell Street Church of Christ Home for Girls in 1930.[16]

As Nashville's oldest and largest boarding home for working girls, the YWCA set the pace for the other homes in Nashville. Its broad mission included "build[ing] Christian character," providing for the "physical, social, mental, and spiritual opportunities to the unprivileged girls" of the city, as well as serving as a "rescue mission for unfortunate girls."[17] In 1909 the YWCA's leaders began specifically addressing the problems faced by Nashville's growing population of white migrant working women. That year the extension department of the YWCA began holding regular devotional services for working women in local workplaces such as McEwen's Laundry, a large commercial laundry, the Nashville Woolen Mills, and the Methodist Publishing House.[18] In 1911 the YWCA moved to new, larger quarters with the construction of its own building at 211 Seventh Avenue North, on the western edge of Nashville's downtown. There it continued reaching out to Nashville's working women. The membership committee sponsored dinners and exhibitions at its pool and gymnasium. In 1912 over 100 saleswomen from local department stores attended a membership drive at the new building. In the winter of 1913, seeking to expand its membership among the city's working women, the YWCA invited the female employees of the Kress department store, the Phillips & Buttorff stoveworks, and the firm of Campbell & Beesley to its new facility for "dinner, [a] swimming exhibition, and [a] demonstration of the advanced gymnasium class of business girls."[19] By 1916 the YWCA had become the primary source of aid for Nashville's migrant women, reporting that "in many instances girls who are without money or friends in the city have stayed at the Association until work could be found."[20]

The very existence of boarding homes like the YWCA indicated the way in which reformers in Nashville responded to the wave of rural women coming to Nashville for work in the 1910s and 1920s. The administrators of these homes were well aware of the rise in the number of wage-earning rural migrants in Nashville. A recounting of the YWCA's early years in Nashville neatly summarized the historical developments in women's work and migration that made such semicharity homes necessary: "New lines of endeavor closed in past generations were rapidly opening up to the womanhood of the world. Industries, factories, and stores were calling many girls and women from the country and surrounding towns to Nashville to take part in this great movement. The Y.W.C.A. was ever ready to meet these young women and work with them in adapting their lives to new and strange ways of living."[21]

The three causes the YWCA championed—women's working-hour reform, the extirpation of forced prostitution or the so-called white slave trade, and women's suffrage—were indicative of the goals of progressive reformers. The leaders of the YWCA saw these reforms as a means to attack the three chief threats to the economic and moral health of working women. In early 1913 the employment department of the "Y" sponsored a number of meetings for local labor unions and "prominent philanthropic and club women" to push for an eight-hour-day law for working women. Interest in limiting the hours of working women grew among the city's reformers in the wake of that year's Christmas shopping season, which had been notorious for the grueling overtime forced upon young saleswomen.[22]

The leaders of Nashville's YWCA saw the "white slave trade" as the leading moral danger facing migrant women. Nationally, concern over the interstate movement of prostitutes culminated in the passage of the Mann Act in 1910.[23] Two years later white slave traders were reported to be active in the city, and a "prominent YWCA worker" informed the local press that "the situation in Nashville is terrible . . . and we know as a positive fact that [white slavery] dealers from Chattanooga and Atlanta have been doing an active business in this city for some time."[24] YWCA officials saw migrant girls, fresh in from the countryside, as particularly vulnerable to prostitution. To address the more immediate problem of country ingenues being swept up by the white slave traders, the YWCA sponsored a branch of the Traveler's Aid Organization in 1912 to meet young migrant women just as they entered the city. By placing "capable women at the [railroad] stations of the city," Traveler's Aid sought to intervene to protect the numerous "young women and girls who, as strangers, arrive at the railroad stations of Nashville" from the white slave traders by offering the services of the YWCA and Nashville's other semicharity homes.[25]

Similarly, the YWCA linked the franchise to promoting the economic interests of working women. The YWCA brought to Nashville regionally and nationally known speakers on the issue and sponsored meetings among the local elite. In 1913 prominent suffragist Laura Clay noted the civil inequality of working women, who were "engaged in all the employments men are" yet could not vote to promote wage and hour legislation for working women. Clay further "emphasized the importance of the franchise to business women and urged them to take an active interest in the work of the local [suffrage] league." By 1916 the Business Women's Equal Suffrage League was holding regular meetings at the YWCA and inviting speakers, such as the Tennessee State Factory and Shop Inspector, to speak on issues concerning working women.[26] Another prominent prosuffrage speaker, Desha Breckenridge, granddaughter of John C. Breckenridge, linked the problems of prostitution, the need for women's labor laws, and suffrage by arguing that "the whole white slave problem is not so much a moral issue as it is an economic question" and that the purpose of women's suffrage was "the protection of working women, married and single."[27]

While the YWCA championed progressive reforms benefiting working women, the lack of affordable housing remained at the core of its and Nashville's other semicharity boarding homes' practical aid to working migrant women. By 1912 the YWCA's dormitory was in full operation, housing "telephone operators, clerks, cash girls, stenographers, typesetters, bookkeepers, laundry workers, seamstresses, milliners and nurses."[28] It charged a variable room rate of $3.00–$5.00 per week, depending upon a resident's income, with $3.75 being the average rate. Newly arriving migrant women depended upon these low room rents, for rooms in private homes could top $20.00 per month, a rate out of reach of most of the YWCA women, whose salaries ranged from $15 to $30 per month. The other semicharity homes charged similar rates.[29]

The YWCA and the other boarding homes in Nashville followed similar restrictive admission and residence policies, with those policies of the YWCA generally emulated by the other homes. The homes limited their housing to young, white, single working women. At the YWCA, for example, women were eligible to stay in the home if they were between the ages of eighteen and thirty and unmarried. Women were allowed a maximum stay in the residence hall of only three years. The Church of Christ homes, the King's Daughters Home, and the YWCA Annex, McGannon Hall, which opened its doors in the 1920s, accommodated older women.[30] The homes were open to only poorly paid women. Women had to be free of communicable disease and prospective residents were interviewed to ascertain their "general attitude" regarding staying in the home and abiding by its rules.[31] Only the YWCA's segregated Blue Triangle League home was open to black women.[32]

Nashville's semicharity homes were a refuge for migrant women, providing a safe, same-sex environment from which boarders could draw strength and mutual support, but this refuge came with a price: Women staying in the boarding homes had to conform to the strict moral regulations established by the homes' administrators. As the YWCA put it, "The moral tone of this institution is in itself a protection to young girls coming to Nashville to work."[33] The rules governing behavior were intended to ensure that the residents maintained "a reputation for good moral conduct." The homes forbade smoking in the building and staying out late. The two Church of Christ homes required attendance at church services and weekly Bible study.[34] Transgressions of the home's moral policies could mean expulsion. At the YWCA, the women "whose reputations . . . become bad are treated with the kindest consideration; every effort is made to save them[,] and only as a last resort are they asked to leave the residence. . . . In no case are they thrown out upon the streets."[35] At the two Church of Christ homes, "cases of violation of regulations of the house are dealt with personally[,] and in some cases girls have been asked to leave the home." At the Girls Christian Home, "indecent conduct is not tolerated."[36]

Meanwhile, the YWCA made a concerted effort to generate a strong sense of community among its members. Its pool, athletic facilities, various clubs, and business training classes drew working migrant women to the center. By 1916 the YWCA had become such a magnet for young working women that an administrator described the residence hall as a "Business Women's University," imbued with a spirit of "sisterhood." The sororal spirit was not complete without maternal advice on how rural women should cope with their new urban jobs, as indicated by part of the credo recited by women in the Girls Work Department: "To labor cheerfully, I must smile in all my work, no matter how disagreeable it may be."[37]

With housing established with family or a semicharity home, Nashville's migrant women soon found that finding a good job was an entirely different matter from finding just any job. Having already taken the initiative to leave their homes in the countryside, migrant women were rarely satisfied "to labor cheerfully" at their first job for long, and they quickly sought better positions. A social survey of white migrant women new to the city conducted in 1933 found that even during the Depression half of the eighty-six employed migrant women interviewed had already shifted from two to five different jobs in the city. Certainly not all these job changes were voluntary. However, even in a slack job market, migrants changed jobs often, coping on their own with temporary unemployment or taking jobs that they liked better or that paid more.[38]

The means by which migrant women obtained work varied with the type of occupation. Just under half of the respondents in the 1933 survey reported obtaining their jobs through direct application to the employer. This was particularly true of women working in factories and restaurants; nearly all of those included in the survey obtained their jobs this way. One migrant woman recounted the process of finding a job as a saleswoman to an interviewer in the early 1930s: "You usually just go in and the manager interviews you. If he likes you, he will let you fill out an application and call you when they need you."[39].

As with finding housing, the aid of family and friends in finding work was helpful, but not essential. Only one-quarter of the migrant women surveyed in 1933 reported obtaining their jobs with the aid of family or friends. Informal networks among other working women, often made through a boarding home, could be just as effective as family connections in finding work. In these cases, knowing an employee in a business was especially helpful in getting hired. One migrant woman described this process when she noted to an interviewer that "sometimes a girl has another girl she knows who works at a place to help her get on." Employers reinforced this practice by requiring references from anyone the applicant might know currently employed by the company. "If [the reference] say[s] you are all right, it helps in getting on," another migrant woman employed as a store clerk reported.[40]

Among whites, religious differences took on increased importance in hiring decisions. By the late 1910s businesses were often requesting that applicants indicate their church affiliation.[41] One migrant woman employed as a sales clerk described how a manager at one local variety store favored members of the Church of Christ. "If a girl has all the necessary qualifications, and if she belongs to that church, she'll most always get on there," she reported. Another migrant woman noted that one's religious affiliation was a standard part of employment applications at retail stores.[42]

All of the migrant women in the survey employed as servants and domestic workers obtained their positions through newspaper advertisements. These women, who were white, however, were atypical, since black women comprised the overwhelming majority of the city's female domestic labor force.[43] Just under a quarter of the migrant women in the survey found positions through employment agencies—critical institutions providing migrant women with jobs. Typically, the most desirable and well-paying clerical and sales positions were almost exclusively acquired through employment agencies, which screened applicants for the proper education and credentials.

The YWCA's Employment Bureau played a critical role in helping migrant women get work in Nashville. Women seeking work registered with the YWCA, providing information about themselves, their qualifications, and the position and wage they desired. The administrators of the Employment Bureau, who served as brokers, "help[ing] the girls . . . seeking employment and at the same time best serv[ing] the employers," then sought to match women with what they judged to be positions appropriate to the woman's education and other qualifications. The bureau was busy; in the first ten months of 1923, it placed 645 women.[44]

Some of the cards that women filed with the YWCA's Employment Bureau survive from the years 1917–18, and the positions to which they aspired say much about these rural women's desire for the newly emerging forms of women's work as well as the difficulties they faced in getting that work. Many of the women who listed with the employment service were fresh in from the country, still identifying towns and hamlets in Nashville's hinterland as their home addresses. Overwhelmingly, they sought clerical or department store positions. Eddie Voss, from Columbia, Tennessee, for example, sought a "clerical" position. Although she listed no experience, she likely would have easily found the position she desired, since she was young (twenty years old) and had recently graduated from Nashville's elite private finishing school for women, Ward-Belmont.[45] Well educated and likely from a middle- or upper-class home, Eddie Voss would have appealed most to the male employers in Nashville's banking and insurance industries who sought women with just her kind of background.

Most rural migrant women seeking work could not boast of the credentials Eddie Voss had. They lacked the proper education and skills, and these shortcomings served as the greatest barriers, after race, to entering the better-paying occupations that were available to migrant women. Women without the proper education—at least a high school diploma and some form of business training on top of that—faced a difficult time getting office positions.[46] Yet women still aspired to these well-paying positions. For example, Anna Altman sought "general office work," even though she had only an eighth-grade education. Tina Sacho, from Jingo, Tennessee, also sought office work, but with only a "grammar school" education, she would have been similarly hindered. There is no record of what positions these women eventually won, but their aspirations for office work show its appeal to a wide social spectrum of rural women who viewed it as providing a definite improvement in their status.[47]

Older migrant women also sought the services of the YWCA's employment bureau. Nannie Jelton, an unmarried, forty-five-year-old recent migrant from the nearby town of Murfreesboro, Tennessee, scrawled, one could interpret as somewhat desperately, on her employment card that she desired "any kind of clerk or cashier or something like that."[48] Addie Cooksey sought employment as a "clerk, saleslady in bookstore[,] cashier or office lady." She described her occupation as "housekeeper" and noted, "[I] am now knitting for soldiers." Another woman who described herself as "middle age" sought "office work," pointing out that she had practiced on the typewriter for one year. Clearly office work held an allure for women. For older women whose opportunities for work were limited, office work was looked upon as particularly promising.[49]

The YWCA viewed clerical and office work as the most viable, and hence desirable, form of employment for women, since it tended to pay the highest wage. The YWCA's Employment Bureau screened women before trying to place them in positions, and women deemed without the proper qualifications, educational or moral, were dissuaded from pursuing certain kinds of jobs. A YWCA administrator expressed concern for one of her residents, writing: "Dessie has become quite a problem to us for she has been out of employment a great deal of the time she has been in the Residence and has not business training so that it is impossible to fit her into a position."[50] In some cases, however, rural women simply could not do the work, and they were forced to find other employment. One young migrant woman staying at the YWCA briefly held a clerical position at one of the city's leading insurance companies, Life and Casualty, but was unable to do the work and was laid off. Whether her education or office skills were inadequate, or whether she simply could not adjust to the regime and pace of office work, we cannot know. However, one month later she found a position at the Washington Shirt Factory.[51]

The Blue Triangle League, the YWCA's branch for black women, also operated an employment service for black women. The Blue Triangle's employment service, however, had to operate within the constraints of the city's segregated employment market. Although one-third of the residents of the home were students at nearby Fisk University, "practically all of the calls [by employers in search of workers] are for domestic help."[52]

The lack of formal education acted as a greater barrier to obtaining better-paying jobs for working-class women than for working-class men. In the skilled trades, men learned much of their craft on the job through the apprentice system. In factories, where semiskilled work predominated, learning on the job was the norm as well. Women who wanted to enter clerical work were expected not only to be fully literate but to be competent in the use of the typewriter, at taking shorthand dictation, at arithmetic, and at simple bookkeeping. All these skills were required for jobs that paid substantially less than men's occupations requiring less formal education.

Since few opportunities existed for women to acquire these skills on the job, the private commercial school took on critical importance—much more so than it did for men.[53] Commercial schools offered migrant women the surest means of obtaining one of the better-paying store or office positions, and they flocked into the classroom. Indeed, Nashville's Women's Commercial Training School, which opened in 1918, understood that a large part of its student body would be comprised of rural migrant women. Announcing its first session, an advertisement for the school read: "To the women of Nashville and the surrounding countryside," a "school has been organized to meet a real need on the matter of training women to take upon themselves the duties and responsibilities of the business world."[54]

The YWCA saw commercial training as the solution to working women's low wages. It would "give the woman the necessary training which will enable her to demand a larger salary or else take her out of the work she is in and train her for a career she seems especially adapted to fill." Elva Sly, general secretary of the YWCA, acknowledged that "many [of Nashville's working women] have been dissatisfied for a long time with the salaries they are getting." Her solution was more training, so that "salesgirls, stenographers, [and] professional women . . . will be enabled to go practically about making themselves more efficient" to their employers, and thus command higher wages. Typical of this emphasis on business training was the YWCA's advice to an unemployed, relief supported resident, who "was prevailed upon to the night school to take typing and shorthand" to solve her dilemma.[55]

By 1920 Nashville counted six commercial training schools. The city's leading commercial training school was the Watkins Institute, located in downtown Nashville in the heart of the city's business district. Like the other five, Watkins was white only. Opened in 1889 through the bequest of Samuel Watkins, a wealthy Nashville brickmaker, the school specialized in day and night adult education. The Watkins Institute charged no tuition, its income being derived from downtown rental property also bequeathed by the benefactor. By 1925 the school enrolled over 1,000 students in its grammar school, high school, and other programs, and had a faculty of forty teachers. Its commercial school included classes in bookkeeping, business law, business arithmetic, and shorthand.[56]

The rise of women's commercial education can be traced through the enrollment patterns of the Watkins Institute's business and commercial classes. In the spring of 1895, Watkins enrolled ninety-four students, of which only seventeen were women, in one general commercial course. By World War I, the Watkins Institute's commercial and business classes had become more specialized and, at the same time, heavily feminized, reflecting changes in the city's economy. By 1918 the school offered courses in shorthand and typewriting, bookkeeping and banking, and commercial law. In the courses that led to strictly clerical positions, women comprised the bulk of the enrollees; the shorthand and typewriting courses enrolled 594 students, of which only 97 were men. The courses on bookkeeping and banking, which imparted broader business skills, enrolled 135 students, of which the majority, 75, were men. The commercial law course was nearly all male; of thirteen enrolled, only two were women. Ten years later courses were similarly divided. Enrollment in the general commercial course in October 1928, which by this time included instruction in shorthand, English, and filing, included 191 students, of whom only 8 were men.[57]

As the enrollment patterns in the commercial courses at the Watkins Institute show, the influx of "businesswomen" into Nashville's offices were businesswomen only in name. The Watkins Institute was in the business of training women clerical workers. Typical of the school's efforts was its sponsorship of "businesswoman's week" which sought to familiarize "the women of Nashville, and especially the girl students [with] the wide variety of vocations that are now open to them." Among the events was a job fair, in which exhibitors "listed the positions which were open to young women, the training necessary to hold them, [and] the salaries to be expected." These fairs connected Watkins' students with employers.[58]

Not all the commercial schools were as well equipped or had such long histories as the Watkins Institute. Robbie Sanford remembered her commercial school, which she entered soon after migrating from Williamson County in the late 1920s, as a private school held in a rented office, with one teacher, who was the sole owner and employee. Yet even this meager business training enabled her to move from a telephone operator's position to a more lucrative office job at the U.S. Tobacco Company in Nashville.[59]

By the 1920s, business education had become standard for most women office workers. Nashville's female clerical workers typically had earned a high school diploma and had taken some type of business course. Sales clerks, also well educated, had an average of at least eleven years of schooling. On the other hand, factory workers and servants had an average of only seven years of schooling. Laundry and restaurant workers were only slightly better educated with an average of eight or nine years of schooling.[60]

But education at commercial schools such as the Watkins Institute offered no guarantee of well-paying positions for migrant women. One investigator noted that many of Nashville's migrant women who took vocational training found that "often the desired occupation is not secured, and many times when a position is secured, the wage is very low."[61] One migrant woman employed as a saleswoman remarked that "I think everyone should take training to improve themselves" but admitted that "as long as one has a job like a chain store job it doesn't help. It didn't help me."[62]

Clerical positions were not the only work that required high educational standards. The city's chain stores "don't employ anyone but high school graduates," one sales worker reported. Women without diplomas were hired only as "Saturday girls" on a temporary and part-time basis.[63] Even in manufacturing, a high school education became increasingly necessary. When DuPont began production of rayon at the site of the former Old Hickory munitions plant in the mid-1920s, it announced its intention to hire 900 women production workers. "It is hoped," the plant supervisor said, "that enough young women with high school training will be available for the company to operate without reducing its qualifications below that point."[64]

How did white migrant women fare compared to native women in entering the city's workforce? Did they land jobs in the city's growing clerical and sales sector? Or were these jobs taken by women native to the city who may have benefited from better connections, experience, and the city's better public schools? Determining exactly the occupations of migrant women in Nashville is quite difficult, as only the most fragmentary evidence remains. Published census statistics offer no means of distinguishing between migrants and natives, and no source comparable to the Selective Service records exists for women.

Two surveys taken during the earliest years of the Great Depression yield the only statistical data on the occupations of migrant women in Nashville. This evidence suggests that rural migrant women were not disproportionately excluded from the better-paying retail and clerical jobs. In one survey of 235 white unmarried migrant women, 31 percent were employed as clerical workers, 16 percent as factory operatives, and 12 percent as saleswomen at department stores and five-and-dime stores. The remaining 42 percent comprised an unspecified catch-all category that included laundry and beauty parlor workers, telephone operators, street vendors, and domestic servants.[65] The other survey, conducted in 1932, showed that of eighty-six employed migrant girls living in Nashville's semicharity homes, 40 percent were employed in some form of office work, 16 percent as waitresses, 14 percent as saleswomen, and 5 percent as factory workers. The remainder were variously employed seamstresses, nurses, a dietitian, a mail inspector, a teacher, and an inspector.[66] When these figures are compared to the distributions of occupations of all women in Nashville in the 1930 census, migrant women were in fact somewhat overrepresented in sales and clerical occupations and underrepresented in factory employment. The 1930 census shows 32 percent of white working women working in clerical occupations, 20 percent as factory operatives, and 6.7 percent as saleswomen and store clerks.[67]

While these statistics provide a general idea of the lines of work that young, single white migrant women entered into, the statistics suffer from a number of limitations, the most important being an undercount of factory workers. By 1933, large numbers of factory women had been laid off and many of them had returned to their families in the countryside. According to investigators, factory operatives tended to be married and thus were not included in the survey. Also, both the surveys used as their sample population residents of Nashville's boarding homes for working women, so those migrant women who were living independently or with families in Nashville were not counted.[68]

However, even the better-paying occupations open to women paid poorly. Contemporary observers recognized that working women's wages, even for the most skilled workers, were inadequate. Organized labor in Nashville decried the fact that employers paid women much less than a living wage and called for female minimum-wage legislation, complaining that "if all employers were fair and just, a minimum wage law for female employees would not be necessary."[69] At a meeting with local employers and the YWCA general secretary, "one fact brought out which was greatly deplored by several of the men and women speakers was that a number of local concerns pay girl employees much less than a living wage." The employers at the meeting agreed that $15.00 was "the lowest living wage which should be paid a girl or women worker." One employer noted that he had on his desk applications from women with several years of experience earning $9.00 a week and that it was not uncommon for typists to earn $5.00 and $6.00 a week.[70]

Systematic data on wages, hours, and working conditions exist for the late 1920s. According to a study of over 800 women wage earners in Nashville, by the late 1920s office and clerical workers earned the highest average wages at just under $18.00 per week. Factory operatives, on the other hand, earned an average of just under $11.00 per week. Store clerks also earned low wages, making an average of $10.25 per week. Earning even less were laundry and restaurant workers, who made an average of $8.74 and $8.53 per week, respectively. Lowest paid were servants, who made an average of $7.20 per week. While a restaurant worker and servant could expect a daily meal, it was hardly adequate compensation for such a low cash wage.[71]

For such wages, working women, and especially those working in the lower-skilled, lower-paying jobs, had to put in long hours. Clerical workers, who not only made the best pay but also had the best working conditions, put in from eight to ten hours a day, with the majority of women putting in nine to ten hours. Store clerks worked from nine to ten hours per day. By 1933, however, according to another study store clerks were putting in an average of eleven hours per day and "many worked overtime without extra pay, and without accurate recording of hours."[72] Factory operatives worked ten to eleven hours per day, as did commercial laundry workers, who typically worked a minimum of ten hours per day. Domestic workers worked even longer hours still. If they lived with their employers, they were basically at work six out of seven days a week, on call from dawn to bedtime. Many servants typically lived with their employers during the week and spent the weekends at home.[73]

Long hours did not ensure steady incomes for migrant women. Seasonal and cyclical unemployment was commonplace, especially for store clerks and factory operatives. While a factory operative could count on a particular hourly wage, when demand slackened, the factory management either reduced hours or laid off workers. In 1929, before the stock market crash, one-third of the women factory workers interviewed by an investigator reported irregular hours and, hence, uncertain earnings. During the holiday season, store clerks worked extended hours but then faced unemployment or shortened hours when the peak shopping season had passed. Clerical workers, on the other hand, worked regular shifts and could count on steady earnings throughout the year. In 1929 only 1 percent of clerical workers reported irregular hours.[74]

Employers were hesitant to pay women a living wage partly because they assumed that women could rely on the earnings of a husband or a father for the bulk of their subsistence. Indeed, employers, one investigator reported, preferred to hire city natives rather than migrant women because they could be sure that they lived with their families and could afford to work for less.[75]

Low wages meant that the subsidized rents at Nashville's boarding homes for working women were important to the economic survival of many migrant women. One "factory girl," after working and trying unsuccessfully to support herself, had moved into one of Nashville's semicharity homes. An orphan with no family to rely upon, she was only working part-time due to slack demand and earning just $3.85 to $5.94 each week. With her subsidized room and board at $3.00 per week at the YWCA, she was barely getting by.[76]

Despite low wages, clerical and department store employers required a standard of employee dress that drained the meager earnings of migrant women. One twenty-one-year-old migrant woman, who earned $5.00 each week as a department store package wrapper, reported that she had to spend "most" of her earnings on clothes, as the store's management required its employees "to look neat and attractive." Also an orphan without relatives, staying at a working women's boarding home allowed her to support herself.[77]

Some migrant women coped with their meager earnings by aiding each other. For example, "Miss G," as an investigator described her, was able to live a bit better than her wages as a physicians' clerk allowed by relying upon her friends by borrowing clothes and money to attend shows.[78]

Dating was also employed as an economic strategy. The same Miss G., for example, had a gentleman friend—described as a "fiancé"—who paid for much of her entertainment. But even more than that, the fiancé made gifts of clothing, which helped Miss G. acquire the dress necessary for her work as well as for her evenings out. While the social surveyor naively stated that her future depended upon the good fortunes of her "fiancé," the nature of the relationship may have been much more pragmatic and reciprocal. A salesclerk, when asked if it was true that working girls in Nashville had "three to four dates a week," responded with exasperation: "a poor working girl's got to do something with her time . . . what do you expect her to do?" Working migrant women, freed of the constraints of family and rural society, struck out in new ways to navigate their new lives in Nashville.[79]

Not all migrant women, however, successfully supported themselves as independent workers through legal means. Some women turned to stealing. Such was the case with Emma Fleeman. She migrated from Hartsville, Tennessee, around 1924 or 1925 and worked at the Werthan Bag Company, one of the city's larger textile mills. By 1930 she had fraudulently charged $231 worth of shoes, coats, dresses, hats, and hosiery to accounts not her own at a number of Nashville department stores. Claudia Stone embezzled money—an amount apparently "in the hundreds"—from the Cain-Sloan department store when she worked there as a sales clerk.[80] Camilla Caldwell, on the other hand, who worked as a social worker during the 1930s, remembered that with the onset of the Depression and the subsequent layoffs at the city's factories, some migrant women ended up in Nashville's red light district and the bawdy houses that lined Crawford Street, near downtown.[81]

Living and working in Nashville did not mean that migrant women were independent of the authority of men. Working women in Nashville typically served under male managers and supervisors, which put them in a vulnerable position, dependent upon their wages yet also seen by male managers as "outside the realm of parental or community protection."[82] Consequently, these superiors could sometimes abuse their substantial authority in the workplace. One saleswomen noted that "some [managers] are just naturally hard on a girl anyhow." She recalled one assistant manager "who just liked to find fault with [whatever] a girl did." She noted that the assistant manager liked public spectacle and humiliating the saleswomen; "he would bawl them out right before a customer."[83]

The close proximity of subordinate women workers and male supervisors could lead to even greater abuses. Migrant women had to walk a fine line between deflecting unwanted advances and keeping their jobs. Robbie Sanford recalled that while working at the U.S. Tobacco factory in the 1920s as a clerical worker she faced what she described as the "usual harassment of the boss." She recalled: "This old guy, he was the manager and he was always calling you in and trying to be sweet, I guess you'd call it. And he would bring me home and sometimes pick me up. But that's as far as it ever got." Sanford understood his intentions, and to deflect his advances and protect her job she cleverly played the role of country ingenue: "I was so country and dumb, purposely."[84]

But after being rebuffed by Robbie Sanford, the supervisor moved on to one of her coworkers. She recalled, "Yeah there was one other girl there [at

U.S. Tobacco]. One day I was off for something and he called her in and she said—how did she have it—he started trying to put his hands on her face or shoulder, and she got up and walked around the chair and he'd walk around behind her."[85] Not all migrant women successfully navigated the sexual hazards of the workplace. One migrant woman from Cummingsville, Tennessee, contracted a venereal disease from an affair with her supervisor at the A&P grocery store where she worked as a clerk.[86] Such harassment was not necessarily tolerated by higher management, however. One female sales clerk stated that it "just sometimes" did happen, "but the company will fire a manager like that as soon as they find it out, and they'll find it out if he does it much."[87]

The difficulties Nashville's working women faced in earning an adequate living and navigating the hazards of city life did not deter the thousands of young rural women who poured into the city in the late 1910s and 1920s. They were attracted by jobs in Nashville's factories, department stores, and offices, as well as the excitement of city life. While semicharity boarding homes for working women, employment agencies, and commercial training schools facilitated the integration of rural women into Nashville's labor force, women only turned to them when it was in their interest to do so. Otherwise, they relied upon other migrant women for help in finding work and making do in the city.

Rural migrant women were motivated by the desire for a measure of independence from the economic, social, and familial constraints of rural life. Historian Joanne Meyerowitz has argued of Chicago's single working women, or "women adrift," that these young, independent women offered a model of rebellion and independence for middle-class women.[88] If her assertion is true, then Nashville's migrant women offered an even more powerful model of rebellion and independence. These women had loosened the bonds of family and of rural community to move to Nashville to pursue independent lives.

Conclusion

Historians agree that rural America underwent a dramatic transformation during the first third of the twentieth century, even if they disagree on the specific causes, the extent, and timing of change. David Danbom branded the efforts of Progressive-era reformers to make farming and farm people "more organized and efficient" according to an urban model as the "resisted revolution." The failure of this resistance ushered in the "first industrial decade" of American agriculture in the 1920s, undermining tradition-bound rural culture. More recently, Hal Barron has explored the "second transformation" of the rural North. Rejecting the dichotomies of "traditional" and "modern," Barron instead explores how rural northerners faced the increasing order and structure of an urban-industrial society through "accommodation as well as resistance" by adapting to change while remaining "both a part of the American mainstream and apart from it." Historians of the rural South concur. Jeanette Keith's study of Tennessee's Upper Cumberland shows how rural people sought to resist and challenge the economic development and reform schemes of urban-based elites. Jack Temple Kirby points to Depression-era federal agricultural policies and World War II as the crucible in which the South's rural social order gave way to an urban and industrial one.[1]

Migration was a critical aspect of the transformation of the rural South. Indeed, the migration from farm to city stands as one of the defining experiences in the social history of the modern South. Over the course of the twentieth century, the exodus of population from the farms and hamlets of the South has transformed the region from one overwhelmingly rural and agricultural to one where most people live in or near cities and work for wages or salaries.

It is ironic that while black and white southerners are imbued with a strong sense of place, they have been among the most mobile Americans in this century. This experience of rural-urban migration is not, of course, unique to the South; it is an experience that rural southerners have shared with migrating populations in eighteenth- and nineteenth-century Europe and with rural people in the developing world in our own times.[2] Indeed, rural-urban migration is a fundamental social process of the modern era.

The prevalence of migration in past and present societies should not obscure the fact that it is a social process deeply embedded in historical contexts. This is not to say that each migration represents a case of historical particularism; rather, migration is the story of people acting in their own interests within larger contexts not of their own making. In the case of Nashville, rural migration emerged from the interaction between patterns of development in rural Middle Tennessee, Nashville, and the South with the traditional mobility strategies of Middle Tennessee farm families. In the South, national and regional patterns of development created a low-wage region within the larger national economy. At the same time, the patterns of Middle Tennessee development tended to concentrate non-farm employment in Nashville while market linkages between the city and its rural hinterland integrated the countryside into the wider economy. A growing population placed harsh pressures on Middle Tennessee's general farming regime, disrupting the social organization of agriculture. In the countryside, limited employment opportunities off the farm meant that rural people would have to search for work in other places.

These broader patterns of regional economic development, however, are only part of the story of rural-urban migration. Temporary, seasonal, and circular rural migration patterns had long been employed by Middle Tennessee farm families. Young, unmarried Middle Tennessee men, in particular, frequently worked as itinerant timber workers or farmhands before settling down and marrying. As opportunities in agriculture declined, rural people extended these seasonal patterns to include migration to Nashville. Nashville migrants followed paths forged by new regional market linkages between city and hinterland, which brought rural people in closer contact with Nashville. More Middle Tennesseans migrating to Nashville in the 1910s and 1920s strengthened personal networks between city and countryside and promoted more migration.

Tennessee progressives' response to outmigration from the countryside unintentionally promoted migration. When progressives responded to what they saw as an alarming exodus from agriculture in the 1910s and 1920s, they sought to increase the appeal of rural life by supporting policies intended to strengthen the social and economic foundations of rural communities, and thus stem the movement. They did this by promoting rural public school reform in the 1910s and 1920s and rural highway construction in the 1920s. However, improved public schools raised the basic level of education among the young, particularly women, making them more easily employed in Nashville's emerging clerical and "pink collar" sector in the 1920s. Modern highways integrated isolated areas of Middle Tennessee into the regional economy and made it easier for rural Middle Tennesseans to leave the countryside and head to places like Nashville.

Nashville's demand for labor influenced the selectivity of migration to the city. The city's failure to develop an extensive manufacturing sector limited the opportunities available to white men, while entrenched employment discrimination limited most black migrants to menial jobs. Black migrant women faced a labor market that increasingly favored white migrant women. Rural women flocked to Nashville to take new jobs in Nashville's factories, department stores, and offices seeking some measure of independence from the authority of male kinsmen and other constraints of rural life. By the 1920s these women dominated the migration to Nashville.

Migration to Nashville was a complex process of adaptation and adjustment in which thousands of rural Middle Tennesseans navigated a period of rapid social and economic change and furthered their own interests. The decisions of thousands of southerners to leave farming and try their fate in the region's cities laid the demographic and social foundations for what is today a modern, urban South.

Middle Tennessee and Nashville
Net Migration Estimates

The Survival-Rate Method of Calculating Net Migration

Net migration measures the change in the size of an area's population due solely to population mobility during a fixed time interval. Net migration is thus a residual measure. The basic method of calculating net migration is to determine the total change in an area's population and then add deaths and subtract births. The residual difference is net migration. Gross migration, one might keep in mind, measures the actual number of migrants in a particular population at a particular time or during a fixed interval.[1]

Since Tennessee did not begin statewide birth and death registration until 1926, reliable data on births and deaths are not available for this study. Demographers have developed the survival-rate method of estimating net migration to overcome such shortcomings. The survival-rate method calculates an expected population over the course of a census decade based on national survival rates and subtracts that figure from the actual population. The survival-rate method takes advantage of the age distribution statistics for states and major cities supplied in each decennial federal census. The standard formula is:

$$M_{x+t} = P_{x+t}^t - sP_x^o$$

where x is an age group
t is the interval between censuses [ten years]
P_x^o is the population age x at the first census
P_{x+t}^t is the population age $x + t$ at the next census
s is the race and sex specific census survival rate

Calculations for five-year age groups were performed separately for native-born populations of white males, white females, black males, and black females. The sum of these calculations yielded the estimate of total net migration for each place and the age-, race-, and sex-specific migration estimates discussed in Chapters 5 and 6. Migration rates were computed by dividing net migration by the population at the beginning of the decade and multiplying by one thousand.

Since the federal census did not begin reporting population by age groups on the county level until 1930, some method of overcoming this lack of data was needed. A solution first proposed by Neil Fligstein was employed. The state-level age structure was applied to county-level native-born population totals (by sex and race) to arrive at estimated age structure values for each county.[2]

Calculating net migration for Nashville posed different problems. Age structure data for the city's population by race and sex obviated the need for the estimation procedure described above. However, changes in Nashville's corporate boundaries made adjustments to the reported census population statistics necessary. Nashville's annexation of populous urbanized districts on its borders in the 1900s and the 1920s would have injected a large degree of error into the calculations. Not correcting the statistics for these boundary changes would have inflated net migration estimates by counting as migrants those who migrated to Nashville merely by virtue of annexation. These boundary changes required the addition to the 1900 population figures of the territory annexed during the decade 1900–1910 in the calculations for the decade 1900–1910, and for 1920 population data for the decade 1920–30. Since published census records listed total population for these outlying districts, the age, sex, and racial structure of the population was assumed to match that of the city as a whole.

The survival-rate method of calculating net migration is an estimation procedure that involves a number of assumptions, and error can creep in at many points. The survival ratios assume standard national mortality rates; higher southern mortality rates in the countryside and in Nashville are not reflected in the calculations. In this regard, the net migration estimates are conservative. In addition, in estimating county-level age structures it is assumed that rural Middle Tennessee's age structure resembled that of the state as a whole, a not unreasonable assumption when one considers that Middle Tennessee accounted for some 40 percent of the state's population.

Table A.1. Net Migration Estimates, Rural Middle Tennessee Counties, 1890–1930

County	1890–1900	1900–1910	1910–1920	1920–1930
Bedford	−4,510	−4,208	−3,259	−4,005
Cannon	−2,129	−2,866	−1,862	−2,593
Cheatham	−532	−1,223	−1,819	−2,007
Clay	−384	−932	−1,075	−1,141
Coffee	−1,019	−2,272	−695	−3,051
Cumberland	1,223	−515	−714	−554
Dekalb	−2,043	−3,377	−2,094	−3,280
Dickson	1,495	−1,733	−2,880	−3,562
Fentress	−193	50	1,204	−1,185
Franklin	−1,946	−2,749	−2,382	−2,176
Giles	−6,857	−5,141	−3,975	−6,443
Grundy	78	−753	123	−1,773
Hickman	−1,005	−2,313	−2,264	−4,206
Houston	−89	−1,119	−776	−1,439
Humphreys	−679	−1,639	−2,118	−2,413
Jackson	−938	−2,547	−2,107	−3,385
Lawrence	312	−605	2,196	−1,224
Lewis	829	632	−1,003	−1,186
Lincoln	−5,126	−4,012	−3,083	−3,997
Macon	−376	−816	−1,667	−3,136
Marion	−1,052	−1,375	−3,428	−2,511
Marshall	−3,156	−4,089	−1,594	−3,899
Maury	−2,530	−6,766	−7,728	−5,769
Montgomery	150	−5,894	−4,267	−5,278
Moore	−1,201	−1,560	−855	−1,031
Overton	−1,102	−343	−844	−2,421
Perry	−566	−1,370	−1,943	−1,679
Pickett	−354	−1,094	−614	−510
Putnam	3	−406	−1,016	−2,297
Robertson	404	−3,085	−2,713	−1,623
Rutherford	−6,539	−4,502	−3,477	−5,108
Smith	−2,588	−3,214	−3,387	−3,874
Stewart	220	−2,518	−2,040	−3,307
Sumner	−2,006	−3,964	−1,402	−3,326
Trousdale	−814	−885	−526	−1,109
Vanburen	−298	−755	−507	273
Warren	−910	−2,387	−1,504	−396
Wayne	−865	−2,669	−968	−2,565
White	−708	−1,269	−1,818	−2,550
Williamson	−3,985	−5,033	−3,123	−3,653
Wilson	−4,373	−5,003	−2,196	−5,507

Table A.2. Net Migration Rates (per 1,000 Population), Rural Middle Tennessee Counties, 1890–1930

County	1890–1900	1900–1910	1910–1920	1920–1930
Bedford	−183	−176	−144	−184
Cannon	−175	−237	−172	−253
Cheatham	−60	−121	−173	−206
Clay	−53	−111	−119	−124
Coffee	−74	−147	−44	−176
Cumberland	231	−63	−77	−55
Dekalb	−131	−205	−136	−213
Dickson	111	−94	−144	−184
Fentress	−38	8	162	−114
Franklin	−104	−136	−116	−105
Giles	−196	−156	−125	−208
Grundy	13	−98	15	−178
Hickman	−70	−142	−137	−259
Houston	−17	−174	−125	−232
Humphreys	−58	−123	−152	−179
Jackson	−70	−168	−140	−226
Lawrence	26	−40	125	−52
Lewis	325	148	−166	−209
Lincoln	−188	−153	−119	−155
Macon	−35	−63	−115	−210
Marion	−70	−80	−182	−144
Marshall	−167	−218	−94	−225
Maury	−67	−159	−191	−163
Montgomery	5	−165	−127	−164
Moore	−201	−274	−178	−230
Overton	−92	−26	−53	−137
Perry	−73	−156	−220	−216
Pickett	−75	−204	−121	−98
Putnam	0	−24	−51	−103
Robertson	20	−124	−107	−63
Rutherford	−187	−134	−105	−155
Smith	−141	−169	−183	−226
Stewart	18	−166	−137	−226
Sumner	−85	−152	−55	−120
Trousdale	−139	−148	−90	−185
Vanburen	−104	−242	−181	104
Warren	−63	−146	−91	−23
Wayne	−75	−207	−80	−199
White	−58	−90	−118	−162
Williamson	−152	−191	−129	−156
Wilson	−161	−185	−86	−210

Table A.3. Net Migration Estimates and Rates (per 1,000 Population), Nashville, Tenn., by Race and Sex, 1890–1930

	1890–1900	1900–1910	1910–1920	1920–1930
White males	450	683	1,572	4,261
Per 1,000	21	23	46	92
White females	502	2,567	2,101	7,925
Per 1,000	23	85	58	161
Black males	−380	−179	416	1,763
Per 1,000	−27	−11	26	92
Black females	1,115	905	1,004	2,552
Per 1,000	67	43	49	111
Total net migration	1,687	3,975	5,092	16,501
Per 1,000	23	41	47	122

Notes

Introduction

1. "Robert Penn Warren: A Reminiscence," in John Egerton, *Nashville: The Face of Two Centuries* (Nashville: PlusMedia, 1979), 205; Paul K. Conkin, *The Southern Agrarians* (Knoxville: University of Tennessee Press, 1988), 19, 58–59; Tracy Campbell, *The Politics of Despair: Power and Resistance in the Tobacco Wars* (Lexington: University Press of Kentucky, 1993); and Suzanne Marshall, *Violence in the Black Patch of Kentucky and Tennessee* (Columbia: University of Missouri Press, 1994) are recent treatments of the Black Patch War.

2. Charles K. Wolfe, *The Grand Ole Opry: The Early Years, 1925–1935* (London: Old Time Music, 1975), 70; Walter D. Haden, ed., *Fiddlin' Sid's Memoirs: The Autobiography of Sidney J. Harkreader*, John Edwards Memorial Foundation Special Series, no. 9 (Los Angeles: John Edwards Memorial Foundation, 1976), 17. Harkreader states in his memoir that he met Macon in 1921, but his recollection of precise dates is poor. Wolfe's account, which places the meeting in 1923, is certainly correct.

3. This apt phrase is coined in Don H. Doyle, *Nashville since the 1920s* (Knoxville: University of Tennessee Press, 1985), 30.

4. The South here includes the eleven states of the Confederacy (Alabama, Arkansas, Florida, Georgia, Louisiana, Mississippi, North Carolina, South Carolina, Tennessee, Texas, and Virginia), with the addition of Kentucky and Oklahoma. The precise figures are 13.4 percent urban in 1890 and 32.1 percent urban in 1930. Urban areas are defined as those with a population of 2,500 or greater. Figures are conveniently reported in T. Lynn Smith, "The Emergence of Cities," in *The Urban South*, ed. Rupert B. Vance and Nicholas J. Demerath (Chapel Hill: University of North Carolina Press, 1954), 33.

5. Don H. Doyle, *New Men, New Cities, New South: Atlanta, Nashville, Charleston, Mobile, 1860–1910* (Chapel Hill: University of North Carolina Press, 1990), 1–21.

6. Twelve Southerners, *I'll Take My Stand: The South and the Agrarian Tradition* (1930; New York: Harper Torchbooks, 1962); Mark G. Malvasi, *The Unregener-*

ate South: The Agrarian Thought of John Crowe Ransom, Allen Tate, and Donald Davidson (Baton Rouge: Louisiana State University Press, 1997).

7 Richard A. Peterson, Creating Country Music: Fabricating Authenticity (Chicago: University of Chicago, 1997).

8 Gerald Capers, "The Rural Lag on Southern Cities," Mississippi Quarterly 21 (Fall 1968): 258; William D. Miller, "Rural Values and Urban Progress, 1900–1917," ibid., 269; David R. Goldfield, Cotton Fields and Skyscrapers: Southern City and Region (Baton Rouge: Louisiana State University Press, 1982), 3.

9 William Cronon, Nature's Metropolis: Chicago and the Great West (New York: W. W. Norton, 1991); Raymond Mohl, "City and Region: The Missing Dimension in U.S. Urban History," Journal of Urban History 25 (November 1998): 3–21; Roberta Balstad Miller, City and Hinterland: A Case Study of Urban Growth and Regional Development (Westport, Conn.: Greenwood Press, 1979); Calvin Goldscheider, "Migration and Rural Social Structure: An Overview," in Rural Migration in Developing Nations: Comparative Studies of Korea, Sri Lanka, and Mali, ed. Calvin Goldscheider (Boulder, Colo.: Westview Press, 1984), 1–19; Sidney Goldstein, "Urbanization, Migration and Development," in Urban Migrants in Developing Nations: Patterns and Problems of Adjustment, ed. Calvin Goldscheider (Boulder, Colo.: Westview Press, 1983), 3–19; Ronald Skeldon, Population Mobility in Developing Countries: A Reinterpretation (London: Belhaven Press, 1990).

10 Joe William Trotter Jr., ed., The Great Migration in Historical Perspective: New Dimensions of Race, Class, and Gender (Bloomington: Indiana University Press, 1991), surveys this literature.

Chapter One

1 George D. Hay, A Story of the Grand Ole Opry (Nashville: Privately published, 1953), 9–10; Curtis W. Ellison, Country Music Culture: From Hard Times to Heaven (Jackson: University Press of Mississippi, 1995), 3, 10; Richard A. Peterson, Creating Country Music: Fabricating Authenticity (Chicago: University of Chicago Press, 1997), 99. Peterson reports that there is no evidence that any of the many radio barn dance programs that arose in the South and across the country in the 1920s and 1930s ever engaged a "caller" to lead an actual barn dance among the live audience.

2 Clipping, "WSM's Fourth Birthday," Radio Digest 23:6, pp. 62, 77, in Grand Ole Opry Files, Country Music Foundation Library and Media Center; Hay, Grand Ole Opry, 1.

3 Donald Davidson, "Current Attitudes toward Folklore," in Still Rebels, Still Yankees and Other Essays (1957; Baton Rouge: Louisiana State University Press, 1972), 134. This essay originally dates from 1940. In 1939 Davidson moved to a home on Fairfax Avenue, near the Vanderbilt University campus, but also just a few blocks from Sixteenth and Seventeenth Avenues, where

Nashville's post–World War II music industry came to settle along what is now known as "Music Row" (Donald Davidson to Ward Allison Dorrence, 27 November 1939, Dorrence Papers, Southern Historical Collection, University of North Carolina, Chapel Hill). Davidson distilled his observations of the music industry into his posthumously published comic novel, *Big Ballad Jamboree* (Jackson: University Press of Mississippi, 1996).

4 David Goldfield, *Cotton Fields and Skyscrapers: Southern City and Region* (Baton Rouge: Louisiana State University Press, 1982), 4.

5 Ellison, *Country Music Culture*, xiii–xxii.

6 John Woodruff Rumble, "Fred Rose and the Development of the Nashville Music Industry, 1942–1954" (Ph.D. dissertation, Vanderbilt University, 1980), remains the best study of the rise of the Nashville recording industry.

7 Bill C. Malone, "The Rural South Moves to the City: Country Music since World War II," in *The Rural South since World War II*, ed. R. Douglas Hurt (Baton Rouge: Louisiana State University Press, 1998), 96.

8 Ellison, *Country Music Culture*; Peterson, *Creating Country Music*, 5–6.

9 Uncle Dave Macon File, NF 1331, and Fiddlin Sid Harkreader File, NF 897, John Edwards Memorial Collection, Southern Historical Collection, University of North Carolina, Chapel Hill; Richard A. Peterson and Paul Di Maggio, "The Early Opry: Its Hillbilly Image in Fact and Fancy," *Journal of Country Music* 4 (Summer 1973): 43.

10 Clipping, "WSM's Fourth Birthday," 62, 77; *Nashville Tennessean*, 4, 5 October 1925; Powell Stamper, *The National Life Story: A History of the National Life and Accident Insurance Company of Nashville, Tennessee* (New York: Appleton-Century-Crofts, 1968), 161.

11 Susan B. Carter and Richard Sutch, "Myth of the Industrial Scrap Heap: A Revisionist View of Turn-of-the-Century American Retirement," *Journal of Economic History* 56 (March 1996): 5–38; Vivian Rothman Zelizer, *Morals and Markets: The Development of Life Insurance in the United States* (New York: Columbia University Press, 1979), 73.

12 "Selling Farmers Life Insurance," *The Shield*, 25 November 1940, 14; "WSM Family Album" [undated promotional booklet from the early 1930s], WSM Grand Ole Opry Files, Country Music Foundation Library and Media Center, Nashville; see also Ronald R. Kline, *Consumers in the Country: Technology and Social Change in Rural America* (Baltimore, Md.: Johns Hopkins University Press, 2000), 55–86, 113–27.

13 Charles K. Wolfe, *Tennessee Strings: The Story of Country Music in Tennessee* (Knoxville: University of Tennessee Press, 1977), 54–55; Charles K. Wolfe, *A Good-Natured Riot: The Birth of the Grand Ole Opry* (Nashville: Country Music Foundation Press and Vanderbilt University Press, 1999), 269–87; Peterson and DiMaggio, "Early Opry," 39–40.

14 *The Shield*, 26 January; 2 March; 2 February 1926.

15 Other examples of this trend are discussed in Pamela Grundy, "'We Always Tried to Be Good People': Respectability, Crazy Water Crystals, and Hillbilly

Music on the Air, 1933–1935," *Journal of American History* 81 (March 1995): 1591–1620, and Pamela Grundy, "From Il Trovatore to the Crazy Mountaineers: The Rise and Fall of Elevated Culture on WBT-Charlotte, 1922–1930," *Southern Cultures* 1 (Spring 1994): 51–73.

16 Sam and Kirk McGee, performers, "Chevrolet Car," in *Nashville Early String Bands*, vol. 1 [sound recording], Charlottesville, Va.: County Records, 2000. In 1930, 34.2 percent of Tennessee farm households owned an automobile, while only 2.7 percent owned a tractor. See University of Tennessee, Agricultural Experiment Station, "Human and Physical Resources of Tennessee, Chapters XIV, XV, Transportation and Communication," by Charles E. Allred, Samuel W. Atkins, and William E. Hendrix, *Rural Research Series*, no. 63 (Knoxville, Tenn., 1939), 247; and "Farm Tenancy in Tennessee," by Charles E. Allred, William E. Hendrix, and Benjamin D. Raskopf. *Rural Research Series*, no. 17 (Knoxville, Tenn., 1936), 12.

17 Alton Delmore, *The Delmore Brothers: Truth Is Stranger Than Publicity*, edited by Charles K. Wolfe (Nashville: Country Music Foundation Press, 1995), 103–17; Rinzler and Cohen, *Uncle Dave Macon*, 16–18. I am grateful to Bill Mansfield for bringing these song lyrics to my attention and explaining their significance in Macon's life. Rural hostility to the new taxes needed for 1920s hard-surfaced road construction is explored in Jeanette Keith, *Country People in the New South: Tennessee's Upper Cumberland* (Chapel Hill: University of North Carolina Press, 1995), 103–17, and Hal S. Barron, *Mixed Harvest: The Second Great Transformation in the Rural North, 1870–1930* (Chapel Hill: University of North Carolina Press, 1997), 19–42.

18 Charles Wolfe, "Uncle Dave Macon," in *Stars of Country Music: Uncle Dave Macon to Johnny Rodriguez*, ed. Bill C. Malone and Judith McCulloh (Urbana: University of Illinois Press, 1975), 42–43; Ralph Rinzler and Norm Cohen, *Uncle Dave Macon: A Bio-Discography*, JEMF Special Series, No. 3 (Los Angeles: John Edwards Memorial Foundation, Inc., 1970), 16–18.

19 See Grace Elizabeth Hale, *Making Whiteness: The Culture of Segregation in the South, 1890–1940* (New York: Pantheon Books, 1998), 8–9.

20 *Nashville Tennessean*, 17 February 1924; 11 August, 6 September 1925; 6 September 1920.

21 Mary Bufwack and Robert K. Oermann, "Adelyne Hood: The Amalgamation of Vaudeville and Folk Traditions in Early Country Music," *JEMF Quarterly* 18 (1982): 116–30; Delmore, *Delmore Brothers*, 71–72.

22 Wolfe, *Good-Natured Riot*, 7–8; George D. Hay, *Howdy Judge* (Nashville: McQuiddy Press, 1926), 3–4, 82, 104–6. The classic description of the "policy" racket is found in St. Clair Drake and Horace R. Cayton, *Black Metropolis: A Study of Negro Life in a Northern City* (New York: Harcourt, Brace and Company, 1945).

23 Wolfe, *Tennessee Strings*, 54–55.

24 See the title page of Hay, *Howdy Judge*.

25 Hay, *Grand Ole Opry*, 17–18; Wolfe, *Good-Natured Riot*, 225–26; undated advertisement reproduced in Jerry Wayne Rinks, "We Shield Millions: A History of WSM, 1925–1950" (Ph.D. dissertation, University of Tennessee, Knoxville, 1993), 172.

26 Lasses White, *Lasses White's Book of Humor and Song: Songs, Parodies, Jokes, Poems* (n.p., 1935), 18; "Jamup and Honey Scrapbook" (n.d., n.p.), in Earl R. Yates Collection, Archives of Appalachia, East Tennessee State University, Johnson City, Tenn.; Lu Ann Jones, "Gender, Race, and Itinerant Commerce in the Rural New South," *Journal of Southern History* 66:2 (2000): 297–320.

27 Wilds is quoted in Jack Hurst, *Nashville's Grand Ole Opry* (New York: Harry N. Abrams, Inc., 1975), 159. See also Eric Lott, *Love and Theft: Blackface Minstrelsy and the American Working Class* (New York: Oxford University Press, 1995), 15–37.

28 Wolfe, *Good Natured Riot*, 45–46, 103; David C. Morton with Charles K. Wolfe, *DeFord Bailey: A Black Star in Early Country Music* (Knoxville: University of Tennessee Press, 1991), 17.

29 Tony Russell, *Blacks, Whites, and Blues* (New York: Stein and Day, 1970), 55. I am indebted to Bill Mansfield for this citation.

30 Hay, *Grand Ole Opry*, 10. Charles K. Wolfe argues that Bailey's dismissal from the Opry occurred because the performer had the misfortune to be caught in the middle of an acrimonious power struggle over the control of song licenses and performance rights. The American Society of Composers, Authors, and Publishers (ASCAP) had instituted a licensing boycott of radio stations in 1941. WSM supported a newly formed rival song-licensing organization, Broadcast Music, Inc. (BMI). Many of Bailey's songs were under ASCAP license and thus could not be performed on WSM. Bailey, apparently unwilling to learn or compose new material, had to go. This explanation would be more convincing if Hay had invited Bailey back on the program after the ASCAP-BMI controversy had been resolved. See Wolfe, *Good-Natured Riot*, 126–27.

31 Morton, *DeFord Bailey*, 12–18; Rebecca Thomas, "There's a Whole Lot o' Color in the 'White Man's Blues': Country Music's Selective Memory and the Challenge of Identity," *Midwest Quarterly* 38:1 (1996): 73–89.

Chapter Two

1 *Nashville Tennessean*, 11 March 1917.

2 David Ralph Meyer, "A Dynamic Model of the Integration of Frontier Urban Places into the United States System of Cities," *Economic Geography* 56 (April 1980): 121–23. On the theory of metropolitan hinterlands see Otis Dudley Duncan et al., *Metropolis and Region* (Baltimore, Md.: Johns Hopkins University Press, 1960); Harvey S. Perloff, *Regions, Resources, and Economic Growth*

(Baltimore, Md.: Johns Hopkins University Press, 1960); and Francis X. Blouin, Jr., *The Boston Region, 1810–1850: A Study of Urbanization* (Ann Arbor, Mich.: UMI Research Press, 1980).

3   *Nashville Tennessean*, 24 March 1917. A brief chronicle of the booster trips is given in ibid., 18 May 1924.

4   *Nashville Banner*, 28 May 1910. Nashville's business leaders were not alone in attributing their city's present and potential economic growth to the productivity of their hinterland. The Atlanta-based *Southern Banker* noted that "Atlanta has grown to its present commanding position among the cities of the South because of the trade and support it has received from the wonderfully productive territory surrounding it" (*Southern Banker*, May 1923, 1).

5   David L. Carlton, "The Revolution from Above: The National Market and the Beginnings of Industrialization in North Carolina," *Journal of American History* 77 (September 1990): 449–50, 459.

6   A recent examination of 123 elites in Nashville in 1880 found that 59, or 48 percent, were primarily engaged in wholesale commerce or finance. See Don H. Doyle, *New Men, New Cities, New South: Atlanta, Nashville, Charleston, Mobile, 1860–1910* (Chapel Hill: University of North Carolina Press, 1990), 99.

7   John Wooldridge, ed., *History of Nashville, Tennessee* (Nashville: Publishing House of the Methodist Episcopal Church, South, 1890), 247–48.

8   Doyle, *New Men, New Cities, New South*, 25–28; Maury Klein, *History of the Louisville & Nashville Railroad* (New York: Macmillan, 1972), 40–42.

9   Klein, *Louisville & Nashville Railroad*, 153–57.

10 *Nashville Banner*, 22 July 1907. By comparison, the total value of products manufactured in the city in 1904 was $21,567,000 (U.S. Census Bureau, *Thirteenth Census of the United States: 1910*, vol. 9, *Manufactures* [Washington: Government Printing Office, 1912], 1190–91).

11 *Nashville Tennessean*, 18 November 1923.

12 Ibid., 4 January 1925.

13 Nashville Board of Trade, *Yearbook, 1908–09* (Nashville, 1909), 14. The *Nashville Tennessean* ran a regular weekly section in the 1910s and 1920s titled "On the Firing Line with Nashville's Army of Commercial Travelers" that chronicled the activities of Nashville's wholesale jobbers and salesmen.

14 *Nashville Tennessean*, 18 November 1923.

15 Ibid., 11 March 1917.

16 Ibid.

17 Ibid., 18 November 1923.

18 Ibid., 25 March 1917.

19 Ibid., 4 January 1925, 29 July 1923.

20 Ibid., 11 March 1917.

21 Ibid., 29 July 1923.

22 Ibid., 18 November 1923.

23 Ibid., 11 March 1917.

24 Ibid., 29 July 1923.

25 Nashville Board of Trade, *Yearbook, 1908–09,* 14.

26 *Nashville Tennessean,* 24 January 1925.

27 Claude A. Campbell, "The Development of Banking in Tennessee" (Ph.D. dissertation, Vanderbilt University, 1932).

28 Michael P. Conzen, "The Maturing Urban System in the United States, 1840–1910," *Annals of the Association of American Geographers* 67 (March 1977): 88–108. See *The Southern Banker,* June 1922 and May 1923, for examples of advertisements by metropolitan banks soliciting correspondent accounts from rural and small-town banks.

29 Calculated from the Tennessee bank listings in R. G. Dun & Company, *Mercantile Agency Reference Book (and Key) Containing Ratings of Merchants, Manufacturers, and Traders Generally, Throughout the Southern States,* vol. 87 (January 1890) (New York: R. G. Dun & Co., 1890).

30 Calculated from the Tennessee bank listings in R. G. Dun & Company, *The Mercantile Agency Reference Book (and Key) Containing Ratings of Merchants, Manufacturers, and Traders Generally,* vol. 143 (January 1904) (New York: R. G. Dun & Co., 1904).

31 Calculated from Tennessee bank listings in Bradstreet Company, *Bradstreet's Book of Commercial Ratings of Bankers, Merchants, Manufacturers, Etc. in a Portion of the United States,* vol. 228 (January 1925) (New York: The Bradstreet Co., 1925).

32 *Nashville Banner,* 22 May 1909.

33 The Nashville Life Insurance Company, "Nashville Life Insurance Company of Nashville, Tennessee, July 1, 1873" (Nashville: Tavel, Eastman & Howell, 1873).

34 There were only three major southern-based life insurance companies in 1900; by 1910 there were forty. See *Proceedings of the Third Annual Convention of the Southern Commercial Congress* (Atlanta, Ga., 1911; Washington: The [Southern Commercial] Congress, 1911), 966.

35 Powell Stamper, *The National Life Story: A History of the National Life and Accident Insurance Company of Nashville, Tennessee* (New York: Appleton-Century-Crofts, 1968), 1–2, 17–18, 31–40; Don H. Doyle, *Nashville in the New South, 1880–1930* (Knoxville: University of Tennessee Press, 1985), 213.

36 Stamper, *National Life Story,* 60–61.

37 *Nashville Banner,* 29 May 1909.

38 *Nashville Tennessean,* 22 July 1923; Doyle, *Nashville in the New South,* 212.

39 *Nashville Banner,* 29 May 1909; *Nashville Tennessean,* 22 July 1923.

40 *Nashville Tennessean,* 22 July 1923.

41 J. B. Killebrew, *Introduction to the Resources of Tennessee* (Nashville: Tavel, Eastman & Howell, 1874), 696, 701.

42 Ira P. Jones, *The City of Nashville: Illustrated* (Nashville: n.p., 1890), 59.

43 Wooldridge, ed., *History of Nashville,* 252.

44 Emory Q. Hawk, *Economic History of the South* (New York: Prentice-Hall,

1934), 301; Robert E. Corlew, *Tennessee: A Short History*, 2nd ed. (Knoxville: University of Tennessee Press, 1981), 118–19, 231–32; Samuel Cole Williams, "Early Iron Works in the Tennessee Country," *Tennessee Historical Quarterly* 6 (March 1947): 39–46.

45 *Nashville Daily American*, 9 February 1881.

46 Herman Hollis Chapman, *The Iron and Steel Industries of the South* (University: University of Alabama Press, 1953), 44, 57–58, 59, map 15.

47 C. Vann Woodward, *Origins of the New South, 1877–1913*, 2nd ed. (Baton Rouge: Louisiana State University Press, 1971), 126–28.

48 William H. Doran, "The Development of the Industrial Spirit in Tennessee, 1910–1920" (Ph.D. dissertation, George Peabody College for Teacher, 1965), 179–83; Gavin Wright, *Old South, New South: Revolutions in the Southern Economy since the Civil War* (New York: Basic Books, 1986), 173–77.

49 Wooldridge, ed., *History of Nashville*, 224; Glenn Rogers, "Localization of a Few Selected Industries in Nashville" (M.A. thesis, George Peabody College for Teachers, 1932), 16–17.

50 Wooldridge, ed., *History of Nashville*, 224–25.

51 Rogers, "Selected Industries," 14–17.

52 Wooldridge, ed., *History of Nashville*, 225–26.

53 Marshall-Bruce-Polk Co., *Nashville City Directory, 1920* (Nashville: Marshall-Bruce-Polk, 1920). The *Nashville Banner*, 22 June 1907, noted the completion of a new textile factory with a capacity of 500 looms and 20,000 spindles employing 400 "men, women, boys and girls."
    Nashville's textile mills in 1920 were Morgan & Hamilton, Werthan Bag, Warrioto Mills, and the May Hosiery Mills. No separate enumeration for the city's textile industry is given in the Manufacturing Census of 1910, 1920, or 1930. See U.S. Census Bureau, *Thirteenth Census*, vol. 9, *Manufactures*; U.S. Census Bureau, *Fourteenth Census of the United States, Taken in the Year 1920*, vol. 8, *Manufactures* (Washington: Government Printing Office, 1923); and U.S. Census Bureau, *Fifteenth Census of the United States: 1930, Manufactures*, vol. 3, *Reports by States* (Washington: Government Printing Office, 1933).

54 Jones, *City of Nashville*, 59.

55 David L. Carlton, "Unbalanced Growth and Industrialization: The Case of South Carolina," in *Developing Dixie: Modernization in a Traditional Society*, ed. Winfred B. Moore Jr. et al. (New York: Greenwood Press, 1988), 115.

56 Minutes of the Industrial Committee, Nashville Chamber of Commerce, 2 March 1925, Chamber of Commerce Records, Tennessee State Library and Archives, Nashville.

57 University of Tennessee, Agricultural Experiment Station, "Development of the Timber Industry in Tennessee and the United States," by Charles E. Allred, S. W. Watkins, and Frank M. Fitzgerald, *Rural Research Series*, no. 92 (Knoxville, 1939), 4.

58 Stanley F. Horn, *This Fascinating Lumber Business* (Indianapolis: Bobbs-Merrill Company, 1943), 109–10. Black walnut was in particular demand for

use in Singer Sewing Machines (University of Tennessee, Agricultural Experiment Station, "Development of the Timber Industry in Tennessee," 4).

59 Horn, *Fascinating Lumber Business*, 110.

60 Ibid.; University of Tennessee, Agricultural Experiment Station, "Development of the Timber Industry in Tennessee," 4; William Lynwood Montell, *Don't Go Up Kettle Creek: Verbal Legacy of the Upper Cumberland* (Knoxville: University of Tennessee Press, 1983), 85–87.

61 Wooldridge, ed., *History of Nashville*, 229; Montell, *Kettle Creek*, 87.

62 Figures calculated from data collected in U.S. Census Office, *Report on Manufacturing Industries in the United States at the Eleventh Census: 1890*, pt. 2, *Statistics of Cities* (Washington: Government Printing Office, 1895); U.S. Census Office, *Twelfth Census of the United States, Taken in the Year 1900*, vol. 8, *Manufactures* (Washington: Government Printing Office, 1902); U.S. Census Bureau, *Thirteenth Census*, vol. 9, *Manufactures*; U.S. Census Bureau, *Fourteenth Decennial Census of the United States, Taken in the Year 1920*, vol. 8, *Manufactures*; U.S. Census Bureau, *Fifteenth Census, Manufactures*, vol. 3, *Reports by States*. The 1900 manufacturing census did not separately report employment figures for furniture manufacturing and lumber products industries.

63 *Nashville Tennessean*, 15 July 1923; University of Tennessee, Agricultural Experiment Station, "Development of the Timber Industry in Tennessee," 4–7. Seeking to minimize Memphis's rise as Tennessee's leading hardwood lumber market, the *Nashville Tennessean* derisively characterized the city as the "Metropolis of the Chips" (15 July 1923).

64 Wooldridge, *History of Nashville*, 222–24.

65 *Nashville Tennessean*, 29 July 1923.

66 Clarence Colton Dawson, "History of the Flour Milling Industry in Nashville, Tennessee" (M.A. thesis, George Peabody College for Teachers, 1931), 53, 55–56, 58.

67 William H. Joubert, *Southern Freight Rates in Transition* (Gainsville: University of Florida Press, 1949), 12, 73, 179–87; Dawson, "Flour Milling Industry," 58–59, 60; U.S. Census Bureau, *Fifteenth Census, Manufactures*, vol. 3, *Reports by States*, 499.

68 Blanche Henry Clark, *The Tennessee Yeomen, 1840–1860* (Nashville: Vanderbilt University Press, 1942), 121, 124–25.

69 University of Tennessee, Agricultural Experiment Station, "The Development and Present Importance of Nashville Livestock Market," by M. J. Danner, B. H. Luebke, and B. D. Raskopf, *Rural Research Series*, no. 205 (Knoxville, 1946), iv, 2–3. The authors cite evidence that in 1878, 47 percent of hogs, 61 percent of cattle, and 67 percent of the sheep entering the Nashville stockyards were reshipped to other southern markets.

70 *Nashville Banner*, 28 May 1910.

71 *Nashville Tennessean*, 2 January 1921.

72 Laura Kate Miller, "Geographical Influences on the Growth of Nashville" (M.A. thesis, George Peabody College for Teachers, 1923), 80; University

of Tennessee, Agricultural Experiment Station, "Nashville Livestock Market," iv.

73 *Nashville Tennessean,* 4 January 1925.

74 Ibid., 2 January 1921.

75 University of Tennessee, Agricultural Experiment Station, "Human and Physical Resources of Tennessee, Chapter V, Minerals and Mining," by Charles E. Allred, Samuel W. Atkins, and William E. Hendrix, *Rural Research Series,* no. 44 (Knoxville, 1937), 61–62.

76 Gunnar Myrdal, *Rich Lands and Poor: The Road to World Prosperity* (New York: Harper, 1957), 27–29.

77 Albert O. Hirschman, *The Strategy of Economic Development* (New Haven: Yale University Press, 1958), 183–89; Myrdal, *Rich Lands and Poor,* 23–38; Niles M. Hansen, *Intermediate Size Cities and Growth Centers* (New York: Praeger, 1971).

   The concept of uneven development has been applied to regions within the South in Carlton, "Unbalanced Growth and Industrialization," 111–30; and in a different context, to Middle Tennessee in John M. Marshall, "Industrialization and Agricultural Productivity," in *Growing Metropolis: Aspects of Development in Nashville,* ed. James F. Blumstein and Benjamin Walter (Nashville: Vanderbilt University Press, 1975), 311–40.

78 David R. Meyer, "Emergence of the American Manufacturing Belt: An Interpretation," *Journal of Historical Geography* 9:2 (1983): 145–74; David R. Meyer, "Midwestern Industrialization and the American Manufacturing Belt in the Nineteenth Century," *Journal of Economic History* 49:4 (December 1989): 921–37; William N. Parker, *Europe, America, and the Wider World: Essays on the Economic History of Western Capitalism,* vol. 2 (New York: Cambridge University Press, 1991), 217–18; David L. Carlton, "The American South and the American Manufacturing Belt," in *The South, the Nation, and the World: Perspectives on Southern Economic Development,* ed. David L. Carlton and Peter A. Coclanis (Charlottesville: University Press of Virginia, 2003), 163–78.

Chapter Three

1 An earlier generation of economists and sociologists acknowledged the role of population pressures in late-nineteenth and early-twentieth-century southern agriculture. Howard Odum summarized their views in stating that the "population problem is *the* problem" and that the region's population "is undoubtedly too large" (Howard W. Odum, *Southern Regions of the United States* [Chapel Hill: University of North Carolina Press, 1936], 461, 462). The case is made more thoroughly in Rupert B. Vance and Nadia Danilevsky, *All These People: The Nation's Human Resources in the South* (Chapel Hill: Univer-

sity of North Carolina Press, 1945). See also Clarence H. Danhof, "Four Decades of Thought on the South's Economic Problems," in *Essays in Southern Economic Development*, ed. Melvin L. Greenhut and W. Tate Whitman (Chapel Hill: University of North Carolina Press, 1964), 15–21.

Recent historical works that acknowledge population pressures in the region's agriculture include Robert Tracy McKenzie, *One South or Many? Plantation Belt and Upcountry in Civil War–Era Tennessee* (Cambridge, Eng.: Cambridge University Press, 1994), and Jack Temple Kirby, *Rural Worlds Lost: The American South, 1920–1960* (Baton Rouge: Louisiana State University Press, 1987), 99–101. Kirby discusses population pressures only in Appalachia and the Ozarks during the Great Depression, however.

For migration in a national historical context see Kathleen Neils Conzen, "A Saga of Families," in *The Oxford History of the American West*, ed. Clyde A. Milner, Carol A. O'Connor, and Martha A. Sandweiss (New York: Oxford University Press, 1994), 325–27, 336, 341.

2 *Nashville Banner*, 28 May 1910.

3 J. B. Killebrew, *Introduction to the Resources of Tennessee* (Nashville: Tavel, Eastman & Howell, 1874), 3–4, 64–65; Emory Q. Hawk, *Economic History of the South* (New York: Prentice-Hall, 1934), 7; Edward T. Luther, *Our Restless Earth: The Geologic Regions of Tennessee* (Knoxville: University of Tennessee Press, 1977), 36–41.

4 U.S. Census Office, *Report of the Statistics of Agriculture in the United States at the Eleventh Census: 1890* (Washington: Government Printing Office, 1895).

5 Tallies from a map of Tennessee and Kentucky in R. G. Dun & Company, *Mercantile Agency Reference Book (and Key) Containing Ratings of Merchants, Manufacturers, and Traders Generally, Throughout the Southern States*, vol. 87 (January 1890).

6 Stephen V. Ash, *Middle Tennessee Society Transformed, 1860–1870: War and Peace in the Upper South* (Baton Rouge: Louisiana State University Press, 1988), 9; Killebrew, *Resources of Tennessee*, 3–4, 64–65, 291, 620–21; Robert E. Corlew, *Tennessee: A Short History*, 2nd ed. (Knoxville: University of Tennessee Press, 1981), 10–11.

7 University of Tennessee, Agricultural Experiment Station, "Human and Physical Resources of Tennessee, Chapter 1, Geology, Topography, Soils," by Charles E. Allred, Samuel W. Atkins, and Benjamin D. Raskopf, *Rural Research Series Monograph*, no. 38 (Knoxville, 1937), 13–15.

8 University of Tennessee, Agricultural Experiment Station, "Human and Physical Resources of Tennessee, Chapters XIV, XV, Transportation and Communication," by Charles E. Allred, Samuel W. Watkins, and William E. Hendrix, *Rural Research Series*, no. 63 (Knoxville, 1939), ii, 225.

9 University of Tennessee, Agricultural Experiment Station, "Geology, Topography, Soils," 13–14; Killebrew, *Resources of Tennessee*, 622; U.S. Census Office, *Statistics of Agriculture at the Eleventh Census: 1890.*

10 Byrd Douglas, *Steamboatin' on the Cumberland* (Nashville: Tennessee Book Co., 1961), 289; University of Tennessee, Agricultural Experiment Station, "Transportation and Communication," 238; *Nashville Tennessean*, 8 May 1922.

11 Jeanette Keith, *Country People in the New South: Tennessee's Upper Cumberland* (Chapel Hill: University of North Carolina Press, 1995), 58–75.

12 Robert Tracy McKenzie, *One South or Many? Plantation Belt and Upcountry in Civil War–Era Tennessee* (New York: Cambridge University Press, 1994); Donald L. Winters, "Farm Size and Production Choices: Tennessee, 1850–1860," *Tennessee Historical Quarterly* 52 (1993): 212–24.

13 The five leading cotton-growing counties in Middle Tennessee in 1889 were Giles (5,595 bales), Rutherford (4,770 bales), Lincoln (2,488 bales), Maury (1,697 bales), and Williamson (861 bales). In 1889 Middle Tennessee produced a total of 17,545 bales of cotton (U.S. Census Office, *Statistics of Agriculture at the Eleventh Census: 1890*).

14 The five leading tobacco-producing counties in Middle Tennessee were Montgomery (9,331,200 lbs.), Robertson (8,605,730 lbs.), Cheatham (1,894,667 lbs.), Stewart (1,803,553 lbs.), and Sumner (1,155,808 lbs.). In 1889 Middle Tennessee produced 22,790,940 lbs. of tobacco (U.S. Census Office, *Statistics of Agriculture at the Eleventh Census: 1890*).

15 Verda Ledbetter interview, 12 July 1979, Tennessee State Parks Folklife Collection, RG 59, Tennessee State Library and Archives, Nashville (hereafter TSPFC).

16 Walter Martin, "Agricultural Commercialism in the Nashville Basin, 1850–1860" (Ph.D. dissertation, University of Tennessee, 1984). The importance of Middle Tennessee corn to the Lower South in the late nineteenth century is suggested by the 1884 annual freight statement issued by the Louisville & Nashville agent at Wetumpka, Alabama, that showed 1,099,100 bushels of corn received, nearly all of it originating from the Central Basin. See "Statement of Freight Forwarded and Received by Wetumpka Station . . . for Fiscal Year Ending June 30, 1884," quoted in James F. Doster, "Wetumpka's Railroad: Its Construction and Early Traffic," *Alabama Review* 3 (July 1950): 180–82.

17 Samuel Dean narrative, n.d., Federal Writers Project Papers, Southern Historical Collection, University of North Carolina, Chapel Hill (hereafter FWPP).

18 U.S. Census Office, *Statistics of Agriculture at the Eleventh Census: 1890*, 31–32, discusses the problems faced by hog producers in Tennessee in 1889.

19 University of Tennessee, Division of University Extension, "Educational, Economic and Community Survey: Bledsoe County," *University of Tennessee Record: Extension Series*, vol. 4, no. 2 (Knoxville, 1927), 15; Lynwood Montell, *Don't Go Up Kettle Creek: Verbal Legacy of the Upper Cumberland* (Knoxville: University of Tennessee Press, 1983), 40; Wayne Clark Moore, "Farm Communities and Economic Growth in the Lower Tennessee Valley: Humphreys

County, Tennessee" (Ph.D. dissertation, University of Rochester, 1990), 210, 274–75; Keith, *Country People*, 16–17; Ledbetter interview.

20 The increase in tenancy in the 1920s occurred largely after 1925. See U.S. Census Bureau, *Fifteenth Census of the United States: 1930, Agriculture*, vol. 2, pt. 2, *The Southern States* (Washington: Government Printing Office, 1932), 869.

21 Tenancy figures calculated from the Integrated Public Use Samples of the 1900, 1910, and 1920 federal population census returns. Figures are for the entire state of Tennessee to allow for an adequate number of cases for analysis. See Steven Ruggles and Matthew Sobek et al., *Integrated Public Use Microdata Series: Version 2.0 (IPUMS)* (Minneapolis: Historical Census Projects, University of Minnesota, 1997), <http://www.ipums.org>.

22 "Reports . . . on Farm Management, Farm Tenancy, Christian Co. Ky., 1915," Bureau of Agricultural Economics, RG 83, National Archives, Washington, in James Grossman, comp., *Black Workers in the Era of the Great Migration, 1916–1929* (Frederick, Md.: University Publications of America, Inc., 1985), reel 22.

23 Keith, *Country People*, 31–31.

24 University of Tennessee, Agricultural Experiment Station, "Types of Tenant Areas in Tennessee," by Charles E. Allred and E. E. Briner, *Rural Research Series*, no. 73 (Knoxville, 1938), 21, 23.

25 U.S. Industrial Commission, *Report of the Industrial Commission on Agriculture and Agricultural Labor*, vol. 10, 57th Cong., 1st sess., doc. 179 (Washington: Government Printing Office, 1901), 449.

26 *Southern Agriculturalist*, 1 February 1920, 34; 1 January 1920, 4.

27 University of Tennessee, Agricultural Experiment Station, "An Economic Analysis of Farming in Overton County, Tennessee," by C. E. Allred, assisted by S. W. Watkins, *Agricultural Economics Survey*, no. 1 (Knoxville, 1927), 41.

28 Middle Tennessee's fertility rates followed wider southern and national trends by declining steadily in the late nineteenth century. This decline stemmed from a number of causes, not the least of which was declining opportunities in agriculture, increasing urbanization of the population, and outmigration. Despite this downward trend, Middle Tennessee fertility remained high throughout the period, and the region's families continued to be large.

The debate over the decline in American fertility rates is concisely summarized in Deanna Lynn Pagnini, "American Fertility in Transition: Rural Family Building Patterns in the Early Twentieth Century" (Ph.D. dissertation, University of North Carolina, Chapel Hill, 1992), 3, 6–10. See also Robert Higgs, *Competition and Coercion: Blacks in the American Economy, 1865–1914* (Chicago: University of Chicago Press, 1980), 18–19.

29 Stewart E. Tolnay, "The Decline of Black Marital Fertility in the Rural South: 1910–1940," *American Sociological Review* 52 (April 1987): 211–17. Middle Tennessee total marital fertility rates are calculated from *IPUMS* census data.

30 Samuel H. Preston and Michael R. Haines, *Fatal Years: Child Mortality in Late-Nineteenth-Century America* (Princeton, N.J.: Princeton University Press, 1991), 128–32.

31 Elbridge Sibley, *Differential Mortality in Tennessee, 1917–1928: A Statistical Study Conducted Jointly by Tennessee State Department of Public Health and Fisk University* (Nashville: Fisk University Press, 1930), 58–59, 110–11.

32 In 1900 the population densities of the Black Belt and the Piedmont were thirty-nine and forty-six persons per square mile, respectively. See Edward L. Ayers, *The Promise of the New South: Life after Reconstruction* (New York: Oxford University Press, 1992), 5, 448.

33 William H. Nicholls, "The Effects of Industrial Development on Tennessee Valley Agriculture, 1900–1950," *Journal of Farm Economics* 38 (November 1956): 1637, 1644–45.

34 David B. Grigg, *Population Growth and Agrarian Change: An Historical Perspective* (Cambridge, Eng.: Cambridge University Press, 1980), 25–26.

35 *Southern Agriculturalist*, 1 April 1924, 3; 1 May 1925, 4.

36 Ibid., 1 April 1921, 11; 15 May 1924, 3; 15 July 1924, 3.

37 All figures apply to forty-one rural counties in the Middle Tennessee study area. Figures are calculated from published U.S. Census data collected in Inter-University Consortium for Political and Social Research, *Historical, Demographic, Economic, and Social Data: The United States, 1790–1970* [Computer file] (Ann Arbor, Mich.: Inter-University Consortium for Political and Social Research, 2001).

38 J. B. Williams interview by John Rumble, 18 May 1981, in author's possession.

39 Grigg, *Population Growth and Agrarian Change*, 22–23, notes that the fragmentation of farmland has been common in agrarian economies suffering from strong population pressures.

40 Ester Boserup, *The Conditions of Agricultural Growth: The Economics of Agrarian Change under Population Pressure* (Chicago: Aldine, 1965). See also Ester Boserup, "The Impact of Scarcity and Plenty on Development," *Journal of Interdisciplinary History* 14:2 (Autumn 1983): 383–407.

41 John S. Otto, "Forest Fallowing in the Southern Appalachian Mountains: A Problem in Comparative Agricultural History," *Proceedings of the American Philosophical Society* 133 (1989): 51–63.

42 *Southern Agriculturalist*, 15 February 1920, 17. Land ratios are calculated from improved and unimproved farmland data in Inter-University Consortium for Political and Social Research, *Historical, Demographic, Economic, and Social Data*.

43 Equivalent figures are not available for 1930 because of changing census definitions.

44 Tennessee State Planning Commission, "Major Land Use Problems in Tennessee," by Brodus F. Lucas and E. P. Callahan, *Report*, no. 30 (Nashville, 1936), 10–12.

45 Willies Rich interview, quoted in Montell, *Don't Go up Kettle Creek*, 51.

46 *Southern Agriculturalist*, 1 September 1920, 6.

47 Charles D. Lewis, "The Changing Mountains," *Mountain Life and Work* (July 1928): 15–19.

48 "The Present Deplorable Indifference of Farmers," pp. 4–6, in Purdue Agricultural Reports, folder 13, Tennessee State Library and Archives, Nashville.

49 Figures calculated from U.S. Census Office, *Statistics of Agriculture at the Eleventh Census: 1890*, and U.S. Census Bureau, *Fifteenth Census, Agriculture*, vol. 2, pt. 2, *The Southern States*.

50 Quoted in Pagnini, "American Fertility in Transition," 35.

Chapter Four

1   Oma Hubbard interview, 27 July 1979, TSPFC.

2   *Tennessee Agriculture* (July 1913), 216–20.

3   Jessie Thomas Sanders, "A Study of Nashville City Markets" (M.A. thesis, George Peabody College for Teachers, 1916), 8.

4   Jeanette Keith, *Country People in the New South: Tennessee's Upper Cumberland* (Chapel Hill: University of North Carolina Press, 1995), 103–17.

5   J. B. Killebrew, *Introduction to the Resources of Tennessee* (Nashville: Tavel, Eastman & Howell, 1874), 633.

6   *Tennessee Agriculture* (January 1915), 7–16, 20; *Nashville Tennessean*, 10 February 1923.

7   Oma Hubbard interview; University of Tennessee, Agricultural Experiment Station, "An Economic Analysis of Farming in Overton County, Tennessee," by C. E. Allred, assisted by S. W. Watkins, *Agricultural Economics Survey*, no. 1 (Knoxville, 1927), 32; University of Tennessee, Division of University Extension, "Educational, Economic and Community Survey: Bledsoe County," *University of Tennessee Record: Extension Series*, vol. 4, no. 2 (Knoxville, 1927), 12, 19; University of Tennessee, Agricultural Experiment Station, "Factors Determining Types of Farming in Tennessee," by Charles E. Allred and Bent T. Latham Jr., *Rural Research Series*, no. 79 (Knoxville, 1938), 15.

8   Sanders, "Nashville City Markets," 1–5, 8, 10, 16, 32–33; Ellis Jones interview by John Rumble, 29 May 1981, in author's possession. The curb market should not be confused with the old City Market, which still stands to the north of the Davidson County courthouse.

9   U.S. Department of Agriculture, *Statistical Bulletin*, no. 7, "Shipments and Unloads of Certain Fruits and Vegetables, 1918–1923" (April 1925), 5, 32, 36.

10 *Nashville Tennessean*, 30 December 1922.

11 *Nashville Labor Advocate*, 19 April 1918; Arch Trawick, "An Old Time Drummer Talks about the Grocery Business, 1846–1946," typescript, 3, 10–12, in Archibald Trawick Papers, Tennessee State Library and Archives, Nashville; *Nashville Tennessean*, 30 December 1922, 11 February, 17 February 1923.

12 *Nashville Tennessean*, 11 February 1923.

13 *Tennessee Agriculture* (July 1921), 8; (December 1922), 7; Tennessee Depart-
    ment of Agriculture, *Biennial Report of the Department of Agriculture, 1921–
    1922* (Nashville, 1922), 11–12.

14 Tennessee State Planning Commission, "Nashville Food Merchandising Sur-
    vey," by Frank J. Ray and John N. Kellog, *Report*, no. 80 (Nashville, 1938), 16–
    18; Tennessee Department of Agriculture, *Biennial Report*, 11–12; James L.
    McCorkle Jr., "Moving Perishables to Market: Southern Railroads and the
    Nineteenth-Century Origins of Southern Truck Farming," *Agricultural His-
    tory* 66 (1992): 42–62; *Nashville Tennessean*, 11 February 1923.

15 Donald J. Pisani, *From the Family Farm to Agribusiness: The Irrigation Crusade
    in California and the West, 1850–1931* (Berkeley: University of California Press,
    1984), 335–439.

16 Claude Leonard Bickford interview, TSPFC; *Nashville Tennessean*, 11 August
    1925; Fred Boyd narrative, 1981, typescript in author's possession.

17 *Nashville Tennessean*, 18 March 1924.

18 Ibid., 21 March 1924.

19 Mary Jean DeLozier, *Putnam County, Tennessee, 1850–1970* (Cookeville, Tenn.:
    Putnam County, 1979), 109–12, 114; *Southern Agriculturalist*, 15 July 1922, 14.

20 *Southern Agriculturalist*, 15 November 1924, 17.

21 DeLozier, *Putnam County*, 221; *Fifteenth Census of the United States: 1930, Agri-
    culture*, vol. 2, pt. 2, *The Southern States* (Washington: Government Printing
    Office, 1932). Prices are in 1930 dollars.

22 *Dixie Poultry Journal* [Nashville, Tenn.] (February 1927), 7.

23 Lynwood William Montell, *Upper Cumberland Country* (Jackson: University
    Press of Mississippi, 1993), 55; *Southern Agriculturalist*, 1 April 1920, 22.

24 *Southern Agriculturalist*, 15 February 1920, 45.

25 *Nashville Tennessean*, 4 February 1923, 17 February 1925.

26 *Southern Agriculturalist*, 1 January 1920, 27; 1 March 1920, 27.

27 Robbie Sanford interview by John Rumble, 21 May 1981, in author's posses-
    sion.

28 Montell, *Upper Cumberland Country*, 38–40, 45; Keith, *Country People*, 17–18;
    Benita J. Howell, "Survey of Folklife along the Big South Fork of the Cumber-
    land River" (Department of Anthropology, University of Tennessee–Knox-
    ville, 1981), 112–13.

29 United States Department of Agriculture, *Statistical Bulletin*, no. 18, "Statis-
    tics of Hogs, Pork, and Pork Products" (January 1927), 14–18; *Nashville Ten-
    nessean*, 2 January 1921.

30 *Tennessee Agriculture* (March 1922), 15.

31 *Nashville Tennessean*, 17 February, 19 July 1925.

32 Ibid., 12 December 1922, 20 January 1923, 3 April 1923.

33 *Southern Agriculturalist*, 1 July 1923, 15.

34 Ibid., 1 March 1920, 42; 15 April 1920, 22–23.

35 *Tennessee Agriculture* (October 1922), 8–10; *Southern Agriculturalist*, 1 March
    1920; Wayne Clark Moore, "Farm Communities and Economic Growth in

the Lower Tennessee Valley: Humphreys County, Tennessee" (Ph.D. dissertation, University of Rochester, 1990), 274–75.

The spirited debate over class conflict and fence laws in the nineteenth-century South can be followed in Shawn Everett Kantor and J. Morgan Kousser, "Common Sense or Commonwealth? The Fence Law and Institutional Change in the Postbellum South," *Journal of Southern History* 59 (May 1993): 202–42; Steven Hahn, "A Response: Common Cents or Historical Sense," ibid., 243–58; and Kantor and Kousser, "A Rejoinder: Two Visions of History," ibid., 259–66. It is notable that none of these authors considers regions of the South such as Middle Tennessee, where the open range was protected well into the twentieth century.

36 Ronald D. Eller, *Miners, Millhands, and Mountaineers: Industrialization of the Appalachian South, 1880–1930* (Knoxville: University of Tennessee Press, 1982), 93–112.

37 Montell, *Upper Cumberland Country*, 10–11; Steven A. Schulman, "The Lumber Industry of the Upper Cumberland Valley," *Tennessee Historical Quarterly* 32 (Fall 1973): 255–64.

38 Everette Rowland interview, TSPFC; Keith, *Country People*, 23–24; William Lynwood Montell, *Don't Go Up Kettle Creek: Verbal Legacy of the Upper Cumberland* (Knoxville: University of Tennessee Press, 1983), 91.

39 Finits Evits narrative, 10 November 1938, Puryear, Tenn., FWPP; Moore, "Farm Communities and Economic Growth," 199–201.

40 J. B. Williams interview by John Rumble, 18 May 1981, in author's possession.

41 Quoted in Keith, *Country People*, 86.

42 University of Tennessee, Agricultural Experiment Station, "Economic Analysis of Farming in Overton County," 41.

43 William Cronon, *Nature's Metropolis: Chicago and the Great West* (New York: W. W. Norton, 1991), 200–206, describes the deforestation of the Great Lakes' white pine forests.

44 *Nashville Banner*, 28 May 1910.

45 University of Tennessee, Agricultural Experiment Station, "Development of the Timber Industry in Tennessee and the United States," by Charles E. Allred, S. W. Watkins, and Frank M. Fitzgerald, *Rural Research Series*, no. 92 (Knoxville, 1939), 17, 33.

46 University of Tennessee, Agricultural Experiment Station, "Economic Analysis of Farming in Overton County," 81.

47 University of Tennessee, Agricultural Experiment Station, "Forest Production Areas: Tennessee and the United States," by Charles E. Allred and Frank Fitzgerald, *Rural Research Series*, no. 93 (Knoxville, 1939), 13–15.

48 Killebrew, *Resources of Tennessee*, 71–75.

49 Finits Evits narrative; Montell, *Don't Go Up Kettle Creek*, 118; Moore, "Farm Communities and Economic Growth," 202; University of Tennessee, Agricultural Experiment Station, "Economic Analysis of Farming in Overton County," 83–84.

50 Anthony M. Tang, *Economic Development in the Southern Piedmont, 1860–1950: Its Impact on Agriculture* (Chapel Hill: University of North Carolina Press, 1958), 179–80.

Chapter Five

1   *Rural Record*, 10 June 1882.
2   Frank L. Owsley, *Plain Folk of the Old South* (Baton Rouge: Louisiana State University Press, 1949), 23–28, 45–47; Michael Tadman, *Speculators and Slaves: Masters, Traders, and Slaves in the Old South* (Madison: University of Wisconsin Press, 1989).
3   Tobe Easterly narrative, n.d., Big Ivy, Tenn.; Idella Woods narrative, 20 December 1938, Whitlock, Tenn., FWPP.
4   James Morgan to William Morgan, 18 December 1870, William Morgan Papers, Southern Historical Collection, University of North Carolina, Chapel Hill.
5   J. B. Killebrew, *Introduction to the Resources of Tennessee* (Nashville: Tavel, Eastman & Howell, 1874), 636, 668.
6   Carter Woodson, *A Century of Negro Migration* (New York: Russell and Russell, 1969), 120–21.
7   Daniel M. Johnson and Rex R. Campbell, *Black Migration in America: A Social Demographic History* (Durham, N.C.: Duke University Press, 1981), 50–52, 61–65. The migration to Hawaii is briefly described in the *Locomotive Fireman's Magazine* 30 (February 1901): 248.
8   Ray Stannard Baker, *Following the Color Line: American Negro Citizenship in the Progressive Era* (New York: Doran & Co., 1908; New York: Harper & Row, 1964), 79.
9   Gainsboro *Sentinel*, 13 November 1903, 12 May 1906, quoted in Jeanette Keith, *Country People in the New South: Tennessee's Upper Cumberland* (Chapel Hill: University of North Carolina Press, 1995), 219.
10 Fleta Cole narrative, 7 November 1938, Puryear, Tenn., FWPP.
11 Ella Paschall narrative, 17 November 1938, Puryear, Tenn., FWPP.
12 Ibid.
13 Gavin Wright, *Old South, New South: Revolutions in the Southern Economy since the Civil War* (New York: Basic Books, 1986), 97–98.
14 University of Tennessee, Agricultural Experiment Station, "Factors Determining Types of Farming in Tennessee," by Charles E. Allred and Bent T. Latham Jr., *Rural Research Series*, no. 79 (Knoxville, 1938), 27–28.
15 Samples sizes were as follows: DeKalb County, 3 percent sample, $N = 38$; Robertson County, 3 percent sample, $N = 65$. See Draft Registration Cards, World War I Selective Service Records, RG 163, National Archives and Records Administration, Southeast Region, East Point, Ga.
16 Robertson County shares its northern border with Kentucky, and six of the

sixty-five registrants in the sample were born in that state. One registrant in the DeKalb sample was from Kentucky. All others were Tennessee born.

17 W. A. V. Clark, *Human Migration* (Beverly Hills, Calif.: Sage Publications, 1986), 21–23.

18 John P. Graves, *Northwest Davidson County: The Land, Its People* (Nashville: Privately printed by author, 1975), 13.

19 Arguments that tenants and sharecroppers were coerced into remaining in one place can be found in Jonathan M. Wiener, *Social Origins of the New South, Alabama, 1860–1885* (Baton Rouge: Louisiana State University Press, 1978), 69–73, and Crandall A. Shifflett, *Patronage and Poverty in the Tobacco South* (Knoxville: University of Tennessee Press, 1982), xii. Recent arguments that debt peonage was a chief means of impeding the mobility of tenants and sharecroppers focus on black farmers and include William Cohen, "Negro Involuntary Servitude in the South, 1865–1900: A Preliminary Analysis," *Journal of Southern History* 42 (February 1976): 31–60; William Cohen, *At Freedom's Edge: Black Mobility and the Southern White Quest for Racial Control, 1861–1915* (Baton Rouge: Louisiana State University Press, 1991); Pete Daniel, "The Metamorphosis of Slavery, 1865–1900," *Journal of American History* 66 (June 1979): 88–99; Pete Daniel, *The Shadow of Slavery: Peonage in the South, 1901–1969* (Urbana: University of Illinois Press, 1972), 3–81; and Daniel A. Novak, *The Wheels of Servitude: Black Forced Labor after Slavery* (Lexington: University Press of Kentucky, 1978).

20 While this statement is generally true, one should not take this assertion too far, as indicated by the experience of Louise Williams, whose father "had to make boys out of his two oldest girls. . . . We did nearly everything that had to be done about tobacco, and we did it the hard way [without] modern machinery." See Louise Williams narrative, 17 March 1981, typescript in author's possession.

21 Santifee Paschall narrative, 11 November 1938, Puryear, Tenn., FWPP.

22 Finits Evits narrative, 10 November 1938, Puryear, Tenn., FWPP; Mary Louise Lillie Glasgow narrative, 21 March 1981, typescript in author's possession.

23 Quoted in Lynwood William Montell, *Upper Cumberland Country* (Jackson: University Press of Mississippi, 1993), 54.

24 Idella Woods narrative.

25 C. O. Brannen, *Relation of Land Tenure to Plantation Organization*, USDA Department Bulletin No. 1269 (Washington, 18 October 1924), 44–45.

26 Ray Bob Lewis interview, TSPFC.

27 Ibid.; Ella Thompson interview, TSPFC; Montell, *Upper Cumberland Country*, 11–14.

28 Finits Evits interview, FWPP.

29 Ibid.

30 Ibid.

31 This study uses a modified version of the forward-survival-rate method to

estimate net migration. Demographers developed this technique to estimate net migration for populations that lack complete birth and death registration data. Tennessee did not begin statewide birth and death registration until 1926.

The forward-survival-rate method estimates net migration by using survival ratios to calculate an area's expected native-born population if there has been no migration between two censuses, and then subtracts that figure from the actual native-born population enumerated at the second census. In practice, calculations are performed on five-year age groups, by sex and race, and then summed to arrive at total net migration. See the Appendix for a fuller discussion of methodology. See also Everette S. Lee et al., *Population Redistribution and Economic Growth, United States, 1870–1950*, vol. 1, *Methodological Considerations and Reference Tables* (Philadelphia: American Philosophical Society, 1957), 15–25; Donald J. Bogue, Kenneth Hinze, and Michael White, *Techniques of Estimating Net Migration* (Chicago: Community and Family Study Center, University of Chicago, 1982), 15–41; and Henry S. Shryock et al., *The Methods and Materials of Demography* (New York: Academic Press, 1976), 378–84. Elbridge Sibley, *Differential Mortality in Tennessee, 1917–1928: A Statistical Study Conducted Jointly by Tennessee State Department of Public Health and Fisk University* (Nashville: Fisk University Press, 1930), 106–7, discusses the incompleteness of Tennessee vital records up through the late 1920s.

32 U.S. Department of Labor, Division of Negro Economics, George Edmund Haynes, Director, *Negro Migration in 1916–17* (Washington: Government Printing Office, 1919; New York: Negro Universities Press, 1969).

33 Everette S. Lee, "A Theory of Migration," *Demography* 3 (1966): 48.

34 See James R. Grossman, *Land of Hope: Chicago, Black Southerners, and the Great Migration* (Chicago: University of Chicago Press, 1989), 38–65, for a discussion of migration and popular attitudes toward agriculture in wider context.

35 "Talking Is My Life," FWPP; University of Tennessee, Agricultural Experiment Station, "An Economic Analysis of Farming in Overton County, Tennessee," by Charles E. Allred, assisted by S. W. Watkins, *Agricultural Economic Survey*, no. 1 (Knoxville, 1927), 39; University of Tennessee, Division of University Extension, "Educational, Economic and Community Survey: Bledsoe County," *University of Tennessee Record: Extension Series*, vol. 4, no. 2 (Knoxville, 1927), 28.

36 *Tennessee Agriculture* (July 1912), 89; (July 1922), 16; *Nashville Tennessean*, 2 January 1923.

37 *Tennessee Agriculture* (July 1922), 5.

38 Ibid., 3; *Nashville Tennessean*, 23 December 1923. Tennessee agricultural reformers followed national trends in advocating cooperative purchasing and marketing organizations as a solution to the economic woes of farmers. See

U.S. Congress, *Report of the Joint Commission of Agricultural Inquiry*, part 4, "Marketing and Distribution," 67th Cong., 1st sess., 1921, House Report No. 408 (Washington: Government Printing Office, 1922), 226–31. Calls for crop diversification were prominent in the southern agricultural press of the 1920s, especially the Nashville-based *Southern Agriculturalist* and *Dixie Poultry Journal*; see also George C. Osborn, "The Southern Rural Press and Some Significant Rural Problems, 1900–1940," *Agricultural History* 29 (July 1955): 116.

39 U.S. Congress, *Report of the Commission on Country Life*, Senate Doc. 705, 60th Cong., 2nd sess., 23 January 1909 (Washington: Government Printing Office, 1909).

40 Tennessee Department of Public Instruction, *Rural School Situation in Tennessee* (Nashville: McQuiddy Printing Co., 1911), 7.

41 This view is extensively developed in Jeanette Keith, *Country People in the New South: Tennessee's Upper Cumberland* (Chapel Hill: University of North Carolina Press, 1995); William A. Link, *The Paradox of Southern Progressivism, 1880–1930* (Chapel Hill: University of North Carolina Press, 1992); and David Danbom, *The Resisted Revolution: Urban America and the Industrialization of Agriculture, 1900–1930* (Ames: Iowa State University Press, 1979).

42 *Tennessee Agriculture* (July 1921), 9.

43 Ibid. (September 1913), 294; (July 1913), 195.

44 Tennessee Department of Public Instruction, *Rural School Situation in Tennessee*, 7.

45 *Tennessee Agriculture* (July 1922), 4–5.

46 *Southern Agriculturalist*, 15 January 1922, 5; 1 July 1924, 4. See also Keith, *Country People*, 131–42, 199–210, for a detailed examination of education reform in the Upper Cumberland and Hal S. Barron, *Mixed Harvest: The Second Great Transformation in the Rural North, 1870–1930* (Chapel Hill: University of North Carolina Press, 1997), 43–77, for an analysis of a similar situation in the rural North.

47 Katherine Atherton Grimes, "A Word for the Little Red Schoolhouse," *Southern Agriculturalist*, 1 February 1920, 31; an editorial critical of Grimes's article is found on page 3 of the same issue. See also Dewey W. Grantham, *Southern Progressivism: The Reconciliation of Progress and Tradition* (Knoxville: University of Tennessee Press, 1983), 332–33.

48 Andrew David Holt, *The Struggle for a State System of Public Schools in Tennessee, 1903–1936* (New York: Bureau of Publications, Columbia University Teachers College, 1938), 255, 263.

49 *Southern Agriculturalist*, 1 July 1921, 4–5.

50 *Tennessee Agriculture* (July 1913), 199–200; (January 1915), 6; University of Tennessee, Division of University Extension, "Educational, Economic and Community Survey: Bledsoe County," 28.

51 *Tennessee Agriculture* (October 1913), 476.

52 Ibid. (July 1921), 11–13. The *Nashville Tennessean* was a strong advocate of good roads. See the 22 December 1922 editorial that called for a "modern state-wide system of good roads . . . connecting each county seat in the state."

53 Holt, *Public Schools in Tennessee*, 263; University of Tennessee, Agricultural Experiment Station, "Human and Physical Resources of Tennessee, Chapter XXVII, Education: Public and Private; Chapter XXVIII, Illiteracy, Reading Habits, Libraries," by Charles E. Allred, Samuel W. Atkins, F. M. Fitzgerald, *Rural Research Series*, no. 81 (Knoxville, 1938), 245.

54 University of Tennessee, Agricultural Experiment Station, "Farm Tenancy in Tennessee," by Charles E. Allred, William E. Hendrix, and Benjamin D. Raskopf, *Rural Research Series*, no. 17 (Knoxville, 1936), 14; University of Tennessee, Agricultural Experiment Station, "Education of Farmers' Wives and Children in Four Counties of Tennessee," by Charles E. Allred and Benjamin D. Raskopf, *Rural Research Series*, no. 27 (Knoxville, 1937), 5. No breakdown of educational attainment by age for men was provided. See also Keith, *Country People*, 196–202.

55 Tennessee Department of Public Instruction, *Rural School Situation in Tennessee*, 50.

56 *Tennessee Market Bulletin* (1 January 1928).

57 University of Tennessee, Division of University Extension, "Educational, Economic and Community Survey: Bledsoe County," 23.

58 *Tennessee Agriculture* (October 1922), 4–5.

59 University of Tennessee, Agricultural Experiment Station, "Human and Physical Resources of Tennessee, Chapters XIV, XV, Transportation and Communication," by Charles E. Allred, Samuel W. Atkins, and William E. Hendrix, *Rural Research Series*, no. 63 (Knoxville, 1939), 247; University of Tennessee, Agricultural Experiment Station, "Farm Tenancy," 12.

60 "Talking Is My Life."

61 Mrs. John C. [Olive Dame] Campbell, "Flame for a New Future for the Highlands," *Mountain Life and Work* 1 (April 1925): 11. Calvin Goldscheider, "Migration and Rural Social Structure: An Overview," in *Rural Migration in Developing Nations: Comparative Studies of Korea, Sri Lanka and Mali*, ed. Calvin Goldscheider (Boulder, Colo.: Westview Press, 1984), 7–9, elaborates on the process of modernization, migration, and cultural diffusion.

62 *Mountain Life and Work* 1 (April 1925): 1; Andrew Nelson Lytle, "The Hind Tit," in Twelve Southerners, *I'll Take My Stand: The South and the Agrarian Tradition* (1930; New York: Harper Torchbooks, 1962), 244.

Chapter Six

1 L. A. Sjaastad, "The Costs and Returns of Human Migration," pt. 2, *Journal of Political Economy* 70 (1962): 80–93, and Michael P. Todaro, "A Model of Labor Migration and Urban Unemployment in Less Developed Countries," *Ameri-*

can Economic Review 59 (1969): 138–48, are seminal works on neoclassical economic theory. Michael Greenwood, "Research in Internal Migration in the United States," *Journal of Economic Literature* 13 (June 1975): 397–433, and Douglas S. Massey et al., "Theories of International Migration: A Review and Appraisal," *Population and Development Review* 19 (September 1993): 431–66, provide useful overviews of the literature on U.S. migration. William Vickery, *The Economics of Negro Migration, 1900–1960* (New York: Arno Press, 1977), and Robert Higgs, *Competition and Coercion: Blacks in the American Economy, 1865–1914* (Chicago: University of Chicago Press, 1980), 26–27, apply neoclassical theory to black migration northward.

2 *Nashville Tennessean*, 23 December 1922; Samuel Dean narrative, 2 November 1938, Nashville, Tenn., FWPP.

3 The importance of periodic market trips to towns and cities in fostering more permanent rural-urban migration is stressed in Ronald Skeldon, *Population Mobility in Developing Countries: A Reinterpretation* (London: Belhaven Press, 1990), 56–57.

4 Everette Rowland interview, TSPFC.

5 Camilla Caldwell interview by John Rumble, 21 May 1981, in author's possession.

6 Everette Rowland interview.

7 Claude Leonard Bickford interview, TSPFC.

8 Fred Boyd narrative, 18 March 1981, in author's possession.

9 Daisy Perry interview by John Rumble, 29 May 1981, in author's possession; Camilla Caldwell interview.

10 Avis Carol Wiggins, "The Migrant Girl" (M.A. thesis, Vanderbilt University, 1933), 78.

11 J. B. Williams interview by John Rumble, 18 May 1981, in author's possession.

12 J. B. Williams interview.

13 *Nashville Tennessean*, 6 May 1917.

14 *Old Hickory News*, 10 August; 14 September; 5, 19 October 1918.

15 David Edward Brand, "Fill the Empty Shell: The Story of the Government Munitions Project at Old Hickory, Tennessee, 1918–1919" (M.A. thesis, Vanderbilt University, 1971), 34–36; *Old Hickory News*, 31 August; 7, 14 September; 5, 12 October; 9 November 1918.

16 LuCretia Owen Diary, 3 December 1918, Tennessee State Library and Archives, Nashville; *Old Hickory News*, 31 August 1918. Figures reported in *Old Hickory News* are approximate.

17 Owen Diary, 11, 13 November 1918.

18 *Old Hickory News*, 12 October 1918; Owen Diary, 8, 31 October; 9 November 1918.

19 Owen Diary, 1 November 1918; *Old Hickory News*, 2 November 1918.

20 Owen Diary, 8 October; 1, 9 November 1918; *Old Hickory News*, 17 August 1918.

21 Owen Diary, 3, 19 December 1918.

22 *Nashville Tennessean*, 20 November 1921.

23 Ibid., 21, 25, 27 November, 1918.

24 Ibid., 24 November 1920.

25 Ibid., 14 July 1923.

26 Don H. Doyle, *Nashville in the New South, 1880–1930* (Knoxville: University of Tennessee Press, 1985), 192–93.

27 See the Appendix for a discussion of the forward-survival-rate method of estimating net migration.

28 *Nashville Tennessean*, 23 December 1922.

29 See Chapter 8 for a detailed examination of working migrant women.

30 The last World War I–era registration, in which all men between the ages of eighteen and twenty-one and thirty-one and forty-five were required to register, took place on 12 September 1918. Unfortunately, this more comprehensive registration recorded minimal data about registrants and thus could not be used for this study. See Draft Registration Cards, World War I Selective Service Records, RG 163, National Archives and Records Administration, Southeast Region, East Point, Ga.; U.S. War Office, *Second Report of the Provost Marshal General to the Secretary of War on the Operations of the Selective Service System to December 20, 1918* (Washington: Government Printing Office, 1919), 582–87.

31 Carole Marks, *Farewell — We're Good and Gone: The Great Black Migration* (Bloomington: Indiana University Press, 1989), 3, 34–41, argues that the World War I migration of black southerners north was dominated by urban workers; this assertion is supported by the overrepresentation of the urban-born among those moving north in the draft registration data.

32 Since this study is concerned with internal migration to Nashville, foreign-born registrants were excluded from calculations using the draft record samples. Overall, the foreign-born comprised 2.5 percent of the 1917 draft sample and 1.6 percent of the 1918 sample.

33 Fisk University Department of Social Science, "A Social Study of Negro Families in the Area Selected for the Nashville Negro Federal Housing Project" (typescript, 1934), 10; Council of Social Agencies [Nashville], "A Social Study of White Families in the Area Selected for the Nashville Federal Housing Project" (typescript, 1934), 4. The survey of white families specified that only heads of households be counted in migration calculations; the survey of black families is vague on this point. However, since both surveys employed the same format and presentation, one can confidently assume that the figures for black migration include only heads of household.

34 Wiggins, "Migrant Girl," 11–12; R. E. Wicker, "A Study of Working Women Residing in Nashville's Four Largest Semi-Charity Homes for Women" (B.D. thesis, Vanderbilt University, 1931), 19.

35 Wiggins, "Migrant Girl," 14–16.

36 J. B. Williams interview.

37 A. C. Jones narrative, 6 January 1938, Nashville, Tenn., FWPP.

38 Daisy Perry interview.

39 A. C. Jones narrative.

40 Fred Boyd narrative.

41 Jones's case is recounted in Danforth Reynolds Ross, "A Study of Insecurity among Rural Relief Families in a Tennessee Urban Community" (M.A. thesis, Vanderbilt University, 1937), 100–103.

42 Samuel Dean narrative, 2 November 1938, Nashville, Tenn., FWPP.

43 Ellis B. Jones interview by John Rumble, 29 May 1981, in author's possession.

44 J. B. Williams interview.

45 Louise Williams narrative, 17 March 1981, in author's possession.

46 Ibid.

47 J. B. Williams interview.

48 Idella Woods narrative, 20 December 1938, Whitlock, Tenn., FWPP. Woods was married in 1904.

49 Mark Austin Hutton, "A Sociological Study of Five and Ten Cent Store Saleswomen in a Southern City" (M.A. thesis, Vanderbilt University, 1936), 120.

50 Wiggins, "Migrant Girl," 79.

51 Mary Brown Casefile, 3 July 1933, YWCA Collection, Tennessee State Library and Archives, Nashville (hereafter YWCAC).

52 Roberta Vick Casefile, [n.d., probably 1928], YWCAC.

53 Nellie Preville Casefile, 15 January 1930, YWCAC.

54 Julia Brown Casefile, 4 October 1928, YWCAC.

55 Billie Nell Banks Casefile, 15 November 1932, YWCAC.

56 Wiggins, "Migrant Girl," 79.

57 Hutton, "Five and Ten Cent Store Saleswomen," 120.

58 Ibid., 120, 134.

59 Wiggins, "Migrant Girl," 78.

60 Fay Fowler, "Economic Adjustment of Rural Unmarried Girls Working in Nashville, 1932–1933" (M.A. thesis, Scarritt College for Christian Workers, 1933), 1.

61 Lela Pearl McClaren Casefile, 11 March 1931, YWCAC.

62 Lillie Pearl (Davis) Shropshire interview by author, 20 August 1991, in author's possession.

63 Robbie Sanford interview by John Rumble, 21 May 1981, in author's possession.

64 Grace Brimm Casefile, 23 February 1933, YWCAC.

65 *Nashville Tennessean*, 20 December 1922, describes the raid on the hotel and subsequent arrests.

66 Cothrom Casefile [no first name given], 5 May 1929, YWCAC.

67 Maude English Casefile, 6 January 1930, YWCAC.

68 Hutton, "Five and Ten Cent Store Saleswomen," 102.

69 Hattie Teal Casefile, 25 June 1929, YWCAC.

70 Valera Pollack Casefile, 21 October 1931, YWCAC.

1   The occupation categories are similar to those in social mobility studies. The categories are high-white-collar and professional positions; low-white-collar and petty entrepreneurial positions; skilled manual labor; semiskilled and unskilled labor. This scheme follows closely the method used to classify occupations in the 1920 census in Olivier Zunz, *The Changing Face of Inequality: Urbanization, Industrial Development, and Immigrants in Detroit, 1880–1920* (Chicago: University of Chicago Press, 1982), 420–34.

2   Richard Davis Smart Jr., "The Economic Condition of Negroes in Nashville, Tenn.," *Vanderbilt University Quarterly* (April 1904), 108–13.

3   James Thomas Hardwick, "The Economic Condition of the Negro in Nashville" (M.A. thesis, YMCA Graduate School, Nashville, 1922), 6.

4   Sterling D. Spero and Abram L. Harris, *The Black Worker: The Negro and the Labor Movement* (New York: Columbia University Press, 1931), 87–115, esp. 87–89.

5   Smart, "Economic Condition of Negroes," 108–13.

6   *Nashville Tennessean*, 29 January 1899.

7   Hardwick, "Economic Condition of the Negro," 20–21.

8   Smart, "Economic Condition of Negroes," 111; Hardwick, "Economic Condition of the Negro," 8–11.

9   *Nashville Labor Advocate*, 12, 19 April 1918.

10 Don H. Doyle, *Nashville in the New South, 1880–1930* (Knoxville: University of Tennessee Press, 1985), 27, 168; Deborah Cooney, ed., *Speaking of Union Station: An Oral History of a Nashville Landmark* (Nashville: Union Station Trust Fund, 1977), 4, 10–18; Hardwick, "Economic Condition of the Negro," 20–21.

11 The Nashville local of the Hod Carriers' Union, No. 531, was very likely formed soon after the organization of the National Hod Carriers Union was formed in 1903. The founding of the national union is discussed in Arch A. Mercey, *The Laborers' Story, 1903–1953: The First Fifty Years of the International Hod Carriers', Building and Common Laborers' Union of America* (Washington: Ransdell, 1954), 23–24.

12 Smart, "Economic Condition of Negroes," 111.

13 *Nashville Labor Advocate*, 29 March 1918; Hardwick, "Economic Condition of the Negro," 11; Gary Fink, ed., *Labor Unions* (Westport, Conn.: Greenwood Press, 1977), 205–7.

14 *Nashville Labor Advocate*, 13 November 1908.

15 Ibid., 13, 20 April 1917; 1, 15 June 1917; 15 July 1921.

16 Hardwick, "Economic Condition of the Negro," 8–11.

17 C. W. McKissack to U.S. Commissioner of Labor, 4 April 1918, "Negro Bricklayers 1918," U.S. Department of Labor 20/659, RG 174, National Archives and Record Administration, James R. Grossman, comp., *Black Workers in the*

Era of the Great Migration, 1916–1929 (Frederick, Md.: University Publications of America, Inc., 1985), microfilm.

18 Nashville Labor Advocate, 14 August 1908.

19 George Edmund Haynes to the Executive Committee on Improving Industrial Conditions among Negroes, 3 November 1909, in George Edmund Haynes Papers, Fisk University, Nashville.

20 "Tennessee Industry Factory Schedules, 1925," Woman's Bureau, U.S. Department of Labor, Research Division Survey Materials, RG 86, National Archives and Record Administration, in Grossman, comp., Black Workers.

21 Black workers also mined the Middle Tennessee phosphate deposits that were the basis of the Nashville fertilizer industry. See Lester C. Lamon, Black Tennesseans, 1900–1930 (Knoxville: University of Tennessee Press, 1977), 133.

22 Glenn Rogers, "Localization of a Few Selected Industries in Nashville" (M.A. thesis, George Peabody College for Teachers, 1932), 15.

23 George S. Schuyler, "Negro Labor and Public Utilities, III," The Messenger 9 (April 1927): 116–17, reprinted in Philip S. Foner and Ronald L. Lewis, eds., The Black Worker: A Documentary History from Colonial Times to the Present, vol. 6, The Era of Post-War Prosperity and the Great Depression, 1920–1936 (Philadelphia: Temple University Press, 1981), 49.

24 "Ganging places" are described in the Nashville Tennessean, 18 October 1936.

25 Gavin Wright, Old South, New South: Revolutions in the Southern Economy since the Civil War (New York: Basic Books, 1986), 177–97.

26 Nashville Board of Trade, Yearbook, 1906 (Nashville, 1906); "West Nashville: Manufacturing Metropolis of the South" (Nashville, 1908), 8.

27 Tennessee Electric Power Company, Waterpower (1 May 1925), p. 49, box 1, folder 3, Tennessee Electric Power Company Papers, Tennessee State Library and Archives, Nashville.

28 David L. Carlton, Mill and Town in South Carolina, 1880–1920 (Baton Rouge: Louisiana State University Press, 1982); C. Vann Woodward, Origins of the New South, 1877–1913, 2nd ed. (Baton Rouge: Louisiana State University Press, 1971), 221–22; Paul M. Gaston, The New South Creed: A Study in Southern Mythmaking (New York: Alfred A. Knopf, 1970).

29 George B. Tindall, The Emergence of the New South, 1913–1945 (Baton Rouge: Louisiana State University Press, 1967), 523.

30 Allen Tullos, Habits of Industry: White Culture and the Transformation of the Carolina Piedmont (Chapel Hill: University of North Carolina Press, 1989), xii–xiv; I. A. Newby, Plain Folk in the New South: Social Change and Cultural Persistence, 1880–1915 (Baton Rouge: Louisiana State University Press, 1989), 519.

31 George Sinclair Mitchell, Textile Unionism and the South (Chapel Hill: University of North Carolina Press, 1931), 21–62; Melton A. McLaurin, Paternalism and Protest: Southern Cotton Mill Workers and Organized Labor, 1875–1905 (Westport, Conn.: Greenwood Press, 1971).

32 Jacquelyn Dowd Hall et al., *Like a Family: The Making of a Southern Cotton Mill World* (Chapel Hill: University of North Carolina Press, 1987); Douglas Flamming, *Creating the Modern South: Millhands and Managers in Dalton, Georgia, 1884–1894* (Chapel Hill: University of North Carolina Press, 1992).

33 Henry M. McKiven Jr., *Iron and Steel: Class, Race, and Community in Birmingham, Alabama, 1875–1920* (Chapel Hill: University of North Carolina Press, 1995), is an important exception.

34 For example, the International Association of Machinists, which figures so prominently in interpretations of workers' responses to scientific management, was founded in Atlanta in 1888 (David Montgomery, *Workers' Control in America: Studies in the History of Work, Technology, and Labor Struggles* [Cambridge, Eng.: Cambridge University Press, 1979], 48–90, 113–38; Fink, ed., *Labor Unions*, 201–3).

35 *Nashville Labor Advocate*, 19 May, 1 September 1922.

36 M. B. Schnapper, *American Labor: A Pictorial Social History* (Washington: Public Affairs Press, 1975), 232, contains an illustration of the delegates to the Nashville convention.

37 Those unions as listed in the *Nashville Labor Advocate*'s Local Union Directory in January 1917 were Barbers' Union, No. 35; Bookbinders' Union, No. 83; Bricklayers' Union, No. 1; Brewery Workers' Union, No. 101; Brotherhood of Boilermakers, Iron and Shipbuilders; United Brotherhood of Leather Workers; Brotherhood of Locomotive Engineers, Rock City, Cumberland, and Jere Baxter Divisions; Brotherhood of Railway Firemen; Cigarmakers' Union, No. 83; Garment Workers' Union, No. 133; Letter Carriers' Union; Machinists' Union, No. 154; Mailers' Union; Molders' Union, No. 55; Moving Picture Operators' Union, No. 626; Painters' Union; Paperhangers Union; Post Office Clerks' Union; Plumbers' Union, No. 352; Printing Pressmens' Union, No. 83; Retail Clerks' Union; Stage Employees' Union; Tailors' Union, No. 85; Stereotypers' and Electrotypers' Union, No. 78; Typographical Union, No. 20.

38 Rabbi Isidore Lewinthal, [Nashville], to Industrial Removal Office, New York City, 8 January 1907; Sam Levy, Nashville, to David Bressler, General Manager of the Industrial Removal Office, New York, 27 January 1907; Phillips & Buttorff Manufacturing Company to S. M. Hirsh, Nashville, 22 April 1912, all folder no. 3., Industrial Removal Office Collection, Jewish Federation Archives, Nashville; *Nashville Labor Advocate*, 7 March 1919, mentions the 1913–14 bookbinders' strike.

39 *Nashville Labor Advocate*, 6 April 1917.

40 David M. Kennedy, *Over Here: The First World War and American Society* (New York: Oxford University Press, 1980), 266–68; Selig Perlman and Philip Taft, *History of Labor in the United States, 1896–1932*, vol. 4, *Labor Movements*, ed. John R. Commons (New York: Macmillan, 1935), 408–9; Valerie Jean Conner, *The National War Labor Board: Stability, Social Justice, and the Voluntary State in World War I* (Chapel Hill: University of North Carolina Press, 1983).

41 *Nashville Labor Advocate*, 4 January 1918.

42   Ibid., 15 March, 19 April 1918.

43   Ibid., 22 March 1918.

44   Ibid., 21 June 1918.

45   Ibid., 17 July, 27 September, 8 November, 3 May 1918.

46   Ibid., 10 May 1918.

47   Ibid., 22 March, 5 April 1918.

48   Ibid., 19 April, 25 May, 27 September, 8 November 1918.

49   Ibid., 21 February 1919.

50   Ibid., 7, 21 March 1919.

51   Ibid., 31 January 1919.

52   Ibid.

53   Ibid., 31 January, 14 February, 7 March 1919.

54   Ibid., 14, 21 March 1919.

55   Ibid., 4 April, 18 April 1919; Waldo Proffitt, "A Study of Social Conditions in Davidson County" (M.A. thesis, Vanderbilt University, 1926), 38.

56   *Nashville Labor Advocate*, 31 January, 14 February 1919.

57   Ibid., 21 February 1919.

58   Ibid., 7, 28 March 1919.

59   Ibid., 13, 27 June, 3 October 1919.

60   Ibid., 22 August 1919; James A. Burran, "Labor Conflict in Urban Appalachia: The Knoxville Streetcar Strike of 1919," *Tennessee Historical Quarterly* 38:1 (Spring 1979): 62–78. Chattanooga streetcar workers had a long history of labor militancy as well. See James B. Jones, "Class Consciousness and Worker Solidarity in Urban Tennessee: The Chattanooga Carmen's Strikes of 1899–1917," *Tennessee Historical Quarterly* 52:2 (Summer 1993): 98–112.

61   *Nashville Labor Advocate*, 28 March, 5 September 1919.

62   Ibid., 12 September 1919.

63   Ibid., 19, 26 September 1919.

64   Ibid., 3 October 1919.

65   Ibid., 31 October, 7 November 1919.

66   Lawson was abducted on 19 November; the officers were acquitted in a trial the following spring; see *Nashville Labor Advocate*, 21 November 1919; 5 March, 30 April 1920. The *Nashville Banner*, 20 November 1919, simply reported that Lawson "left hurriedly" after being "escorted from the city and warned on leaving not to return again."

67   The meeting is described in "Minutes of Meeting of Law and Order Committee, 7 January 1929," Nashville Chamber of Commerce Minutes, Chamber of Commerce Records, Tennessee State Library and Archives, Nashville.

68   *Nashville Labor Advocate*, 21 May, 4 June, 2 July 1920.

69   Ibid., 11, 18 June 1920.

70   Ibid., 16 July, 7 August, 10, 24 September 1920; 25 January, 11 February, 15 April 1921; *Nashville Tennessean*, 26 August 1920; 22 April 1924. The typographers struck on 1 May 1921 and stayed out until November 1922 (*Nashville Labor Advocate*, 10 November 1922).

1   *Nashville Tennessean*, 31 January 1924; Don H. Doyle, *Nashville in the New South, 1880–1930* (Knoxville: University of Tennessee Press, 1985), 69.

2   *Nashville Tennessean*, 14 February 1924.

3   Ibid., 10 February 1924. See O. Latham Hatcher et al., *Rural Girls in the City for Work: A Study Made for the Southern Women's Educational Alliance* (Richmond, Va.: Garret & Massie, 1930), for an example of a wider interest in southern female rural-urban migration.

4   *Nashville Tennessean*, 10 February 1924.

5   Gavin Wright, *Old South, New South: Revolutions in the Southern Economy since the Civil War* (New York: Basic Books, 1986), 150–53.

In 1907 the Tennessee legislature passed legislation that prohibited the employment of women and children under the age of sixteen for more than sixty-two hours per week, with the maximum allowable hours reduced to sixty-one in 1909 and sixty in 1910. Further legislation in 1911 prohibited the employment of children under the age of fourteen "in, about or in connection with any mill, factory, workshop, laundry, telegraph, or telephone office, or in the distribution or transmission of merchandise or messages." The act also prohibited the employment of children under fourteen in any manner that interfered with school attendance, agriculture and domestic service excepted. The 1911 legislation also reduced the maximum work week for women and children under sixteen to fifty-eight hours per week. See Tennessee Bureau of Workshop and Factory Inspection, *Labor Laws of the State of Tennessee* (Nashville: Williams Printing Company, 1921), 20, 27, 40–45; Dewey W. Grantham, *Southern Progressivism: The Reconciliation of Progress and Tradition* (Knoxville: University of Tennessee Press, 1983), 197, 401.

6   U.S. Census Bureau, *Fourteenth Census of the United States, Taken in the Year 1920*, vol. 4, *Population: 1920 Occupations* (Washington: Government Printing Office, 1923); U.S. Census Bureau, *Fifteenth Census of the United States: 1930, Population*, vol. 4, *Occupations by States* (Washington: Government Printing Office, 1933).

7   U.S. Department of Labor, Women's Bureau, *The Occupational Progress of Women, 1910 to 1930*, bulletin no. 104 (Washington: Government Printing Office, 1933), 13.

8   *Nashville Tennessean*, 18 December 1922.

9   Ibid., 9 March 1924.

10 Ibid., 17, 24 March 1924. See also Tera Hunter, *To 'Joy My Freedom: Southern Black Women's Lives and Labors after the Civil War* (Cambridge, Mass.: Harvard University Press, 1997), 187–218.

11 Anna Fay Fowler, "Economic Adjustment of Rural Unmarried Girls Working in Nashville, 1932–1933" (M.A. thesis, Scarritt College for Christian Workers, 1933), 6.

12 Lillie Pearl (Davis) Shropshire interview by author, 20 August 1991, in author's possession.

13 Fowler, "Rural Unmarried Girls," 1.

14 Wiggins, "Migrant Women," 5; R. E. Wicker, "A Study of the Working Women Residing in Nashville's Four Largest Semi-Charity Homes for Women" (B.D. thesis, Vanderbilt University, 1931), 16; Joanne Meyerowitz, *Women Adrift: Independent Wage Earning Women in Chicago, 1880–1930* (New York: Oxford University Press, 1988), 48–50.

15 Carole Stanford Bucy, *Women Helping Women: The YWCA of Nashville, 1898–1998* (Nashville: The YWCA of Nashville and Middle Tennessee, 1998), 38–65; Josie B. Sellar, "The Blue Triangle League [of] the Young Women's Christian Association" typescript, 1931, Fisk University, W. D. Weatherford Papers, Southern Historical Collection, University of North Carolina, Chapel Hill; Wiggins, "Migrant Girl," 5; Wicker, "Working Women," 16. Wicker reports there were 206 residents in Nashville's white semicharity homes in 1931.

16 "The Young Woman's Christian Association of Nashville, 1898–1928," 3–5, box 9, YWCAC; Wiggins, "Migrant Girl," 63–67.

17 "The Young Woman's Christian Association of Nashville, 1898–1928," 3–5.

18 "Prospectus, 1909–1910," and untitled newspaper clipping, 4 October 1909, both in Scrapbooks, box 9, YWCAC.

19 Undated, untitled newspaper clipping, 1912; *Nashville Banner*, 3 February 1913; and *Nashville Democrat*, 28 February 1913, all Scrapbooks, box 9, YWCAC.

20 "Y.W.C.A. News," October 1916, box 9, YWCAC.

21 "The Young Woman's Christian Association of Nashville, 1898–1928," 7.

22 *Nashville Banner*, 3 January 1913, Scrapbooks, box 9, YWCAC.

23 Paul Boyer, *Urban Masses and Moral Order in America, 1820–1920* (Cambridge: Harvard University Press, 1978), 191.

24 *Nashville Democrat*, 27 June 1912, Scrapbooks, box 9, YWCAC.

25 *Nashville Tennessean*, 27 June 1912, Scrapbooks, box 9, YWCAC.

26 *Nashville Banner*, 3 January, 10 January; and untitled newspaper clipping, 22 March 1916, Scrapbooks, box 9, YWCAC.

27 *Nashville Banner*, 12 February 1913, Scrapbooks, box 9, YWCAC; see also Marjorie Spruill Wheeler, *New Women of the New South: The Leaders of the Woman Suffrage Movement in the Southern States* (New York: Oxford University Press, 1993).

28 Undated, untitled newspaper clipping, 1912, Scrapbooks, box 9, YWCAC.

29 Ibid.; "Rooms to Rent File," ca. 1918, box 13, YWCAC.

30 Wicker, "Working Women," 9, 24.

31 Ibid., 2–3; Wiggins, "Migrant Girl," 63–64.

32 Sellers, "Blue Triangle League," 14.

33 "Y.W.C.A. News."

34 Wiggins, "Migrant Girl," 64–65.

35 Wicker, "Working Women," 4–5.

36 Wiggins, "Migrant Girl," 63–67.

37 Untitled clipping, 20 October 1909, Scrapbooks, box 9, YWCAC; "Y.W.C.A. News."

38 Wiggins, "Migrant Girl," 42; Fowler, "Rural Unmarried Girls," 6.

39 Mark Austin Hutton, "A Sociological Study of Five and Ten Cent Store Sales-women in a Southern City" (master's thesis, Vanderbilt University, 1936), "Interview A," 76.

40 Hutton, "Five and Ten Cent Store Sales Women," "Interview G," 130.

41 Thus was worded a typical classified advertisement: "Wanted—Two Ladies for order department . . . give age, church, present employment," *Nashville Tennessean*, 7 March 1917.

42 Hutton, "Five and Ten Cent Store Sales Women," 119, 128.

43 Fowler, "Rural Unmarried Girls," 5.

44 *Nashville Banner*, 7 November 1923, in Scrapbooks, 1924, United Givers Fund Papers, Tennessee State Library and Archives, Nashville.

45 Doyle, *Nashville in the New South*, 209–11.

46 Aline Mayne Cavanagh, "Women Workers in Nashville: A Wage Study" (M.A. thesis, Vanderbilt University, 1929), 29.

47 "Position Desired Cards," 1917–1918, box 13, YWCAC.

48 Ibid.

49 Ibid.

50 F. K. Roberts [YWCA] to Dr. L. Ross Lynn, Thornwell Orphanage, Clinton, S.C., 3 September 1930, Dessie Padget Casefile, box 11, YWCAC. The Nash-ville YWCA's enthusiasm for placing women in clerical positions differed from that of other YWCAs, such as Chicago's, which "only reluctantly ac-cepted the new work role for women as clerical workers." See Lisa Fine, *Souls of the Skyscraper: Female Clerical Workers in Chicago, 1870–1930* (Philadelphia: Temple University Press, 1990), 131.

51 Hester Shepard Casefile, 4 June, 13 July 1929, box 11, YWCAC.

52 Sellers, "Blue Triangle League," 1–28.

53 Susan B. Carter and Mark Prus, "The Labor Market and the American High School Girl, 1890–1928," *Journal of Economic History* 42 (March 1982): 163–71; Leslie Woodcock Tentler, *Wage Earning Women: Industrial Work and Fam-ily Life in the United States, 1900–1930* (New York: Oxford University Press, 1979), 93–107.

54 *Nashville Labor Advocate*, 5 July 1918.

55 Ibid., 19 July 1912, in Scrapbooks, box 9, YWCAC; "Y.W.C.A. News"; Ina Shorrebeck to Fulton County, Georgia Relief Administration, 24 April 1935, Caseworker Letters, box 11, YWCAC.

56 *Nashville Tennessean*, 29 August 1926. The Watkins Institute was comprised of the following departments: Americanization School, Grammar School, High School, Commercial School, Trade School, Home Arts School, Art School, Music School, Continuation School, Economics and Government,

and Library ("Watkins Institute: Free Night School, Thirty-Eighth Session, 1926–1927," Watkins Institute Records, Nashville).

57　"Report for Month ending March 5, 1895"; "Rollbook, 1890–1902"; "Monthly Class Reports, 1918–1921"; "Monthly Class Reports, 1928–1929," Watkins Institute Records, Watkins Institute, Nashville.

58　*Nashville Tennessean*, 16 March 1929.

59　Robbie Sanford interview by John Rumble, 21 May 1981, in author's possession.

60　Cavanagh, "Women Workers," 29, 33–35.

61　Wiggins, "Migrant Girl," 56.

62　Hutton, "Five and Ten Cent Store Sales Women," "Interview B," 83.

63　Hutton, "Five and Ten Cent Store Sales Women," 128.

64　*Nashville Tennessean*, 11 January 1925.

65　Fowler, "Rural Unmarried Girls," v, 5.

66　Wiggins, "Migrant Girl," 40.

67　U.S. Census Bureau, *Fifteenth Census: Occupations*, 1541.

68　Fowler, "Rural Unmarried Girls," iv–v.

69　*Nashville Labor Advocate*, 2 February 1917.

70　*Nashville Banner*, 7 November 1923, in Scrapbooks, 1924, United Givers Fund Papers, Tennessee State Library and Archives, Nashville.

71　Cavanagh, "Women Workers," 8–9.

72　Fowler, "Rural Unmarried Women," 6–7. This was before the implementation of National Recovery Administration codes, which improved wages and working conditions somewhat.

73　Fowler, "Rural Unmarried Women," 6–7; Cavanagh, "Women Workers," 36.

74　Cavanagh, "Women Workers," 50.

75　Wiggins, "Migrant Girl," 56–57.

76　Fowler, "Rural Unmarried Girls," 1.

77　Ibid., 2. For similar evidence of the economic burden of dress regulations among saleswomen in New York and Chicago, see Susan Porter Benson, *Counter Culture: Saleswomen, Managers, and Customers in American Department Stores* (Urbana: University of Illinois Press, 1986), 194.

78　Wiggins, "Migrant Girl," 59.

79　Ibid., 58–59. The use of dating and romance by women workers in New York to enhance living standards is described in Kathy Lee Peiss, *Cheap Amusements: Working Women and Leisure in Turn-of-the-Century New York* (Philadelphia: Temple University Press, 1986), 51–55.

80　Emma Fleeman Casefile, 22 September 1930, and Claudia Stone Casefile [n.d., likely 1929], box 11, YWCAC.

81　Camilla Caldwell interview by John Rumble, 21 May 1981, in possession of author.

82　Peiss, *Cheap Amusements*, 51.

83　Hutton, "Five and Ten Cent Store Sales Women," "Interview A," 80.

84　Robbie Sanford interview.

85 Ibid.

86 Pearl Hale Casefile, 10 August 1931, box 11, YWCAC.

87 Hutton, "Five and Ten Cent Store Sales Women," 80.

88 Meyerowitz, *Women Adrift*.

Conclusion

1 David Danbom, *The Resisted Revolution: Urban America and the Industrialization of Agriculture, 1900–1930* (Ames: Iowa State University Press, 1979), v, 120; Hal S. Barron, *Mixed Harvest: The Second Great Transformation in the Rural North, 1870–1930* (Chapel Hill: University of North Carolina Press, 1997), 9, 16; Jeanette Keith, *Country People in the New South: Tennessee's Upper Cumberland* (Chapel Hill: University of North Carolina Press, 1995); Jack Temple Kirby, *Rural Worlds Lost: The American South, 1920–1960* (Baton Rouge: Louisiana State University Press, 1987).

2 See James H. Jackson Jr. and Leslie Page Moch, "Migration and the Social History of Modern Europe," *Historical Methods* 22 (Winter 1989): 27–36, and Ronald Skeldon, *Population Mobility in Developing Countries: A Reinterpretation* (London: Belhaven Press, 1990), for useful reviews of the literature on migration.

Appendix

1 The following discussion draws from Donald J. Bogue, Kenneth Hinze, and Michael White, *Techniques of Estimating Net Migration* (Chicago: Community and Family Study Center, University of Chicago, 1982), 15–30; Everette S. Lee et al., *Population Redistribution and Economic Growth, United States, 1870–1950*, vol. 1, *Methodological Considerations and Reference Tables* (Philadelphia: American Philosophical Society, 1957), 15–34; and Henry S. Shryock et al., *The Methods and Materials of Demography* (New York: Academic Press, 1976), 379–84.

2 Neil Fligstein, *Going North: Migration of Blacks and Whites from the South, 1900–1950* (New York: Academic Press, 1981).

Bibliography

PRIMARY SOURCES

Manuscripts

Archives of Appalachia, East Tennessee State University, Johnson City, Tenn.
    Earl R. Yates Collection
Country Music Foundation Library and Media Center, Nashville, Tenn.
    Alcyon Bate Beasley Scrapbook
    Sidney J. Harkreader Scrapbook
    WSM Grand Ole Opry Files
Fisk University, Nashville, Tenn.
    George Edmund Haynes Papers
    Charles S. Johnson Papers
Jewish Federation Archives, Nashville, Tenn.
    Industrial Removal Office Collection
Nashville Public Library, Nashville, Tenn.
    Union Station Oral History Collection
National Archives and Records Administration, Southeast Region, East
    Point, Ga.
    World War I Selective Service Records, RG 163
Southern Historical Collection, University of North Carolina, Chapel Hill, N.C.
    Ward Allison Dorrence Papers
    John Edwards Memorial Collection
    Federal Writers Project Papers
    Archie Green Papers
    William Morgan Papers
    Howard W. Odum Papers
    Rupert Vance Papers
    W. D. Weatherford Papers
Tennessee State Library and Archives, Nashville, Tenn.
    Chamber of Commerce Records
    LuCretia Owen Diary
    Purdue Agricultural Reports

Tennessee Electric Power Company Papers
Tennessee State Parks Folklife Collection
Archibald Trawick Papers
United Givers Fund Scrapbooks
YWCA Collection
Watkins Institute, Nashville, Tenn.
Watkins Institute Records

Musical Recordings

Nashville Early String Bands, vol. 1 [sound recording]. Charlottesville, Va.: County
Records, 2000.

Machine-Readable Data

Inter-University Consortium for Political and Social Research. *Historical, Demo-graphic, Economic, and Social Data: The United States, 1790–1970* [Computer
file]. Ann Arbor, Mich.: Inter-University Consortium for Political and Social
Research, 2001.
Ruggles, Steven, and Matthew Sobek et al. *Integrated Public Use Microdata Series:
Version 2.0.* Minneapolis: Historical Census Projects, University of Minne-sota, 1997. <http://www.ipums.org>.

Interviews and Narratives

Boyd, Fred. Narrative, 1981. Typescript in author's possession.
Caldwell, Camilla. Interview by John Rumble, 21 May 1981. Tape recording in
author's possession.
Glasgow, Mary Louise Lillie. Narrative, 21 March 1981. Typescript in author's
possession.
Jones, Ellis. Interview by John Rumble, 21 May 1981. Tape recording in author's
possession.
Perry, Daisy. Interview by Jonn Rumble, 29 May 1981. Tape recording in au-thor's possession.
Sanford, Robbie. Interview by John Rumble, 21 May 1981. Tape recording in
author's possession.
Shropshire, Lillie Pearl (Davis). Interview by author, 20 August 1991. Tape
recording in author's possession.
Williams, J. B. Interview by John Rumble, 18 May 1981. Tape recording in au-thor's possession.
Williams, Louise. Narrative, 17 March 1981. Typescript in author's possession.

Newspapers and Periodicals

Dixie Poultry Journal
Locomotive Fireman's Magazine
Mountain Life and Work
Nashville Banner
Nashville Globe
Nashville Labor Advocate
Nashville Tennessean
Nashville This Week
Old Hickory News
Rural Record
The Shield
Southern Agriculturalist
Southern Banker
Tennessee Agriculture
Tennessee Market Bulletin

State Documents

Tennessee Bureau of Workshop and Factory Inspection. Labor Laws of the State of Tennessee. Nashville: Williams Printing Company, 1921.

Tennessee Department of Agriculture. *Biennial Report of the Department of Agriculture, 1921–1922.* Nashville, 1922.

Tennessee Department of Public Instruction. *Rural School Situation in Tennessee.* Nashville: McQuiddy Printing Co., 1911.

Tennessee State Planning Commission. "Major Land Use Problems in Tennessee." By Brodus F. Lucas and E. P. Callahan. *Report*, no. 30. Nashville, 1936.

———. "Nashville Food Merchandising Survey." By Frank J. Ray and John N. Kellog. *Report*, no. 80. Nashville, 1938.

University of Tennessee. Agricultural Experiment Station. "The Development and Present Importance of Nashville Livestock Market." By M. J. Danner, B. H. Luebke, and B. D. Raskopf. *Rural Research Series*, no. 205. Knoxville, 1946.

———. "Development of the Timber Industry in Tennessee and the United States." By Charles E. Allred, S. W. Watkins, and Frank M. Fitzgerald. *Rural Research Series*, no. 92. Knoxville, 1939.

———. "An Economic Analysis of Farming in Overton County, Tennessee." By Charles E. Allred, assisted by S. W. Watkins. *Agricultural Economics Survey*, no. 1. Knoxville, 1927.

———. "Education of Farmers' Wives and Children in Four Counties of Tennessee." By Charles E. Allred and Benjamin D. Raskopf. *Rural Research Series*, no. 27. Knoxville, 1937.

———. "Factors Determining Types of Farming in Tennessee." By Charles E. Allred and Bent T. Latham Jr. *Rural Research Series*, no. 79. Knoxville, 1938.

———. "Farm Tenancy in Tennessee." By Charles E. Allred, William E. Hendrix, and Benjamin D. Raskopf. *Rural Research Series*, no. 17. Knoxville, 1936.

———. "Forest Production Areas: Tennessee and the United States." By Charles E. Allred and Frank Fitzgerald. *Rural Research Series*, no. 93. Knoxville, 1939.

———. "Human and Physical Resources of Tennessee, Chapter I, Geology, Topography, Soils." By Charles E. Allred, Samuel W. Atkins, and Benjamin D. Raskopf. *Rural Research Series Monograph*, no. 38. Knoxville, 1937.

———. "Human and Physical Resources of Tennessee, Chapter V, Minerals and Mining." By Charles E. Allred, Samuel W. Atkins, and William E. Hendrix. *Rural Research Series*, no. 44. Knoxville, 1937.

———. "Human and Physical Resources of Tennessee, Chapters XIV, XV, Transportation, Communication." By Charles E. Allred, Samuel W. Atkins, and William E. Hendrix. *Rural Research Series*, no. 63. Knoxville, 1939.

———. "Human and Physical Resources of Tennessee, Chapter XVII and XXVIII, Education: Public and Private; Illiteracy, Reading Habits, Libraries." By Charles E. Allred, Samuel W. Atkins, F. M. Fitzgerald. *Rural Research Series*, no. 81. Knoxville, 1938.

———. "Types of Tenant Areas in Tennessee." By Charles E. Allred and E. E. Briner. *Rural Research Series*, no. 73. Knoxville, 1938.

University of Tennessee. Division of University Extension. "Educational, Economic and Community Survey: Bledsoe County." *University of Tennessee Record: Extension Series*, vol. 4, no. 2. Knoxville, 1927.

Federal Documents

Brannen, C. O. *Relation of Land Tenure to Plantation Organization.* USDA Department Bulletin No. 1269. Washington, 18 October 1924.

U.S. Census Bureau. *Thirteenth Census of the United States: 1910.* Vol. 9, *Manufactures*. Washington: Government Printing Office, 1912.

———. *Thirteenth Census of the United States Taken in the Year 1910.* Vol. 3, *Population, 1910. Reports by States.* Washington: Government Printing Office, 1913.

———. *Thirteenth Census of the United States, Taken in the Year 1910.* Vol. 4, *Population, 1910. Occupation Statistics.* Washington: Government Printing Office, 1914.

———. *Thirteenth Decennial Census of the United States, 1910.* Vol. 7, *Agriculture. Reports by States.* Washington Government Printing Office, 1913.

———. *Fourteenth Census of the United States, Taken in the Year 1920.* Vol. 4, *Population: 1920 Occupations.* Washington: Government Printing Office, 1923.

———. *Fourteenth Census of the United States, Taken in the Year 1920.* Vol. 6, pt. 2, *Agriculture: The Southern States.* Washington: Government Printing Office, 1922.

————. *Fourteenth Decennial Census of the United States, Taken in the Year 1920.* Vol. 8, *Manufactures: 1919.* Washington: Government Printing Office, 1923.

————. *Fifteenth Census of the United States: 1930. Agriculture.* Vol. 2, pt. 2, *The Southern States.* Washington: Government Printing Office, 1932.

————. *Fifteenth Census of the United States: 1930. Manufactures.* Vol. 3, *Reports by States.* Washington: Government Printing Office, 1933.

————. *Fifteenth Census of the United States: 1930. Population.* Vol. 3, pt. 2, *Reports by States.* Washington: Government Printing Office, 1932.

————. *Fifteenth Census of the United States: 1930. Population.* Vol. 4, *Occupations by States.* Washington: Government Printing Office, 1933.

U.S. Census Office. *Report on Manufacturing Industries in the United States at the Eleventh Census: 1890.* Pt. 2, *Statistics of Cities.* Washington: Government Printing Office, 1895.

————. *Report on Population of the United States at the Eleventh Census: 1890.* Pts. 1 and 2. Washington: Government Printing Office, 1895.

————. *Report of the Statistics of Agriculture in the United States at the Eleventh Census: 1890.* Washington: Government Printing Office, 1895.

————. *Twelfth Census of the United States, Taken in the Year 1900.* Vol. 8, *Manufactures.* Washington: Government Printing Office, 1902.

————. *Twelfth Census of the United States, Taken in the Year 1900. Population.* Pts. 1 and 2. Washington: Government Printing Office, 1902.

————. *Twelfth Census of the United States, Taken in the Year 1900. Special Reports: Employees and Wages.* By Davis R. Dewey. Washington: Government Printing Office, 1903.

————. *Twelfth Decennial Census of the United States, Taken in the Year 1900.* Vol. 5, *Agriculture.* Washington: Government Printing Office, 1902.

U.S. Commission of Agricultural Inquiry. *Report of the Joint Commission of Agricultural Inquiry,* Pt. 4. "Marketing and Distribution," 67th Cong., 1st sess., 1921, House Report No. 408. Washington: Government Printing Office, 1922.

U.S. Congress. *Report of the Commission on Country Life.* Senate Doc. No. 705, 60th Cong., 2nd sess., 23 January 1909. Washington: Government Printing Office, 1909.

————. *Report of the Joint Commission of Agricultural Inquiry,* Part 4. "Marketing and Distribution," 67th Cong., 1st sess., 1921, House Report No. 408. Washington: Government Printing Office, 1922.

U.S. Department of Agriculture. *Statistical Bulletin,* no. 7, "Shipments and Unloads of Certain Fruits and Vegetables, 1918–1923." April 1925.

————. *Statistical Bulletin,* no. 18, "Statistics of Hogs, Pork, and Pork Products." January 1927.

U.S. Department of Labor, Division of Negro Economics, George Edmund Haynes, Director. *Negro Migration in 1916–17.* Washington: Government Printing Office, 1919; New York: Negro Universities Press, 1969.

————. Women's Bureau. *The Occupational Progress of Women, 1910 to 1930.*
Bulletin No. 104. Washington: Government Printing Office, 1933.

U.S. Industrial Commission. *Report of the Industrial Commission on Agriculture
and Agricultural Labor.* Vol. 10, 57th Cong., 1st sess., doc. 179. Washington:
Government Printing Office, 1901.

U.S. War Office. *Second Report of the Provost Marshal General to the Secretary
of War on the Operations of the Selective Service System to December 20, 1918.*
Washington: Government Printing Office, 1919.

Works Progress Administration. "Rural Migration in the United States." By
C. E. Lively and Conrad Taeuber. *WPA Research Monograph* 19. Washington:
Government Printing Office, 1939.

Contemporary Unpublished Reports, Theses, and Social Surveys

Cavanagh, Aline Mayne. "Women Workers in Nashville: A Wage Study." M.A.
thesis, Vanderbilt University, 1929.

Council of Social Agencies [Nashville]. "A Social Study of White Families in the
Area Selected for the Nashville Federal Housing Project." Typescript, 1934.

Fisk University Department of Social Science. "A Social Study of Negro Families in the Area Selected for the Nashville Negro Federal Housing Project."
Typescript, 1934.

Foster, Susie P. "Leisure-Time Activities of Industrial Girls in Nashville." M.A.
thesis, Vanderbilt University, 1930.

Fowler, Fay. "Economic Adjustment of Rural Unmarried Working Girls in Nashville, 1932–1933." M.A. thesis, Scarritt College, 1933.

Gilmore, Harlan W. "Racial Disorganization in a Southern City." Ph.D. thesis,
Vanderbilt University, 1931.

Hardwick, James T. "The Economic Condition of the Negro in Nashville." M.A.
thesis, YMCA Graduate School, Nashville, 1922.

Hutton, Mark A. "A Sociological Study of Five and Ten Cent Store Saleswomen
in a Southern City." M.A. thesis, Vanderbilt University, 1936.

Johnson, Julia M. "The Standard of Living of 100 Negro Families in Nashville."
M.A. thesis, Fisk University, 1933.

Kennamer, Lorrin G. "The Woodworking Industries of Nashville." M.A. thesis,
George Peabody College for Teachers, 1922.

Kennel, Archile C., Jr. "A Statistical Study of a Settlement Area in Nashville."
M.A. thesis, Vanderbilt University, 1930.

McConnell, John P. "Population Problems in Nashville, Tennessee: Based on
United States Census Reports for 1920 and 1930 and Other Related Local
Data." Typescript, YMCA Graduate School, 1933.

Miller, Laura Kate. "Geographical Influences on the Growth of Nashville." M.A.
thesis, George Peabody College for Teachers, 1923.

Proffitt, Waldo. "A Study of Social Conditions in Davidson County." M.A. thesis, Vanderbilt University, 1926.

Rogers, Glenn. "Localization of a Few Selected Industries in Nashville." M.A. thesis, George Peabody College for Teachers, 1932.

Ross, Danforth Reynolds. "A Study of Insecurity among Rural Relief Families in a Tennessee Urban Community." M.A. thesis, Vanderbilt University, 1937.

Sanders, Jessie Thomas. "Study of Nashville City Markets." M.A. thesis, George Peabody College for Teachers, 1916.

Stone, Andrew P. "Primitive Religion among Negroes in Tennessee." M.A. thesis, Fisk University, 1932.

Wicker, R. E. "A Study of the Working Women Residing in Nashville's Four Largest Semi-Charity Homes for Women." B.D. thesis, Vanderbilt University, 1931.

Wiggins, Avis C. "The Migrant Girl." M.A. thesis, Vanderbilt University, 1933.

Wyche, Ruth. "A Community Survey of a Factory District in Nashville, Tennessee." M.A. thesis, Scarritt College, 1931.

Contemporary Published Sources

Beaumont, Henry Francis. *West Nashville: Manufacturing Metropolis of the South.* Nashville: Beaumont, 1908.

The Bradstreet Company. *Bradstreet's Book of Commercial Ratings of Bankers, Merchants, Manufacturers, Etc. in a Portion of the United States.* Vol. 228 (January 1925). New York: Bradstreet Co., 1925.

Jones, Ira P. *The City of Nashville: Illustrated.* Nashville: n.p., 1890.

Killebrew, J. B. *Introduction to the Resources of Tennessee.* Nashville: Tavel, Eastman & Howell, 1874.

Marshall-Bruce-Polk Co. *Nashville City Directory.* Nashville: Marshall-Bruce-Polk, 1899–1930.

Nashville Board of Trade. *Yearbook, 1906.* Nashville: n.p., 1906.

————. *Yearbook, 1908–09.* Nashville: Marshall & Bruce Co., 1909.

Nashville Life Insurance Company. "Nashville Life Insurance Company of Nashville, Tennessee, July 1, 1873." Nashville: Tavel, Eastman & Howell, 1873.

Proceedings of the Third Annual Convention of the Southern Commercial Congress. Atlanta, Ga., 1911. Washington: The (Southern Commercial) Congress, 1911.

R. G. Dun & Company. *Mercantile Agency Reference Book (and Key) Containing Ratings of Merchants, Manufacturers, and Traders Generally, Throughout the Southern States.* Vol. 87 (January 1890). New York: R. G. Dun & Co., 1890.

————. *The Mercantile Agency Reference Book (and Key) Containing Ratings of Merchants, Manufacturers, and Traders Generally.* Vol. 143 (January 1904). New York: R. G. Dun & Co., 1904.

Sibley, Elbridge. *Differential Mortality in Tennessee, 1917–1928: A Statistical Study*

Conducted Jointly by Tennessee State Department of Public Health and Fisk University. Nashville: Fisk University Press, 1930.

Smart, Richard Davis, Jr. "The Economic Condition of Negroes in Nashville, Tenn." *Vanderbilt University Quarterly* (April 1904): 108–13.

Weatherford, Willis D., ed. *A Survey of the Negro Boy in Nashville, Tennessee.* New York: Association Press, 1932.

White, Lasses. *Lasses White's Book of Humor and Song: Songs, Parodies, Jokes, Poems.* N.p., 1935.

Wooldridge, John, ed. *History of Nashville, Tennessee.* Nashville: Publishing House of the Methodist Episcopal Church, South, 1890.

SECONDARY SOURCES

Books and Articles

Anderson, Barbara A. *Internal Migration during Modernization in Late-Nineteenth-Century Russia.* Princeton, N.J.: Princeton University Press, 1980.

Ash, Stephen V. *Middle Tennessee Society Transformed, 1860–1870: War and Peace in the Upper South.* Baton Rouge: Louisiana State University Press, 1988.

Ayers, Edward L. *The Promise of the New South: Life after Reconstruction.* New York: Oxford University Press, 1992.

Barron, Hal S. *Mixed Harvest: The Second Great Transformation in the Rural North, 1870–1930.* Chapel Hill: University of North Carolina Press, 1997.

Benedict, Murray R. *Farm Policies of the United States, 1790–1950.* New York: Twentieth Century Fund, 1953.

Blouin, Francis X., Jr. *The Boston Region, 1810–1850: A Study of Urbanization.* Ann Arbor, Mich.: UMI Research Press, 1980.

Bogue, Donald J., Kenneth Hinze, and Michael White. *Techniques of Estimating Net Migration.* Chicago: Community and Family Study Center, University of Chicago, 1982.

Boserup, Ester. *The Conditions of Agricultural Growth: The Economics of Agrarian Change under Population Pressure.* Chicago: Aldine, 1965.

———. "The Impact of Scarcity and Plenty on Development." *Journal of Interdisciplinary History* 14:2 (Autumn 1983): 383–407.

Boyer, Paul. *Urban Masses and Moral Order in America, 1820–1920.* Cambridge: Harvard University Press, 1978.

Bucy, Carole Stanford. *Women Helping Women: The YWCA of Nashville, 1898–1998.* Nashville: The YWCA of Nashville and Middle Tennessee, 1998.

Bufwack, Mary, and Robert K. Oermann. "Adelyne Hood: The Amalgamation of Vaudeville and Folk Traditions in Early Country Music." *John Edwards Memorial Foundation Quarterly* 18 (1982): 116–30.

Burran, James A. "Labor Conflict in Urban Appalachia: The Knoxville Streetcar Strike of 1919." *Tennessee Historical Quarterly* 38:1 (Spring 1979): 62–78.

Byrd, Douglas. *Steamboatin' on the Cumberland*. Nashville: Tennessee Book Company, 1961.

Campbell, Tracy. *The Politics of Despair: Power and Resistance in the Tobacco Wars*. Lexington: University Press of Kentucky, 1993.

Capers, Gerald. "The Rural Lag on Southern Cities." *Mississippi Quarterly* 21 (Fall 1968): 253–62.

Carlton, David L. "The American South and the American Manufacturing Belt." In *The South, the Nation, and the World: Perspectives on Southern Economic Development*, edited by David L. Carlton and Peter A. Coclanis, 163–78. Charlottesville: University Press of Virginia, 2003.

———. *Mill and Town in South Carolina, 1880–1920*. Baton Rouge: Louisiana State University Press, 1982.

———. "The Revolution from Above: The National Market and the Beginnings of Industrialization in North Carolina." *Journal of American History* 77 (September 1990): 445–75.

———. "Unbalanced Growth and Industrialization: The Case of South Carolina." In *Developing Dixie: Modernization in a Traditional Society*, edited by Winfred B. Moore Jr. et al., 111–30. New York: Greenwood Press, 1988.

Carter, Susan, and Mark Prus. "The Labor Market and the American High School Girl, 1890–1928." *Journal of Economic History* 42 (March 1982): 163–71.

Carter, Susan B., and Richard Sutch. "Myth of the Industrial Scrap Heap: A Revisionist View of Turn-of-the-Century American Retirement." *Journal of Economic History* 56 (March 1996): 5–38.

Chapman, Herman Hollis. *The Iron and Steel Industries of the South*. University: University of Alabama Press, 1953.

Chapman, Murray, and R. Mansell Prothero. "Themes on Circulation in the Third World." In *Circulation in Third World Countries*, edited by R. Mansell Prothero and Murray Chapman, 1–26. London: Routledge & Kegan Paul, 1985.

Clark, W. A. V. *Human Migration*. Beverly Hills, Calif.: Sage Publications, 1986.

Cobb, James C. *The Selling of the South: The Southern Crusade for Industrial Development, 1936–1980*. Baton Rouge: Louisiana State University Press, 1982.

Conner, Valerie Jean. *The National War Labor Board: Stability, Social Justice, and the Voluntary State in World War I*. Chapel Hill: University of North Carolina Press, 1983.

Conzen, Kathleen Neils. "A Saga of Families." In *The Oxford History of the American West*, edited by Clyde A. Milner, Carol A. O'Connor, and Martha A. Sandweiss, 315–57. New York: Oxford University Press, 1994.

Conzen, Michael P. *Frontier Farming in an Urban Shadow: The Influence of Madison's Proximity on the Agricultural Development of Blooming Grove, Wisconsin*. Madison: State Historical Society of Wisconsin, 1971.

———. "The Maturing Urban System in the United States, 1840–1910." *Annals of the American Association of American Geographers* 67 (March 1977): 88–108.

Cooney, Deborah, ed. *Speaking of Union Station: An Oral History of a Nashville Landmark*. Nashville: Union Station Trust Fund, 1977.

Corlew, Robert E. *Tennessee: A Short History*. 2nd ed. Knoxville: University of Tennessee Press, 1981.

Cronon, William. *Nature's Metropolis: Chicago and the Great West*. New York: W. W. Norton, 1991.

Dalton, Robert E. "Montgomery Bell and the Narrows of the Harpeth." *Tennessee Historical Quarterly* 35 (Spring 1976): 3–28.

Danbom, David B. *The Resisted Revolution: Urban America and the Industrialization of Agriculture, 1900–1930*. Ames: Iowa State University Press, 1979.

Danhof, Clarence H. "Four Decades of Thought on the South's Economic Problems." In *Essays in Southern Economic Development*, edited by Melvin L. Greenhut and W. Tate Whitman, 15–21. Chapel Hill: University of North Carolina Press, 1964.

Daniel, Pete. *Breaking the Land: The Transformation of Cotton, Tobacco, and Rice Cultures since 1880*. Urbana: University of Illinois Press, 1985.

Davenport, David Paul. "Migration to Albany, New York, 1850–1855." *Social Science History* 13 (Summer 1989): 159–85.

Davidson, Donald. *Big Ballad Jamboree*. Jackson: University Press of Mississippi, 1996.

———. *Still Rebels, Still Yankees and Other Essays*. 1957. Baton Rouge: Louisiana State University Press, 1972.

Davis, Kingsley. "The Effect of Out-Migration on Regions of Origin." In *Internal Migration: A Comparative Perspective*, edited by Alan Brown and Egon Neuberger, 147–66. New York: Academic Press, 1977.

Delmore, Alton. *The Delmore Brothers: Truth Is Stranger Than Publicity*. Edited by Charles K. Wolfe. Nashville: Country Music Foundation Press, 1995.

DeLozier, Mary Jean. *Putnam County, Tennessee, 1850–1970*. Cookeville, Tenn.: Putnam County, 1979.

Dickson, Robert E. *City and Region: A Geographical Interpretation*. London: Routledge & Kegan Paul, 1964.

Doster, James F. "Wetumpka's Railroad: Its Construction and Early Traffic." *Alabama Review* 3 (July 1950): 180–82.

Doyle, Don H. *Nashville in the New South, 1880–1930*. Knoxville: University of Tennessee Press, 1985.

———. *Nashville since the 1920s*. Knoxville: University of Tennessee Press, 1985.

———. *New Men, New Cities, New South: Atlanta, Nashville, Charleston, Mobile, 1860–1910*. Chapel Hill: University of North Carolina Press, 1990.

Drake, St. Clair, and Horace R. Cayton. *Black Metropolis: A Study of Negro Life in a Northern City*. New York: Harcourt, Brace and Company, 1945.

Dublin, Thomas. "Rural-Urban Migrants in Industrial New England: The Case of Lynn, Massachusetts, in the Mid-Nineteenth Century." *Journal of American History* 73 (Fall 1986): 623–44.

Duncan, Otis Dudley, et al. *Metropolis and Region*. Baltimore, Md.: Johns Hopkins University Press, 1960.

Eller, Ronald D. *Miners, Millhands, and Mountaineers: Industrialization of the Appalachian South, 1880–1930*. Knoxville: University of Tennessee Press, 1982.

Ellison, Curtis W. *Country Music Culture: From Hard Times to Heaven*. Jackson: University Press of Mississippi, 1995.

Fine, Lisa M. *The Souls of the Skyscraper: Female Clerical Workers in Chicago, 1870–1930*. Philadelphia: Temple University Press, 1990.

Fink, Gary, ed. *Labor Unions*. Westport, Conn.: Greenwood Press, 1977.

Fite, Gilbert C. *Cotton Fields No More: Southern Agriculture, 1865–1980*. Lexington: University Press of Kentucky, 1984.

Flamming, Douglas. *Creating the Modern South: Millhands and Managers in Dalton, Georgia, 1884–1894*. Chapel Hill: University of North Carolina Press, 1992.

Fligstein, Neil. *Going North: Migration of Blacks and Whites from the South, 1900–1950*. New York: Academic Press, 1981.

Flynt, J. Wayne. *Dixie's Forgotten People: The South's Poor Whites*. Bloomington: Indiana University Press, 1979.

Foner, Philip S., and Ronald L. Lewis, eds. *The Black Worker: A Documentary History from Colonial Times to the Present*. Vol. 6, *The Era of Post-War Prosperity and the Great Depression, 1920–1936*. Philadelphia: Temple University Press, 1981.

Gaston, Paul M. *The New South Creed: A Study in Southern Mythmaking*. New York: Alfred A. Knopf, 1970.

Glasco, Laurence. "Migration and Adjustment in the Nineteenth-Century City: Occupation, Property and Household Structure of Native-Born Whites, Buffalo, New York, 1855." In *Family and Population in Nineteenth-Century America*, edited by Tamara K. Hareven and Maris A. Vinovskis, 154–78. Princeton, N.J.: Princeton University Press, 1978.

Goldfield, David R. *Cotton Fields and Skyscrapers: Southern City and Region*. Baton Rouge: Louisiana State University Press, 1982.

———. "The Urban South: A Regional Framework." *American Historical Review* 86 (December 1981): 1009–34.

Goldscheider, Calvin. "Migration and Rural Social Structure: An Overview." In *Rural Migration in Developing Nations: Comparative Studies of Korea, Sri Lanka, and Mali*, edited by Calvin Goldscheider, 1–19. Boulder, Colo.: Westview Press, 1984.

Goldstein, Sidney G. "Urbanization, Migration and Development." In *Urban Migrants in Developing Nations: Patterns and Problems of Adjustment*, edited by Calvin Goldscheider, 3–19. Boulder, Colo.: Westview Press, 1983.

Goodrich, Carter, et al. *Migration and Economic Opportunity: The Report of the Study of Population Redistribution*. Philadelphia: University of Pennsylvania Press, 1936.

Gottlieb, Peter. *Making Their Own Way: Southern Blacks' Migration to Pittsburgh, 1916–1930*. Urbana: University of Illinois Press, 1987.

Grantham, Dewey W. *Southern Progressivism: The Reconciliation of Progress and Tradition*. Knoxville: University of Tennessee Press, 1983.

Gras, N. S. B. "The Development of Metropolitan Economies in Europe and America." *American Historical Review* 27 (July 1922): 695–708.

Graves, John P. *Northwest Davidson County: The Land, Its People*. Nashville: Privately printed by author, 1975.

Gregory, James N. *American Exodus: The Dust Bowl Migration and Okie Subculture in California*. New York: Oxford University Press, 1989.

Greenwood, Michael. "Research in Internal Migration in the United States." *Journal of Economic Literature* 13 (June 1975): 397–433.

Grigg, David B. *Population Growth and Agrarian Change: An Historical Perspective*. Cambridge, Eng.: Cambridge University Press, 1980.

Grindle, Merilee S. *Searching for Rural Development: Labor Migration and Employment in Mexico*. Ithaca, N.Y.: Cornell University Press, 1988.

Grossman, James R. *Land of Hope: Chicago, Black Southerners, and the Great Migration*. Chicago: University of Chicago Press, 1989.

Grossman, James R., comp. *Black Workers in the Era of the Great Migration, 1916–1929*. Frederick, Md.: University Publications of America, Inc., 1985. Microfilm.

Grundy, Pamela. "From Il Trovatore to the Crazy Mountaineers: The Rise and Fall of Elevated Culture on WBT-Charlotte, 1922–1930." *Southern Cultures* 1 (Spring 1994): 51–73.

———. "'We Always Tried to Be Good People': Respectability, Crazy Water Crystals, and Hillbilly Music on the Air, 1933–1935." *Journal of American History* 81 (March 1995): 1591–1620.

Hahn, Steven. *The Roots of Southern Populism: Yeoman Farmers and the Transformation of the Georgia Upcountry, 1850–1890*. New York: Oxford University Press, 1983.

———. "The 'Unmaking' of the Southern Yeomanry: The Transformation of the Georgia Upcountry, 1860–1890." In *The Countryside in the Age of Capitalist Transformation: Essays in the Social History of Rural America*, edited by Jonathan Prude and Steven Hahn, 179–203. Chapel Hill: University of North Carolina Press, 1985.

Hale, Grace Elizabeth. *Making Whiteness: The Culture of Segregation in the South, 1890–1940*. New York: Pantheon Books, 1998.

Hale, Will T. *History of DeKalb County, Tennessee*. Nashville: Paul Hunter Publishers, 1915.

Hall, Jacquelyn Dowd, et al. *Like a Family: The Making of a Southern Cotton Mill World*. Chapel Hill: University of North Carolina Press, 1987.

Hansen, Niles M. *Intermediate Size Cities and Growth Centers*. New York: Praeger, 1971.

Hay, George D. *Howdy Judge*. Nashville: McQuiddy Press, 1926.

————. *A Story of the Grand Ole Opry*. Nashville: Privately published, 1953.

Hedstrom, Margaret L. "Beyond Feminisation: Clerical Workers in the United States from the 1920s through the 1960s." In *The White Blouse Revolution: Female Office Workers since 1870*, edited by Gregory Anderson, 145–69. Manchester, Eng.: Manchester University Press, 1988.

Henretta, James. "The Study of Social Mobility: Ideological Assumptions and Conceptual Bias." *Labor History* 18 (Spring 1977): 164–78.

Hershberg, Theodore, and Robert Dockhorn. "Occupational Classification." *Historical Methods* 9 (March–June 1976): 59–98.

Higgs, Robert. *Competition and Coercion: Blacks in the American Economy, 1865–1914*. Chicago: University of Chicago Press, 1980.

Hirschman, Albert O. *The Strategy of Economic Development*. New Haven, Conn.: Yale University Press, 1958.

Hohenberg, Paul M., and Lynn Hollen Lees. *The Making of Urban Europe, 1000–1950*. Cambridge: Harvard University Press, 1985.

Holt, Andrew David. *The Struggle for a State System of Public Schools in Tennessee, 1903–1936*. New York: Bureau of Publications, Columbia University Teachers College, 1938.

Horn, Stanley F. *This Fascinating Lumber Business*. Indianapolis: Bobbs-Merrill Company, 1943.

Howell, Benita J. "Survey of Folklife along the Big South Fork of the Cumberland River." Department of Anthropology, University of Tennessee–Knoxville, 1981.

Hunter, Tera. *To 'Joy My Freedom: Southern Black Women's Lives and Labors after the Civil War*. Cambridge, Mass.: Harvard University Press, 1997.

Hurst, Jack. *Nashville's Grand Ole Opry*. New York: Harry N. Abrams, Inc., 1975.

Jackson, James H., Jr., and Leslie Page Moch. "Migration and the Social History of Modern Europe." *Historical Methods* 22 (Winter 1989): 27–36.

Janiewski, Dolores E. *Sisterhood Denied: Race, Gender, and Class in a New South Community*. Philadelphia: Temple University Press, 1985.

Johnson, Daniel M., and Rex R. Campbell. *Black Migration in America: A Social Demographic History*. Durham, N.C.: Duke University Press, 1981.

Jones, James B. "Class Consciousness and Worker Solidarity in Urban Tennessee: The Chattanooga Carmen's Strikes of 1899–1917." *Tennessee Historical Quarterly* 52:2 (Summer 1993): 98–112.

Jones, Lu Ann. "Gender, Race, and Itinerant Commerce in the Rural New South." *Journal of Southern History* 66:2 (2000): 297–320.

Joubert, William H. *Southern Freight Rates in Transition*. Gainesville: University of Florida Press, 1949.

Kantor, Shawn Everett, and Morgan J. Kousser. "Common Sense or Commonwealth? The Fence Law and Institutional Change in the Postbellum South." *Journal of Southern History* 49 (May 1993): 202–42.

Keith, Jeanette. *Country People in the New South: Tennessee's Upper Cumberland*. Chapel Hill: University of North Carolina Press, 1995.

Kennedy, David M. *Over Here: The First World War and American Society*. New York: Oxford University Press, 1980.

Kirby, Jack Temple. *Rural Worlds Lost: The American South, 1920–1960*. Baton Rouge: Louisiana State University Press, 1987.

———. "The Southern Exodus, 1910–1960: A Primer for Historians." *Journal of Southern History* 49 (November 1983): 585–600.

Klein, Maury. *History of the Louisville & Nashville Railroad*. New York: Macmillan, 1972.

Kline, Ronald R. *Consumers in the Country: Technology and Social Change in Rural America*. Baltimore, Md.: Johns Hopkins University Press, 2000.

Lamon, Lester C. *Black Tennesseans, 1900–1930*. Knoxville: University of Tennessee Press, 1977.

Lee, Everette. "A Theory of Migration." *Demography* 3 (1966): 47–57.

Lee, Everette S., et al. *Population Redistribution and Economic Growth: United States, 1870–1950*. 3 vols. Philadelphia: American Philosophical Society, 1957–64.

Lewis, Earl. "Afro-American Adaptive Strategies: The Visiting Habits of Kith and Kin among Black Norfolkians during the First Great Migration." *Journal of Family History* 12 (1987): 407–20.

Link, William A. *The Paradox of Southern Progressivism, 1880–1930*. Chapel Hill: University of North Carolina Press, 1992.

Lott, Eric. *Love and Theft: Blackface Minstrelsy and the American Working Class*. New York: Oxford University Press, 1995.

Edward T. Luther. *Our Restless Earth: The Geologic Regions of Tennessee*. Knoxville: University of Tennessee Press, 1977.

Mahoney, Timothy R. *River Towns in the Great West: The Structure of Provincial Urbanization in the American Midwest, 1820–1870*. New York: Cambridge University Press, 1990.

Malone, Bill C. "The Rural South Moves to the City: Country Music since World War II." In *The Rural South since World War II*, edited by R. Douglas Hurt, 96. Baton Rouge: Louisiana State University Press, 1998.

Malone, Bill C., and Judith McCulloh, eds. *Stars of Country Music: Uncle Dave Macon to Johnny Rodriguez*. Urbana: University of Illinois Press, 1975.

Marks, Carole. *Farewell—We're Good and Gone: The Great Black Migration*. Bloomington: Indiana University Press, 1989.

Marshall, John M. "Industrialization and Agricultural Productivity." In *Growing Metropolis: Aspects of Development in Nashville*, edited by James F. Blumstein and Benjamin Walter, 311–40. Nashville: Vanderbilt University Press, 1975.

Marshall, Suzanne. *Violence in the Black Patch of Kentucky and Tennessee*. Columbia: University of Missouri Press, 1994.

McKenzie, Robert Tracy. *One South or Many? Plantation Belt and Upcountry in Civil War–Era Tennessee*. Cambridge, Eng.: Cambridge University Press, 1994.

McKiven, Henry M., Jr. *Iron and Steel: Class, Race, and Community in Birming-*

ham, Alabama, 1875–1920. Chapel Hill: University of North Carolina Press, 1995.

McLaurin, Melton A. *Paternalism and Protest: Southern Cotton Mill Workers and Organized Labor, 1875–1905*. Westport, Conn.: Greenwood Press, 1971.

Mercey, Arch A. *The Laborers' Story, 1903–1953: The First Fifty Years of the International Hod Carriers', Building and Common Laborers' Union of America*. Washington: Ransdell, 1954.

Meyer, David Ralph. "A Dynamic Model of the Integration of Frontier Urban Places into the United States System of Cities." *Economic Geography* 56 (April 1980): 120–40.

———. "Emergence of the American Manufacturing Belt: An Interpretation." *Journal of Historical Geography* 9:2 (1983): 145–74.

———. "Midwestern Industrialization and the American Manufacturing Belt in the Nineteenth Century." *Journal of Economic History* 49:4 (December 1989): 921–37.

Meyerowitz, Joanne. *Women Adrift: Independent Wage Earning Women in Chicago, 1880–1930*. New York: Oxford University Press, 1988.

———. "Women and Migration: Autonomous Female Migrants to Chicago, 1880–1930." *Journal of Urban History* 13 (February 1987): 147–68.

Miller, Roberta Balstad. *City and Hinterland: A Case Study of Urban Growth and Regional Development*. Westport, Conn.: Greenwood Press, 1979.

Miller, William D. "Rural Values and Urban Progress, 1900–1917." *Mississippi Quarterly* 21 (Fall 1968): 263–74.

Mitchell, George Sinclair. *Textile Unionism and the South*. Chapel Hill: University of North Carolina Press, 1931.

Moch, Leslie Page. *Paths to the City: Regional Migration in Nineteenth-Century France*. Beverly Hills, Calif.: Sage Publishers, 1983.

Mohl, Raymond. "City and Region: The Missing Dimension in U.S. Urban History," *Journal of Urban History* 25 (November 1998): 3–21.

Montell, William Lynwood. *Don't Go Up Kettle Creek: Verbal Legacy of the Upper Cumberland*. Knoxville: University of Tennessee Press, 1983.

———. *Upper Cumberland Country*. Jackson: University Press of Mississippi, 1993.

Montgomery, David. *Workers' Control in America: Studies in the History of Work, Technology, and Labor Struggles*. Cambridge, Eng.: Cambridge University Press, 1979.

Morton, David C., with Charles K. Wolfe. *DeFord Bailey: A Black Star in Early Country Music*. Knoxville: University of Tennessee Press, 1991.

Murphy, Raymond E. "Land Values in the Blue Grass and Nashville Basin." *Economic Geography* 6 (April 1930): 191–203.

Myrdal, Gunnar. *Rich Lands and Poor: The Road to World Prosperity*. New York: Harper, 1954.

Newby, I. A. *Plain Folk in the New South: Social Change and Cultural Persistence, 1880–1915*. Baton Rouge: Louisiana State University Press, 1989.

Nicholls, William H. "The Effects of Industrial Development on Tennessee Valley Agriculture, 1900–1950." *Journal of Farm Economics* 38 (November 1956): 1636–49.

Odum, Howard W. *Southern Regions of the United States.* Chapel Hill: University of North Carolina Press, 1936.

Osborn, George C. "The Southern Rural Press and Some Significant Rural Problems, 1900–1940." *Agricultural History* 29 (July 1955): 115–22.

Otto, John S. "Forest Fallowing in the Southern Appalachian Mountains: A Problem in Comparative Agricultural History." *Proceedings of the American Philosophical Society* 133 (1989): 51–63.

Parker, William N. *Europe, America, and the Wider World: Essays on the Economic History of Western Capitalism.* Vol 2. New York: Cambridge University Press, 1991.

———. "The South in the National Economy, 1865–1970." *Southern Economic Journal* 46 (April 1980): 1019–48.

Perlman, Selig, and Philip Taft. *History of Labor in the United States, 1896–1932.* Vol. 4, *Labor Movements.* Edited by John R. Commons. New York: Macmillan Co., 1935.

Perloff, Harvey S., et al. *Regions, Resources, and Economic Growth.* Baltimore, Md.: Johns Hopkins University Press, 1960.

Persky, Joseph. "The Dominance of the Rural-Industrial South, 1900–1930." *Journal of Regional Science* 13 (1973): 409–19.

Peterson, Richard A. *Creating Country Music: Fabricating Authenticity.* Chicago: University of Chicago Press, 1997.

Peterson, Richard A., and Paul Di Maggio. "The Early Opry: Its Hillbilly Image in Fact and Fancy." *Journal of Country Music* 4 (Summer 1973): 39–51.

Pisani, Donald J. *From the Family Farm to Agribusiness: The Irrigation Crusade in California and the West, 1850–1931.* Berkeley: University of California Press, 1984.

Poston, Dudley L., and Robert H. Weller. *The Population of the South: Structure and Change in Social Demographic Context.* Austin: University of Texas Press, 1981.

Pred, Allan. *The External Relations of Cities during "Industrial Revolution" with a Case Study of Goteborg, Sweden, 1869–1890.* University of Chicago Department of Geography Research Paper, no. 76. Chicago: University of Chicago Department of Geography, 1962.

Preston, Samuel H., and Michael R. Haines. *Fatal Years: Child Mortality in Late-Nineteenth-Century America.* Princeton, N.J.: Princeton University Press, 1991.

Rinzler, Ralph, and Norm Cohen. *Uncle Dave Macon: A Bio-Discography.* JEMF Special Series, no. 3. Los Angeles: John Edwards Memorial Foundation, Inc., 1970.

Russell, Tony. *Blacks, Whites, and Blues.* New York: Stein and Day, 1970.

Schulman, Steven A. "The Lumber Industry of the Upper Cumberland Valley." *Tennessee Historical Quarterly* (Fall 1973): 255–64.

Schwarzweller, Harry K., James S. Brown, and J. J. Managalam. *Mountain Families in Transition: A Case Study of Appalachian Migration*. University Park: Pennsylvania State University Press, 1971.

Sewell, William H., Jr. *Structure and Mobility: The Men and Women of Marseille, 1820–1870*. Cambridge, Eng.: Cambridge University Press, 1986.

Shryock, Henry S., et al. *The Methods and Materials of Demography*. New York: Academic Press, 1976.

Skeldon, Ronald. *Population Mobility in Developing Countries: A Reinterpretation*. London: Belhaven Press, 1990.

Spero, Sterling D., and Abram L. Harris. *The Black Worker: The Negro and the Labor Movement*. New York: Columbia University Press, 1931.

Stamper, Powell. *The National Life Story: A History of the National Life and Accident Insurance Company of Nashville, Tennessee*. New York: Appleton-Century-Crofts, 1968.

Steckel, Richard H. "The Economic Foundations of East-West Migration during the 19th Century." *Explorations in Economic History* 20 (January 1983): 14–36.

Tang, Anthony M. *Economic Development in the Southern Piedmont, 1860–1950: Its Impact on Agriculture*. Chapel Hill: University of North Carolina Press, 1958.

Thomas, Rebecca. "There's a Whole Lot o' Color in the 'White Man's Blues': Country Music's Selective Memory and the Challenge of Identity." *Midwest Quarterly* 38:1 (1996): 73–89.

Tindall, George B. *The Emergence of the New South, 1913–1945*. Baton Rouge: Louisiana State University Press, 1967.

Todaro, Michael P. "A Model of Labor Migration and Urban Unemployment in Less Developed Countries." *American Economic Review* 59 (1969): 138–48.

Tolnay, Stewart E. "The Decline of Black Marital Fertility in the Rural South: 1910–1940." *American Sociological Review* 52 (April 1987): 211–17.

Trotter, Joe William, Jr., ed. *The Great Migration in Historical Perspective: New Dimensions of Race, Class, and Gender*. Bloomington: Indiana University Press, 1991.

Twelve Southerners. *I'll Take My Stand: The South and the Agrarian Tradition*. 1930. New York: Harper Torchbooks, 1962.

Vance, James. *The Merchants World: The Geography of Wholesaling*. Englewood Cliffs, N.J.: Prentice Hall, 1970.

Vance, Rupert B. *Human Geography of the South: A Study in Regional Resources and Human Adequacy*. Chapel Hill: University of North Carolina Press, 1935.

Vance, Rupert B., and Nadia Danilevsky. *All These People: The Nation's Human Resources in the South*. Chapel Hill: University of North Carolina Press, 1945.

Vance, Rupert B., and Nicholas J. Demerath, eds. *The Urban South*. Chapel Hill: University of North Carolina Press, 1954.

Ward, David. *Cities and Immigrants: A Geography of Change in Nineteenth-Century America*. New York: Oxford University Press, 1971.

Ward, Frank Bird. "The Industrial Development of Tennessee." *Annals of the American Academy of Political and Social Sciences* 153 (January 1931): 141–47.

Warren, George F., and Frank A. Pearson. *Prices*. New York: Wiley, 1933.

Wells, Robert V. *Uncle Sam's Family: Issues in and Perspectives on American Historical Demographic History*. Albany: State University of New York Press, 1985.

Wheeler, Marjorie Spruill. *New Women of the New South: The Leaders of the Woman Suffrage Movement in the Southern States*. New York: Oxford University Press, 1993.

Winters, Donald L. "Farm Size and Production Choices: Tennessee, 1850–1860." *Tennessee Historical Quarterly* 52 (1993): 212–24.

Williams, Samuel Cole. "Early Iron Works in the Tennessee Country." *Tennessee Historical Quarterly* 6 (March 1947): 39–46.

Wolfe, Charles K. *A Good-Natured Riot: The Birth of the Grand Ole Opry*. Nashville: Country Music Foundation and Vanderbilt University Press, 1999.

———. *Tennessee Strings: The Story of Country Music in Tennessee*. Knoxville: University of Tennessee Press, 1977.

Woodson, Carter. *A Century of Negro Migration*. New York: Russell and Russell, 1969.

Woodward, C. Vann. *Origins of the New South, 1877–1913*. 2nd ed. Baton Rouge: Louisiana State University Press, 1971.

Woofter, Thomas Jackson, Jr. *Negro Migration: Changes in Rural Organization and Population of the Cotton Belt*. New York: W. D. Gray, 1920.

Wright, Gavin. *Old South, New South: Revolutions in the Southern Economy since the Civil War*. New York: Basic Books, 1986.

Zelinsky, Wilbur. "Changes in the Geographic Patterns of Rural Population in the United States, 1790–1960." *Geographic Review* 52 (1962): 492–524.

Zelizer, Vivian Rothman. *Morals and Markets: The Development of Life Insurance in the United States*. New York: Columbia University Press, 1979.

Zunz, Olivier. *The Changing Face of Inequality: Urbanization, Industrial Development, and Immigrants in Detroit, 1880–1920*. Chicago: University of Chicago Press, 1982.

Theses and Dissertations

Brand, David Edward. "Fill the Empty Shell: The Story of the Government Munitions Project at Old Hickory, Tennessee, 1918–1919." M.A. thesis, Vanderbilt University, 1971.

Dawson, Clarence Colton. "History of the Flour Milling Industry in Nashville, Tennessee." M.A. thesis, George Peabody College for Teachers, 1931.

Doran, William H. "The Development of the Industrial Spirit in Tennessee, 1910–1920." Ph.D. dissertation, George Peabody College for Teachers, 1965.

Kirby, Russell Stephen. "Urban Growth and Economic Change in the Nine-

teenth-Century South: The Hinterland of Memphis Tennessee, 1830–1900."
Ph.D. dissertation, University of Wisconsin, 1981.

Martin, Walter. "Agricultural Commercialism in the Nashville Basin, 1850–
1860." Ph.D. dissertation, University of Tennessee, 1984.

Moore, Wayne Clark. "Farm Communities and Economic Growth in the Lower
Tennessee Valley: Humphreys County, Tennessee." Ph.D. dissertation, University of Rochester, 1990.

Pagnini, Deanna Lynn. "American Fertility in Transition: Rural Family Building
Patterns in the Early Twentieth Century." Ph.D. dissertation, University of
North Carolina, Chapel Hill, 1992.

Rinks, Jerry Wayne. "We Shield Millions: A History of WSM, 1925–1950." Ph.D.
dissertation, University of Tennessee, Knoxville, 1993.

Rumble, John Woodruff. "Fred Rose and the Development of the Nashville
Music Industry, 1942–1954." Ph.D. dissertation, Vanderbilt University, 1980.

Index

Agriculture: corn production, 41, 42, 44, 56, 178 (n. 16); cotton production, 44, 178 (n. 13); farming practices, 54–56; moonshine production, 62; out-of-state competition, 60–61; population crisis consequences, 39–40, 49–56, 158, 176 (n. 1), 180 (n. 39); tobacco production, 38, 42, 44, 178 (n. 14); transportation of goods, 41–43, 71; wheat production, 36, 44–45. *See also* Farm families; Farm tenancy; Livestock production; Sharecropping system
Altman, Anna, 147
Alven, P. E., 67
Automobile ownership, 12–13, 93–94, 170 (n. 16)

Bailey, DeFord, 7, 10, 16–17, 171 (n. 30)
Baker, Ray Stannard, 75
Banks, Billie Nell, 112
Barbers' Union, 118
Barron, Hal, 157
Bate, Humphrey ("Doctor"), 10
B. G. Wood, 32
Bickford, Claude, 97
Black Patch region, 28, 42, 44
Black Patch War, 1
Bookbinders' and Bindery Women's Union, 130
Bookbinders' Union, 128
Booster Club of Nashville, 19–20, 29, 126

Boosterism, 19–20, 23–25, 29, 31, 126–27
Boot and Shoe Workers' Union, 133
Boserup, Ester, 54
Boxmakers' Union, 130–31
Boyd, Fred, 98, 110
Breckenridge, Desha, 143
Bricklayers' Union, 117–19
Bridge and Structural Iron Workers' Union, 132
Brimm, Grace, 113
Brown, Julia, 112
Brown, Mary, 112
Burton, A. M., 33–34
Business Women's Equal Suffrage League, 143

Caldwell, Camilla, 98, 154
Campbell, G. S., 47–48
Campbell, Olive Dame, 94
Car cleaners' union, 118
Carpenters' Union, 117, 129, 130
Carter Shoe Company, 133
Central Basin region agriculture, 41, 44, 45, 54
Central Church of Christ Home for Girls, 141, 144
Child labor: legislation limiting, 196 (n. 5); in manufacturing industries, 138; outplacement for family survival, 78–79, 111–13, 185 (n. 20)
Circular migration patterns, 75, 79–80, 84, 96–97, 108–10
Clay, Laura, 143

Cole, Fleta, 75
Colored Carpenters' Union, 118, 129
Conditions of Agricultural Growth, The
    (Boserup), 54
Consumerism, 15–16, 94
Cooksey, Addie, 147
Craig, Edwin, 10
Cumberland Plateau: agriculture, 42–
    45, 54, 63, 68; natural resources,
    31–32, 79–80
Cumberland River, 41–43, 69, 71
Curtis, Ward, 79

Dalhart, Vernon, 14
Damrosch, Walter, 7
Danbom, David, 157
Davidson, Donald, 8, 168 (n. 3)
Davidson, Joel, 9
Dean, Samuel, 96, 110
Delmore, Alton and Rabon, 14
DuPont Engineering Company, 98–
    102, 128–29, 150
Dyer, A. J., 132

Early-Cain Co., 131
Edgefield and Nashville Manufactur-
    ing Company, 35
Education: by gender in farm families,
    90–91; of men, 148, 149; outmigra-
    tion linked to, 92–93, 158–59; road
    improvement in reform of, 91–92;
    school reform measures, 87–92; of
    women, 147, 148–50
Ellison, Curtis, 8–9
English, Maude, 113
Everett, Rowland, 97
Evits, Finits, 78, 80
Exoduster movement, 74–75

Farm families: automobile owner-
    ship by, 94; children as economic
    resources in, 78–79, 111–13, 185
    (n. 20); economic security of, 10–11;
    education levels by gender, 90–91;
    size of, 49–50, 179 (n. 28)
Farm family income supplements,
    58–59; barter trade, 65; cured
    meat sales, 66; dairy production,

45, 64–65; hog farming, 45, 66–
    68; logging, 34, 68–72; market
    garden crops, 59–62; moonshine
    production, 62; out-of-state compe-
    tition for, 60–61, 66–67; poultry
    production, 45, 62–64
Farm ownership: land values and, 51–
    53; means of, 48–49, 70; migration
    patterns and, 77–79; security in, 72,
    75
Farm tenancy, 45–47, 52–53, 76–78,
    94. *See also* Agriculture
Federal Chemical, 120
Finley, W. W., 59
Firemen's Union, 119
Fleeman, Emma, 154

Gazin, Beryl, 101
Girls Christian Home, 141
Grand Ole Opry, 1, 7–18
Graves, John, 77
Gray & Dudley Company, 25, 32, 134
Great Migration, 2, 81–82. *See also*
    Migration

Hale, Elizabeth, 13
Hard-Stone Masons' Union, 119
Harkreader, Sidney (Fiddlin' Sid), 1, 3,
    10
Hay, George D., 7–9, 14–15, 17
Haynes, George Edmund, 119
Helpers' and Laborers' Union, 118
Highland Rim: agriculture, 41–42,
    44–45, 54–56, 70–72; natural re-
    sources, 31–32, 42
Hill, H. G., 60–63
Hod Carriers' Union, 118, 192 (n. 11)
Hood, Adelyne, 14
Hotel and Restaurant Employees'
    Union, 130
Hubbard, Oma, 58

Independent Life Insurance Company,
    30
International Association of Machin-
    ists, 194 (n. 34)
International Brotherhood of Electri-
    cal Workers, 130

Jackson, John, 16
Jakes Foundry, 33, 120
Jamup and Honey, 15–16
Jelton, Nannie, 147
John Beachard & Sons, 32
John B. Ransom & Co., 130–31
Johnson, Jordenia, 97
Jones, A. C., 109
Jones, Ben, 110
Jones, Ellis, 110–11

Keith, Jeanette, 157
Kiger, Gus, 133–34
Killebrew, Joseph B., 31, 71
King's Daughters Home, 141, 144
Kirby, Jack Temple, 157
Kittrell, Richard, 118
Knights of Labor, 127

Labor movement. *See* Unions
Lasses and Honey, 15–16
Lawson, J. B., 133
Leather Workers' Union, 131–32
Lewis, Ray Bob, 79
Lieberman, Loveman & O'Brian, 35
Life and Casualty Company, 30
Life insurance rural expansion, 10–11, 30
Lincoln Fire Insurance Company, 30
Livestock production: dairy, 45, 64–65; hog farming, 45, 66–68; out-of-state competition, 66–67; poultry, 45, 62–64; statistics, 36–37; transportation of goods, 63. *See also* Agriculture
Louisville & Nashville Railroad (L&N), 22–23, 35–36, 120, 129
Louisville banking industry, 27–28
Lytle, Andrew, 2–3, 8, 95

Machinists' Union, 129
Macon, Uncle Dave, 1, 9–10, 12–13, 16
Maintenance of Way Union, 129
"Making whiteness," 13
Mann Act, 143
Manufacturing: child labor in, 138; development disparities, 38–39; discriminatory practices, 119–21, 193 (n. 21); migration patterns and, 38
Manufacturing industries of Nashville: banking, 27–29; fertilizer production, 37; flour milling, 35–36; grocery retail, 60–61; insurance, 29–30, 33, 173 (n. 34); iron-products manufacturing, 31–33; lumber and wood products, 34–35, 70–71, 174 (n. 58); meat processing, 36–37, 66–67, 175 (n. 69); textiles, 33–34, 126–27, 132–33, 174 (n. 53); wholesale trade, 172 (n. 6), 172 (n. 10)
May Hosiery Mill, 119
McClaren, Lela, 113
McEwen's Laundry, 139
McKissack, C. W., 119
Middle Tennessee: child mortality, 50; farm tenancy by region, 45–46; hinterland areas defined, 25–27, 40; manufacturing development disparities, 38–39; mining industry, 79–80; natural resources (*see* Natural resources, Middle Tennessee); population data, 50, 83; road conditions in, 59–60. *See also* Tennessee
—link to Nashville growth, 19–21; in agricultural production, 36–37; in livestock production, 36–37; in natural resources, 31, 34–35, 37; small merchants, 25
Migrants: illness/malnourishment in, 100; labor unions and culture of, 126–28; poverty of, 99–100
Migrants, female
—black: domestic work for, 103, 147, 148; education opportunities, 149; employment agencies for, 144; and manufacturing industries' discriminatory practices, 119–20; semicharity homes for, 141, 144; traditional work decline, 139–40. *See also* Migration—patterns of
—white: vs. city natives employed, 153; city natives employment compared, 150–51; economic survival

Migrants, female (*continued*)
strategies, 153–54; education of,
148–50; motivations of, 97, 111–14,
136–37, 140, 155; older, 144, 147;
progressive reformers' goals for,
136, 142; semicharity homes for,
141–45, 153; sexual harassment of,
154–55; suffrage movement and,
143; white slave trade danger to,
142–43; working-hour reform, 142–
43. *See also* Migration—patterns of;
Women
—work opportunities for: age and,
146–47; church affiliation and, 146;
domestic, 103, 147, 148; education
and, 147, 148–50; employment
agencies for, 144, 146–47; and
job search, 139–40, 145–46; by
job type, 151; and wartime labor
recruitment, 100–101
Migrants, male
—white: birthplace size in employment ranking, 124–26; city natives
in employment ranking compared,
115–16; education and work opportunities, 148, 149; nonwhites in
employment ranking compared,
115–18; region of birth in employment ranking, 122–24. *See also*
Migration—patterns of
—black: birthplace size in employment ranking, 124–26; city natives
in employment ranking compared,
121–22; ganging places, 120–21;
manufacturing industries discriminatory practices, 119–21, 193 (n. 21);
region of birth in employment
ranking, 122–24; union discriminatory practices, 117–19; whites in
employment ranking compared,
115–18, 120. *See also* Migration—
patterns of
Migration: exoduster movement, 74;
industrial development in patterns
of, 38–39; interstate distribution,
82–83; intracounty, 75–80, 122;
motivation for, 96–97, 111–14, 136–

37, 140, 155; western, 73–75. *See also*
Nashville inmigration
—patterns of: age structure in, 73,
83–85, 103; circular, 75, 79–80,
84, 96–97, 108–10; gender and,
84, 102–3, 106–8; industrial development in, 38–39; racial, 74–75,
81–85, 106–7; southern, 157–58;
western, 73–75
—rural to urban: destinations, 106;
economics of, 73–75; education role
in, 92–93, 158–59; foundations of,
2; Grand Ole Opry as metaphor,
17–18; net-migration estimates, 80–
82, 185 (n. 31); contributing factors,
19–22, 58–59, 72; road improvement in, 74, 88–89, 92, 93–94,
159; school reform measures and,
87–92, 186 (n. 38); statistics, 50.
See also Nashville inmigration
Miller, G. H., 67
Millmen's Union, 131
Modernity-tradition tensions, 2–3, 8,
12–13, 17–18, 167 (n. 4)
Morgan, James, 74
Morgan, Jo B., Jr., 132–33
Morgan, R. Perry, 63
Morgan & Hamilton Mills, 33, 132–33
Music Row, 169 (n. 3)

Nashville, Chattanooga & St. Louis
Railroad (NC&StL), 22–23, 120, 129
Nashville & Chattanooga Railroad, 22
Nashville & Decatur Railway, 23
Nashville Bridge Company, 132
Nashville Cotton Mills, 33
Nashville development: boosterism
in, 19–20, 29, 31; commercial travelers' role, 23–25, 37; hinterland
areas defined, 25–27; limitations,
21–22, 31–33, 39; rail transport role,
22–23, 32, 43; wholesale trade in,
21–25, 29. *See also* Manufacturing
industries of Nashville
—hinterland contribution to, 19–21;
agricultural production, 35–36, 59–
62, 181 (n. 8); livestock production,

36–37; natural resources availability, 31, 34–35; small merchants,
25
Nashville inmigration: attractions
of, 97–98; beginnings, 96–97;
origination data, 107–8; railroad
role, 98; wartime labor in, 98–102,
107, 128–30. *See also* Migration
—patterns of: age structure in, 103;
circular, 97, 108–10; gender and,
102–3, 106–8, 159; racial, 102
Nashville Life Insurance Company, 29
Nashville outmigration, 103, 106
Nashville Railway & Light Company,
120, 129, 132
Nashville Saddlery Co., 131
Nashville Woolen Mills, 33
National Life and Accident Insurance
Company, 10–11, 30
National Manufacturing Company, 33
Natural resources, Middle Tennessee: coal, 31, 42, 79–80; forests,
34–35, 42–43, 68–72; iron ore, 31;
phosphate deposits, 37

Oklahoma, migration to, 75
Orman-Partee Co., 131
Outmigration. *See* Migration—rural to
urban
Owen, LuCretia, 99, 100, 101

Paperhangers' Union, 129
Paschall, Ella, 75–76
Paschall, Santifee, 78
Peck, Thomas F., 86, 89, 92
Perry, Daisy, 98, 109
Peterson, Richard, 9
Pettifer, Robert, 131
Phillips & Buttorff, 25, 32, 128, 134
Plasterers' Union, 117–18
Pollack, Valera, 114
Preville, Nellie, 112

Racial discrimination: by manufacturing industries, 119–21, 193 (n. 21);
by railroads, 120; by unions, 117–19.
See also Migration—patterns of

Racial segregation, 119, 141, 144
Railroads: discriminatory practices,
120; Nashville growth linked to,
22–23, 32; and transport of goods,
41–43, 63; unions in, 118–19, 129
Reddick, Walter N., 130
Reed Fertilizer Company, 120
River transport of goods, 41–43, 69, 71
Road construction: economy of rural
farm and, 59–60; education reform
linked to, 91–92; outmigration and,
74, 88–89, 92, 93–94, 159; taxation
for, 13, 171 (n. 17)
Russell Street Church of Christ Home
for Girls, 141

Sacho, Tina, 147
Sanford, Robbie, 65, 113, 154–55
School reform. *See* Education
Sharecropping system, 47–48, 53,
76–78. *See also* Agriculture
Short-distance migration, 75–80, 122
Shropshire, Lillie, 113, 140
Sly, Elva, 148
Smith, Mrs. Alvie O., 64–65
South & North Railway, 23
Southern Agrarians, 2–3
Southern Insurance Company, 30
Standard Furniture Company, 119
Stokley, W. B., 89
Stone, Claudia, 154
Stone Masons' Union, 117
Street Carmen's Union, 129, 132, 134

Teal, Hattie, 113–14
Tenant farmers. *See* Farm tenancy
Tennessee: banking industry, compari-
sons by city, 27–29; lumber produc-
tion data, 70–71; road conditions in,
59–60; western migration to, 74.
See also Middle Tennessee; *names of
specific cities*
Tennessee Central Railroad, 32, 43,
63, 98, 120, 129
Tennessee Chemical, 120
Tennessee Coal, Iron & Railroad
Company, 32

Tennessee Department of Agriculture, 63, 67
Trawick, Mrs. Arch, 136
Typographical Union, 128, 134

Unions: discriminatory practices of, 117–19; migrant culture and, 126–28; Open Shop Movement, 134; police intimidation tactics, 133–35; postwar conflicts, 130–35; in textile industries, 126–27, 132–33; wartime labor needs and, 128–30
United Textile Workers' Union, 132
Upper Cumberland natural resources, 34–35

Vick, Roberta, 112
Voss, Eddie, 146

Warren, Robert Penn, 1
Warrioto Cotton Mill, 119, 132–33
Watkins Institute, 149
Wendle, Harriet, 64
Werthan Bag Company, 119
Weyman & Bruton Company, 38, 133
White, Lee Roy "Lasses," 15–16
Wilds, Lee David "Honey," 15–16

Williams, J. B., 70, 98, 111
Williams, Louise, 111, 185 (n. 20)
WLS National Barn Dance, 14
Women's Commercial Training School, 148
Women, white: education of rural, 90–91; farm income strategies, 62–65; unions and, 130, 132. *See also* Migrants, female
Women of Nashville
—black: employment for city natives, 137–39; occupational distribution by race, 138–39
—white: change in percentage employed, 137–38; income levels, 151–53; vs. migrant women employed, 150–51, 153; occupational distribution by race, 138–39
Women's suffrage, 143
Woods, Idella, 111
WSM radio, 10–11, 14–15

YWCA (Young Women's Christian Association), 113–14, 141–45, 148–49
YWCA Blue Triangle League, 144, 148
YWCA Employment Bureau, 146–47